*Flexible Design*
*Revisionary Poetics in Blake's* Vala *or* The Four Zoas

*Vala* or *The Four Zoas* is one of William Blake's few surviving manuscripts and affords a unique opportunity to examine a significant evolution in his poetic practice. While the poem itself exhibits a consistent thematic interest, the modes and methods of representing these interests underwent a radical change in the ten or more years in which Blake wrote and reworked the poem. *Flexible Design* offers an extended and detailed treatment of the gradual shift that took place in Blake's poetics during the composition, transcription, and revision of *Vala* or *The Four Zoas*.

Using the idea of a "flexible design," John Pierce examines the ways in which Blake's mythology and his poem possess a flexibility that allows for significant change to characters, symbols, and poetic techniques within a previously constructed framework. Pierce traces how, in the process of revision, Blake experimented with characterization, increased the importance of Christian symbolism, and developed a mode of narrative presentation controlled less by chronological sequence than by the use of thematic juxtaposition and typology.

JOHN B. PIERCE is associate professor of English, Queen's University.

# Flexible Design

*Revisionary Poetics in Blake's*
Vala *or* The Four Zoas

JOHN B. PIERCE

McGill-Queen's University Press
Montreal & Kingston · London · Buffalo

Legal deposit second quarter 1998
Bibliothèque nationale du Québec

Printed in Canada on acid-free paper

This book has been published with the help of a grant from the Humanities and Social Sciences Federation of Canada, using funds provided by the Social Sciences and Humanities Research Council of Canada.

**Canadian Cataloguing in Publication Data**

Pierce, John Benjamin, 1957–
Flexible design: revisionary poetics in Blake's Vala or the four Zoas
Includes bibliographical references and index.
ISBN 0-7735-1682-4
1. Blake, William, 1757–1827. Four Zoas. 1. Title.
PR4144.V33P53 1998    821'.7    C97-900875-1



Typeset in Adobe Caslon 10.5/13
by Caractéra inc., Quebec City

Now Los & Enitharmon walkd forth on the dewy Earth
Contracting or expanding their all flexible senses
At will to murmur in the flowers small as the honey bee
At will to stretch across the heavens & step from star to star
Or standing on the Earth erect, or on the stormy waves
Driving the storms before them or delighting in sunny beams
While round their heads the elemental Gods kept harmony   (34:9–15)

Then those in Great Eternity met in the Council of God
As one Man for Contracting their Exalted Senses
They behold Multitude or Expanding they behold as one
As One Man all the Universal family & that One Man
They Call Jesus the Christ & they in him & he in them
Live in Perfect harmony in Eden the land of life
Consulting as One Man above the Mountain of Snowdon
   Sublime   (21:1–7)

# Contents

# Acknowledgments

Perhaps one of the disguised blessings of struggling with this book in many different versions over more than ten years can be found in recounting and thanking some of the individuals who have had an influence, both direct and indirect, in its production. Special thanks go to the late Professor Vince De Luca, who guided me in the early stages of writing the dissertation that was later to evolve into this book. I will remember him as a scholar whose dedication to Blake studies and whose depth of understanding of Blake's wall of words stand as a benchmark of possible achievement in literary scholarship. His initial guidance has profoundly affected the whole course of this study.

Professor G.E. Bentley, Jr, offered kind and generous advice at various points in the early stages of this work. He vigorously challenged many commonly held assumptions about the manuscript and has made me think twice about making easy critical statements not supported by the evidence of the manuscript. Morris Eaves also offered valuable commentary on the manuscript as a whole and has always been encouraging in the various stages of its development. Peter Otto's specific encouragements are not forgotten here. Our discussions about the *Vala* manuscript have helped to sustain my belief that the complexity of the *Vala* manuscript, however daunting, was worth extended and close examination. Credit also goes to Andrew Lincoln for his reassurance that there is a great deal of room for further study of the poem.

I would also like to thank the readers for McGill-Queen's University Press and for the Canadian Federation for the Humanities for their helpful commentaries on the manuscript.

Two portions of this book have appeared in print before. Chapter 2 first appeared as "The Changing Mythic Structure of Blake's *Vala* or *The Four Zoas*: A Study of the Manuscript, Pages 43–84" in *Philological Quarterly* 68 (1989): 485–508. Part of chapter 3 was previously published as "The Shifting Characterization of Tharmas and Enion in Pages 3–7 of Blake's *Vala* or *The Four Zoas*" in *Blake: An Illustrated Quarterly* 22 (Winter 1988–89): 93–102.

A research grant from the Social Sciences and Humanities Research Council of Canada enabled me to make several visits to the British Library to check my work and ideas against the original manuscript. Viewing the manuscript itself only reinforced my sense of the importance of the physical aspects of Blake's textuality. The staff at the Manuscript Room in the British Museum were consistently generous in allowing me access to Blake's manuscript and are deserving of sincere thanks.

Finally, I would like to thank my parents for their continued support over the long years of work on this book, and Shelley King for her comments, her reading (and rereading) of my manuscript, and her constant encouragement.

# Textual Note

For many of the difficult cruxes in the manuscript and for the preparation of my edition of the copperplate text (Appendix A) I have consulted the original manuscript of *Vala* or *The Four Zoas* in the British Museum. However, unless otherwise stated, all quotations from Blake's *Vala* or *The Four Zoas* are taken from G.E. Bentley, Jr's facsimile edition *Vala or The Four Zoas: A Facsimile of the Manuscript, a Transcript of the Poem and a Study of Its Growth and Significance* (Oxford: Clarendon 1963). Brackets around material in quotations indicate matter added by me or one of Blake's editors. I have indicated text deleted by Blake with italics in brackets [*thus*]. Text in angle brackets <> is that either written over erasures or added to an already transcribed portion of text. Citations in parentheses give Blake's page and line numbers. References to Bentley's commentary and analysis of the poem's development are indicated by a "B" followed by the page number in his edition. Where it is relevant to my discussion, I have given Bentley's (or on occasion Erdman's) readings of erased or cancelled words; however, I have not included erasures or cancellations where they might needlessly complicate a passage under discussion.

Quotations from Blake's other works are taken from *The Complete Poetry and Prose of William Blake*, ed. David V. Erdman, newly rev. ed. (Berkeley: University of California Press 1982), and are also cited parenthetically in my text. Citations for Blake's poetry give an abbreviated title followed by plate and line number and a page number preceded by an "E" to indicate the Erdman edition. Citations for prose works refer to the page number in Erdman's edition. References to Erdman's textual notes are noted parenthetically by an "E" followed by a page number.

## ABBREVIATIONS

*A*   *America*
*BA*   *Book of Ahania*
*BL*   *Book of Los*
*BU*   *Book of Urizen*
*EG*   *The Everlasting Gospel*
*FR*   *The French Revolution*
*J*   *Jerusalem*
*M*   *Milton*
*MHH*   *Marriage of Heaven and Hell*
*SL*   *Song of Los*
*V*   *Vala* or *The Four Zoas*
*VLJ*   *A Vision of the Last Judgment*

# Preface

The proliferation of studies of *Vala* or *The Four Zoas* over the past two decades marks discussion of the poem as a new locus of interest in Blake research. The appearance of the new facsimile by Erdman and Magno, books by Wilkie and Johnson, Ault, Rosso, and Lincoln and a host of articles examining the intricacies of the manuscript, its composition, and its complications mark the poem as an important site of discussion and debate. While it is difficult to locate a specific moment of origin for this developing interest, two important but very different kinds of publications devoted exclusively to *Vala* or *The Four Zoas* appeared in 1978, marking an important point of departure and development for the study of the poem. The first was Brian Wilkie and Mary Lynn Johnson's *Blake's Four Zoas: The Design of a Dream*. Besides being the first book-length study of the poem, it cut through the compressed symbolism, the allusive characterization, the sometimes tortured and often ambiguous syntax, the narrative disjunctions, and the constant rewritings of major texts of Western thought, including Milton, the Bible, Young, Locke, Newton, Rousseau, and Voltaire (and others), to offer an accessible reading of the poem that became essential for anyone attempting to understand its basic narrative. From the perspective of contemporary criticism Wilkie and Johnson's study may appear to be a fairly direct and uncomplicated reading of the poem. Yet it creates the feeling that the act of paraphrase is not a heresy but a heroic action, and it prepared the way for Donald Ault's *Narrative Unbound* in 1987 and George Anthony Rosso's *Blake's Prophetic Workshop* in 1993.

The second notable event of 1978 was the appearance of a special issue of the *Blake Quarterly* devoted entirely to *Vala*,[1] particularly the textual cruxes arising from the incompletenesses and uncertain readings occasioned by the physical state of the manuscript itself. The importance of these articles in the history of the poem's reception cannot be emphasized too strongly. Together they generated a set of debates about the handling of the two Nights VII[2] and a reliable text for Night 1,[3] for example, that informed the production of Erdman's presentation of *Vala* in his revised edition of the *Complete Poems* in 1982. (As the standard edition of Blake's works, Erdman exerts what might be considered an undue influence on subsequent critical readings of the poem.)[4] Continuing in this tradition, articles devoted to consideration of the material condition of the manuscript have sustained a series of debates in the *Blake Quarterly* about whether the poem is incomplete or unfinished and about what other material form the manuscript might have been destined for (although these debates tend to be more general than particular in their discussion of the state of the manuscript).[5]

One legacy of these two publications from 1978 is the degree to which they have entrenched two separate approaches to the poem: those that concern themselves with the minutiae of manuscript revision, and those devoted to a sustained, coherent, and complete reading of the poem. Perhaps even more intriguing is the separation of these two approaches into different forms of publication. Treatments of the material difficulties of the poem occasioned by its status as a manuscript appear most notably only in article form, continuing in the tradition of the *Blake Quarterly* special issue. Interpretive readings of the poem appear in book form with an obligatory nod of a few pages in preface or introduction to the difficulty occasioned by the state of the manuscript, and an appendix (almost a convention by now) on the "problem" of the two Nights VII. The tireless attempt by Bentley (back in 1963) to record types of paper, stitch marks, variations in the use of pen, pencil, and crayon, writing styles, and other aspects of the poem's physical make-up (along with Erdman's extensive reworking and critiques of Bentley's findings) have had limited visible impact on the construction of arguments by recent critics of *Vala*. I do not mean to say that these critics have not considered such matters fully and carefully in their private studies, rather that the critical arguments following upon these private researches do not make full use of the material complexity of the manuscript. While these books have offered, and continue to offer, new avenues into the study of the thematic, contextual, and narrative difficulties of the poem, none has yet fully embraced the material resistances of the poem – its state as manuscript with alternate readings, cancelled possibilities, uncertainties in direction, and variations in pen, ink, crayon, colour wash, stitch marks, writing styles, paper, and so on. These matters mark the poem as graphically as its characters, themes, and narrative complexities.

The exception to this trend is Andrew Lincoln's *Spiritual History* (1995), which offers a reading of the poem in light of its layered construction. My book follows on Lincoln's in its attempt to bring the interpretive concerns of previous books on *Vala* within the scope of the bibliographic complexities hitherto the domain of articles on the poem. The focus of my study is almost exclusively on *Vala*, and while this might at first seem narrow, the proliferation of studies mentioned at the outset of this Preface suggests that in recent years *Vala* has assumed a central position in Blake's canon and in the critical discourse surrounding Blake. Its growing centrality makes it an important site of discussion and debate, a site that is in no way isolated but that, when more fully explored, should influence other aspects of Blake study. My critical approach here is driven primarily by the physical state of the manuscript, with its many erasures, additions, and complex rearrangements, which require careful, focused, and detailed scrutiny. The method best suited to such scrutiny is that of a largely formalist reading, but one that also attempts to take account of recent theoretical movements. In adopting this approach I do not therefore mean to ignore the recent application of Marxist, feminist, deconstructionist, and a host of post-Saussurean theories to Blake but to emphasize that this early stage of bringing the material force of the manuscript into play with an interpretive approach necessitates a study weighted towards a close reading of textual detail.

It should be noted at the outset that I intend to focus more directly on the poetic than on the pictorial development of *Vala*. Any serious critic of Blake will inevitably feel uneasy about making such a separation between text and design in his works. My approach has been dictated partly by the general incompleteness of many of the drawings. While Magno and Erdman's facsimile offers helpful reconstructions of many of the erased drawings, the unfinished state of all but the drawings on the first few pages leaves the viewer lost in a field of conjecture with no firm basis for argument. In addition, the drawings do not readily lend themselves to the developmental discussion usually possible with a written text. John E. Grant summarizes the difficulties inherent in a discussion of the pictorial aspects of *Vala*:

the fact that a picture in *Vala* has been altered tells nothing about when the alteration was done. Blake might in the space of a day or two have tried out several versions of the picture; thus the amount of ascertainable connection between any text – any *surviving* text, we must constantly recall, in this much-altered manuscript – and any version of the picture is much more likely to have an intellectual or aesthetic cause than to be the result of a Blakean stylistic or organizational predilection. Often it is possible to speak meaningfully about "early" and "late" alterations of the text, but no principle is in sight for comparable assertions about the pictures.[6]

Thus it becomes exceedingly difficult to use the designs in *Vala* to support or refute any argument about the development of the text.[7] Therefore, although I will not entirely ignore the pictorial element, I believe that the exceedingly complicated textual matters in *Vala* merit a full-length study on their own and afford a unique opportunity to investigate an important period in the evolution of Blake's poetic thought.

Perhaps one of the most difficult aspects of this study for a post-Saussurean, poststructuralist reader resides in the questions of intentionality circling about the discussion of any manuscript. A full analysis of the relationship between manuscripts, intentionality, and poststructuralist theory would require a very different book, but I admit that in this discussion of the manuscript intentionality seems as unavoidable as it is unprovable, since the design of my book is to trace the process of change and development of the manuscript under the direction of one individual over a course of several years. I should point out here, however, that I am not attempting to reconstruct Blake's subjective thought processes, rather to trace out the evolution of a poetic construct. Intentionality is thereby a function of the manuscript rather than of an individual consciousness. I do, to some extent, construct a narrative about Blake's process of composition, and while all narratives are fictional, they also seem unavoidable and entirely necessary in this kind of critical project. I use narrative as a fundamental tool of the didactic work that makes the manuscript accessible without compromising its underlying complexities. I take seriously the possibility that the poststructuralist and formalist dimensions of my own work are in visible tension. Indeed, I think this tension is unavoidable. Close reading is essential to opening up this new way of looking at *Vala*, and provides a distinct complement to any post-structuralist observations about it. The powerful undercurrent of cultural materialism in Blake studies by Essick, Viscomi, and Eaves has drawn attention to the importance of the material condition of Blake's writing, and my close readings attempt to incorporate the material condition of the manuscript with theoretical concerns about poetic construction.

This book departs from a central tradition in Blake criticism in its attempt to approach his work as a developing form, in this case as exemplified in the manuscript of *Vala* or *The Four Zoas*. Essential to my argument is the assertion that Blake's poetics underwent a gradual shift during composition, transcription, and revision of the poem, a shift accompanied by a growing emphasis on synoptic and synchronic tendencies. The extensive accretion of new materials over the life of the poem's construction brings it into alignment with *Milton* and *Jerusalem*. The shared relationship of individual lines, characters, and whole passages creates a sense of parallelism with these later works, and in many cases the additions to *Vala* would make little or no sense without them. *Vala* thus gains an increasingly synoptic quality as it is revised.

Emerging in the late 1770s, synoptic studies involved setting the three Synoptic Gospels, Matthew, Mark, and Luke, in parallel columns "to facilitate the study of mutual dependence and difference."[8] Like the Synoptic Gospels, *Vala*, *Milton*, and *Jerusalem* have a "mutual dependence" in the way they overlap and share stories about the Fall. While Blake's poems cannot be presented in parallel columns as the synoptics can, Blake did see his three works as complementary and sought to bring *Vala* into closer alignment with the other two in terms of narrative and character. My concern here is not so much to compare *Vala* with *Milton* and *Jerusalem* but to demonstrate how the synoptic tendencies in Blake's revisions to *Vala* changed the fundamental poetics of narrative and character in the poem. Initially structuring the work along a roughly continuous, sequentially determinate, and diachronic narrative ranging from Fall to Redemption to Judgement, with only the conventional strategy of beginning *in medias res* to disrupt this sequence, Blake gradually altered the shape of the poem and its essential narrative poetics to highlight the discontinuous, the indeterminate, and the synchronic. Character also underwent a shift as it moved from a developmental coherence through engagement with temporal conflict to the transcendent constancy of symbolic attributes.

My essential argument is that the synoptic and synchronic tendencies of Blake's poetics are the result of conscious revision and correction of an essentially diachronic narrative. The synoptic allows for a build-up of diverse but related materials, the synchronic for alignment and association of these elements in vertical rather than horizontal relationship. I should emphasize at this point, however, that I see the synoptic and synchronic as tendencies emerging in the revision of *Vala* rather than in the original conception and early transcription of it.

In this argument I depart to some extent from one of the most influential critical statements made by Northrop Frye about Blake's work as a whole: "We have pointed out the unusual organic consistency of Blake's symbolism: we cannot trace it back to a time when its main outlines were not clear to him."[9] This statement has been taken to argue for a coherence of vision extending from the *Poetical Sketches* published in 1783 to *Jerusalem*, still in progress well after the 1804 date on the title-page. While there do seem to be points of consistent concern throughout Blake's career, all too often discussion of the "organic consistency" in the "main outlines" of his work overshadows points of experiment and development. Thus experiments connecting the "direful monster" of "To Winter" from the *Poetical Sketches* with the Urizen of the middle to late prophecies elide fundamental principles of poetic development and evolution.[10]

Essick's exemplary treatment of Blake as printmaker argues that his "technical experiments in a wide range of graphic media testify to his deep concern with the methods by which images are communicated,"[11] and Joseph Viscomi's *Blake and the Idea of the Book* continues this concern with Blake's developing relationship with these graphic media.[12] Moreover, the recent Trianon Press–Princeton reproductions show us a Blake intrigued with a broad range of variations within the main outlines of his own prints. Given this evidence of his graphic experimentation, scholars are at last moving to consider the subject of Blake's textuality, particularly as it is manifest in his illuminated and typographically produced work. In addition, two recent collections of essays, *Unnam'd Forms: Blake and Textuality* and *Critical Paths: Blake and the Argument of Method*, along with Mark Bracher's *Being Form'd* and Molly Anne Rothenberg's *Rethinking Blake's Textuality*, have complicated our understanding of experimentation in Blake, directing critical attention away from archetypal syntheses to poststructuralist textuality.

When we turn to Blake's manuscripts, however, they tell an even more complex tale of experiment and textuality. It is in the manuscripts that we see textual experiment most vitally enacted. They often evidence a tentativeness at odds with the more familiar idea of Blake, an idea associated with a highly assertive poetic voice. The extensive revisions in "The Tyger," for instance, depict what Martin Nurmi describes as a "dialectical struggle in which Blake strives to bring his emblematic tiger's two 'contraries' ... into ... 'fearful symmetry.'"[13] The painstaking revisions to this poem both large and small, the manifest evidence of "struggle," point to a dedication to development and experiment with verbal variation, syntax, and form. Looked at from this perspective, the manuscripts in particular exist as testaments to the incongruities that emerge in composition.

Perhaps nowhere in Blake's work is "struggle" more evident than in *Vala* or *The Four Zoas*. Flanked by the concise compression of the Lambeth prophecies on one side and the sprawling epics *Milton* and *Jerusalem* on the other, *Vala* or *The Four Zoas* stands as the record of transition and experiment in symbolism, characterization, theme, and especially in narrative method. Incomplete from the perspective of the illuminated work, unwieldy from the perspective of editorial containment, it offers a nearly complete view of poetic process and the turmoil of composition and revision. *Vala* or *The Four Zoas* – even the generally accepted double title suggests some kind of change somewhere – does not seem to have emerged fully formed from Blake's head with all the attendant characters and events that appear in the final manuscript. Characters were added; Christian imagery became more pronounced; the strife among characters generally increased as Blake revised the work. Vincent De Luca points out that "most of Blake's revisions are indeed re-*visions*; they register the eruption of new or deeper conceptions of a subject already rendered, and the fact of the re-seeing may form as much an element of what Blake wishes to impart as the conception seen anew."[14]

Only through a massive act of suppression does the manuscript fully conform to the notion of the unified text or mythic cohesiveness within a "canon" of work. While it is true that Blake seems intent on bringing the poem into alignment with the larger concerns of his mythology, particularly the mythology of the later phases, much in the manuscript is only part of a tentative revision in this direction. Often the synthesizing impulse of criticism – the tendency to create organic wholes at any cost – compromises the inherent stresses within the incomplete manuscript. Indeed, this synthesizing tendency emerges even within the editorial work of David Erdman. In an otherwise admirable edition of Blake's work, Erdman chooses to incorporate Night vii[b] within Night vii[a] despite a total lack of evidence in the manuscript for such a choice.

The work of the Santa Cruz Blake Group offers an essential corrective to the kind of editorial completion offered by Erdman; as they point out, "what the manuscript exhibits in the most graphologically explicit fashion is an ongoing, unfinished process of self-editing, a process which print ordinarily shuts down."[15] This statement acts as a background to my own methodology.

Since the publication of G.E. Bentley Jr's facsimile of the poem in 1963, little critical work (with the exception of several articles in *Blake Quarterly* and, more recently, Lincoln's *Spiritual History*) has been directed towards the impact of the physical manuscript on the interpretation of the poem. Most studies offer valuable exegesis of the work but often gloss over the implications of specific textual changes and the many complicated (even unresolvable) cruxes. Even Ault's seemingly exhaustive *Narrative Unbound*, while acknowledging the "veritable textual labyrinth"[16] of Blake's revisions, does not sustain a full-fledged investigation of the effects of these revisions. Ault tends to focus instead on conceptual patterns such as text as "flight" or as "woven pattern," as if these textual structures were constant in all layers of Blake's manuscript. While offering useful discussions of the historical and literary contexts within which Blake composed the poem and a valuable synthesis of the history of the reception of the poem to the present day, Rosso's book, *Blake's Prophetic Workshop*, has similar limitations. Rosso acknowledges that the "manuscript poses formidable obstacles to reading and comprehension,"[17] but he offers little direct discussion of the obstacles themselves or the way they shift in the course of revision.

The alternate critical path represented by critics such as Bentley, Erdman, and Andrew Lincoln[18] leads to the poem as a more composite form, sometimes as a pastiche of elements not all necessarily brought into conformity with a central design. The composite approach offers pieces of evidence, however uncertain at times, with which to trace Blake's process of composition in great detail. Lincoln's *Spiritual History* does much to restore the balance between an interpretive reading and attention to the impact of the manuscript on such readings. In its attempt to return this equilibrium to an analysis of the poem, it is very much a precursor of what I am attempting here. However, I am not as fully committed to the coherences within layers of the text as Lincoln is, and I also do not attempt a reading of the poem from start to finish. The textual revisions I discuss more extensively are examined as exemplary instances of wide-ranging practices in *Vala*. I do sense that the poem was evolving to a point of coherence, but one that was based on a notion of narrative structure radically different from that with which it began. Essentially, however, I am interested in the fluidity and occasional uncertainties evidenced in revision, leaving the poem as a monument to process rather than product, a literal palimpsest offering an analogy with what De Quincey described as the "natural and mighty palimpsest [of] ... the human brain."[19]

Even allowing for De Quincey's characteristic hyperbole, his mental palimpsest offers an apt description of the layering effect of the poem read as a manuscript rather than as a typographic text:

Everlasting layers of ideas, images, feelings have fallen upon your brain softly as light. Each succession has seemed to bury all that went before. And yet in reality not one has been extinguished. And if, in the vellum palimpsest, lying amongst the other *diplomata* of human archives or libraries, there is any thing fantastic or which moves to laughter, as oftentimes there is in the grotesque collisions of those successive themes, having no natural connection, which by pure accident have consecutively occupied the roll, yet, in our own heaven-created palimpsest, the deep memorial palimpsest of the brain, there are not and cannot be such incoherencies.[20]

In qualifying De Quincey's statement, I would not assert that all layers of the palimpsest can be recovered, or that anything approaching a complete account of all aspects of the manuscript's layering is possible. Undoubtedly certain incoherencies will remain. Any narrative of growth is bound to be selective; mine is no exception. Even a cursory glance at a reproduction of the manuscript reveals a process of revision that is at best daunting and at worst paralysing to anyone trying to see sense in this chaos of additions and deletions. Viewing the original manuscript in the British Library only confirms the complexity of the endeavour, bringing to light layers of palimpsest whose existence simultaneously tantalizes and frustrates. The complexity of the manuscript seems to dictate strategies of containment for any approach to its textual variants.

I strike a balance between a view of the poem as composite and coherent entity. Weighted towards the composite palimpsest on the one side, such a study might drown in a recitation of changing accidentals and other textual minutiae fated to cause the eyes of even the most dedicated Blake critic to glaze over; weighted towards the argument of coherence, on the other, such a study might lead to generalizations that fail to do justice to the subtlety and complexity of Blake's modifications. My evidence is therefore admittedly selective but attempts to be representative also.

As a further strategy of containment, I have chosen to approach the work in terms of two cental categories of poetics, narrative and character. Since at least the time of Aristotle these aspects of poetics have been considered central "qualitative" or defining features of literary form. While Aristotle described plot as the soul of tragedy and therefore the more important of the two, their interrelationship has often been noted.[21] Henry James's famous question, "What is character but the determination of incident? What is incident but the illustration of character?"[22] only reinforces the inextricable nature of these two elements. More recently, Shlomith Rimmon-Kenan has challenged the hierarchical relation of narrative and character, offering instead a model of interdependence.[23] This interdependence is relevant to my own discussion of *Vala* since shifts in narrative shape and character construction often seem interconnected, and it is often virtually impossible to say which came first. As Blake works on the poem, a tension emerges between the early desire to weave a number of narrative units, often derived from the earlier Lambeth works, into a coherent whole and the emerging tendency to use a disjunctive narrative to advance what Ault calls "anti-Newtonian" strategies or what I will call (following Morton Paley) a synchronous narrative often observed in the later works.[24] The shifting of narrative strategies gives the poem a flexible design, one whose outline as suggested in the subtitle – "the Death and Judgement of the Eternal Man" – gains its flexibility through conscious adaptations of sequential disruptions as a fundamental element in narrative experiment. In accord with these changes in narrative are those in characterization.

Given the extensive recent work in narrative, simple definitions are, not surprisingly, elusive at best.[25] In a polemic aimed against Russian Formalist and French narratological definitions, Barbara Herrnstein Smith distinguishes between narrative as structure and narrative as act.[26] My tendency is to opt for the former context (the latter is the main province of Ault's book). In this choice I do not move to the narratological extreme of Prince, Greimas, or Genette, but I am interested in outlining the way structural units shift from place to place in Blake's text and in how temporal sequences are interrupted or disrupted by additions and deletions in the manuscript. These disruptions change the shape and signifying power of narrative on both a micro- and a macrocosmic level. Increasingly the horizontal sequence of narrative is disrupted by insertions that direct attention to vertical significances, and these horizontal and vertical clashes intensify over the course of Blake's revisions. Narrative meaning, as Barthes points out generally, becomes as elusive as the purloined letter in Poe's tale: "the 'search' carried out over a horizontal set of narrative relations may well be as thorough as possible but must still, to be effective, also operate 'vertically': meaning is not 'at the end' of the narrative, it runs across it; just as conspicuous as the purloined letter, meaning eludes all unilateral investigation."[27]

The teleology of Blake's revisions seems ultimately to run in the direction of this vertically oriented perspective, and, as most commentators attest, the revision so directing the narrative structure "eludes all [or nearly all] unilateral investigation." While throughout this study I rely loosely, then, on binary oppositions developed in Russian Formalism and structuralism between vertical and horizontal, synchronic and diachronic, paradigmatic and syntagmatic, combinative and associative,[28] I attempt to avoid the totalizing and abstracting tendencies of these theoretical movements (to the degree that such avoidance is ever possible.) Derrida reminds us that "every transgressive gesture reencloses us" and also that "breaks are always, and fatally, inscribed in an old cloth that must continually, interminably be undone. This interminability is not an accident or contingency; it is essential, systematic, and theoretical."[29] Therefore I have attempted to use these elements from structuralist poetics to gain a point of entry into what Barthes calls the plurality of the text.

While the theoretical and critical discussion of narrative has been extensive, that devoted to character has been relatively limited and almost always attached to lengthy examination of narrative.[30] With the demise or splitting of the subject in poststructuralism, studies in poetics have not led to many full-scale studies of the verbal representation of character. At times it seems as if James's attempt to suggest an equipoise between the two terms has had limited impact on the development of a poetics of character. Again, however, my use of character arises from the suggestions offered by Barthes in *S/Z* that character "is an adjective, an attribute, a predicate," or, more in keeping with "the ideology of the person," "the sum, the point of convergence" of a set of signifying elements (what Barthes calls "semes") that cluster around a proper name.[31] The difficulty caused by Blake's revisions is that the clustering of "adjectives" can lead to a set of apparent contradictions in character attributes with each reworking of the poem. Take what appears to be a very simple instance: Enitharmon is described as "smiling / Bright" in the base transcription of page 10 (lines 1–2); the adjectives are revised to become "frowning / Dark." The change, if not producing a contradictory sense of the whole idea of stability in characterization, suggests a remarkable degree of freedom on Blake's part. There is no essential personality that he fears violating in such revisions; character shifts with the flexibility of context and narrative situation to enter into a new set of emerging designs.

One instance of the "flexible design" I noted a moment ago emerges from reading the physicality of Blake's manuscript in a self-reflexive moment on pages 44 and 45 (see Plate 6). These pages form a facing pair just beyond a moment of change in the kind of paper used for transcription, the density and style of handwriting, and the manner of binding the pages. (I will return to the technical details of these matters in my introduction.) They also appear at a crucial moment in the narrative, when Urizen's world collapses and Tharmas emerges from the wreckage to assert his new authority over the ruined universe:

> from the Dolorous Groan [of Urizen and his hosts] one like a shadow of
>    smoke appeard
> And human bones rattling together in the smoke & stamping
> The nether Abyss & gnasshing in fierce despair. panting in sobs
> Thick short incessant bursting sobbing. deep despairing stamping struggling
> Struggling to utter the voice of Man struggling to take the features of Man.
>    Struggling
> To take the limbs of Man at length emerging from the smoke
> Of Urizen dashed in pieces from his precipitant fall
> Tharmas reard up his hands & stood on the affrighted Ocean
> The dead reard up his Voice & stood on the resounding shore   (44:14–22)

The stamping, sobbing and struggling, the overall impression of indistinctness trying to shape itself into an articulate form of signification, offers an obvious moment of self-reflection in verbal creation. The illustration at the bottom of the page shows a human figure enacting this verbal emergence, its outlines incomplete, with only the expression of discomfort, perhaps horror, as part of the impression conveyed by the male figure's face. His body, particularly his left side – the lower bounding contours – remains unsketched except for a few seemingly random pencil strokes suggesting rather than confirming an act of completion. He looks out and up to see no one, to communicate to no one his anguish at struggling into form. The accompanying figure gracing the left margin seems impassive at best; she is even less defined than the prostrate figure, except for the "triptich or Gothic chapel outlined in her genital zone."[32] Critics find a degree of certainty in the prostrate figure; he is usually identified as Tharmas, sobbing, despairing, and struggling to take human form.[33] The standing figure's identity is less certain. She may be Vala; she may be Enitharmon; but nowhere in *Vala* is a female figure depicted or described as having a "genital tabernacle."[34] Whatever degree of certainty (or relief) we may find in identifying one sketchy figure as Tharmas is qualified by the enigmatic potentialities in the female figure. The basic incompletenesses and enigmas in Blake's transcription become points of departure for additional layerings (not always leading to more certainty themselves).

This general indistinctness jars against the facing-page transcription made on a proof for Edward Young's *Night Thoughts*. The supine figure offers a mirrored posture to the indistinct supine pencil sketch on page 44. The mirroring posture has him exhibiting facial features indicating some distress (perhaps not as intensely as the sketched figure) and looking and reaching up. A significant variation, however, shows a point of connection with the other human figure in the design, this time a male figure. The engraved bodily outlines of these two figures are distinct, complete, and sharpened into relief by a darkened background. The sharpness of definition is the sharpness of the engraving technique – the antithesis of the tentativeness and freely shifting boundaries of the pencil sketches. Still, the sharp definition in outline is belied by the potential uncertainties in the figures' identities. The standing figure is usually taken to be Christ, although Christ is not part of this section of the poem (nor, I might add, was he likely part of the poem at this stage in its transcription). And the supine figure? Is it Tharmas? Perhaps. But identity crises multiply for the interpreter since this proof was originally designed for Night IV of *Night Thoughts*. Here the supine figure is clearly Young's narrator, the standing figure a metaphorical extension of "That Touch with charm celestial, [that] heals the soul."[35] This particular allusion hints at an intertextual matrix in which Blake's and Young's poems potentially intersect with an indeterminacy that opens the text to the literary designs emerging from narrative and character. This intertextual matrix calls into question matters of origination – the conventional relationship of allusion and source – since the design for *Night Thoughts* was created before that for *Vala*, but the reader's experience of the text in this narrative order seems to establish the sketch as the source for the engraved design. As such the sketch seems to inscribe an alternate (or perhaps overlapping) vertical equivalence between the pictured experience of Tharmas and that of Young's narrator.

In a sense the two modes of production define the central antitheses experienced in reading the manuscript: at times sharply edged, clearly defined, certain in its direction as, for example, it describes Urizen's movement through the sixth Night; at others ill-defined, sketchy, uncertain in its messages about what lines are to be included or excluded or how pages are to be ordered in relation to one another (as in the case of the final pages of Night 1).

It is my contention that the only way to understand the poem as we have it is to engage directly with these inherently contradictory modes in the manuscript. I call these contradictory modes part of a "flexible design": the poem struggles with central aspects of literary design, aspects such as plot and character, narrative teleology, and verbal representation, attempting to enact an intelligible form at the same time as it struggles against this design. The struggle against articulation, however, is one that emerges in the process of revision rather than in the initial stages of composition. Repeated examination of the manuscript shows that the flexibility of Blake's design asserts itself against the central conventions of poetics within which the poem itself would logically seem to make sense. As a result, the poem is revised to enact its own meaning through emergent forms while it resists critical struggles to extract a comprehensive or satisfactory statement of its thematic relevance.

What I offer here is neither a return to the organic formalism of New Criticism nor the commitment to total indeterminacy of American deconstruction but a reading of Blake's manuscript that seeks to take fully into account the material form (and the material failure) of the manuscript as part of the critical reading process. Any critical reading will necessarily add to an already layered palimpsest of interpretations; the manuscript itself cannot be ignored as the most important layer in this palimpsest.

*Vala* or *The Four Zoas* is a distinctly layered event. Its meaning exists in the stages of development of the poem, not in its organic unity. This supposition has been too little registered in the field of Blake criticism, and it is this supposition the book attempts to explore.

This book is divided into two main parts. After an introductory section, including a description of the manuscript and a discussion of my hypotheses about Blake's methods of revision and recomposition, I turn to the narrative strategies that emerged in the process of revision. In particular, chapter 1 examines the problems Blake had in deciding how and where to start the poem; chapter 2 moves on to the cruxes of the two Nights VII and Night VIII. In Part 2 I turn to the poetics of character, beginning in chapter 3 with an examination of the way revisions to the copperplate transcription change the nature of some of the central figures in the poem. The following chapter looks at the development of Tharmas and the Spectre of Urthona in the middle transcription, and the final chapter examines the emergence of Rahab in the final stages of the manuscript's development. I conclude with a general discussion of the implications of this revisionary poetics to our reading of Blake's other works. Variants of a slightly different nature appear in the typographic and illuminated forms of Blake's works; reading these as a layered signifying event compromises the assertion of a stable textual form for critical examination.

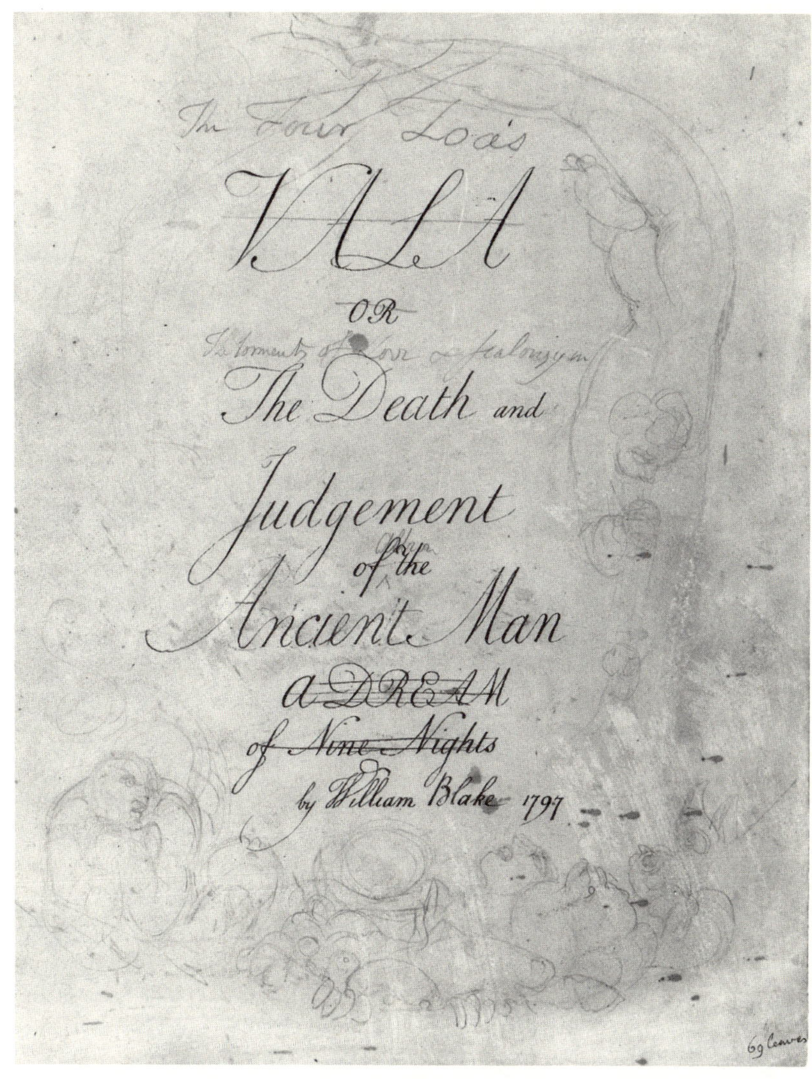

Plate 1   Page 1 of Blake's manuscript. The title changes are easily visible, even the rather tentative addition of "The Four Zoas."

Plate 2   Page 5. One of the most heavily revised pages in the entire manuscript. The copperplate transcription is completely erased, and the page contains much text added after the entire poem was transcribed.

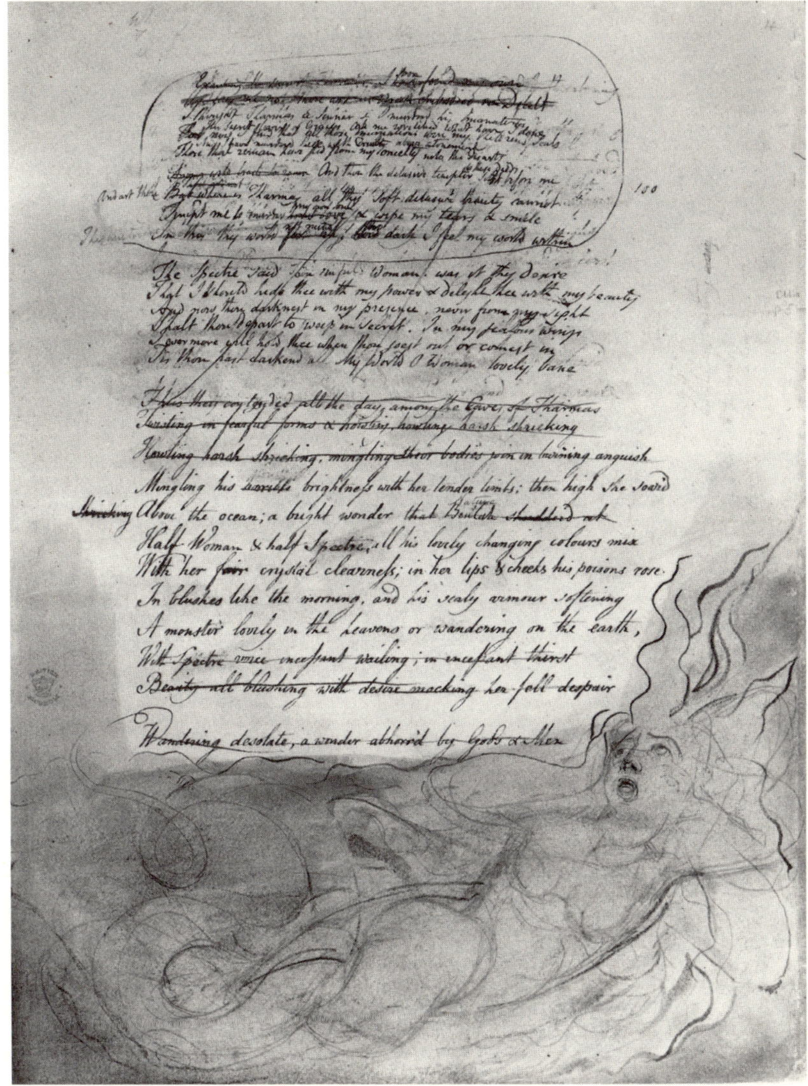

Plate 3   Page 7. The start of the copperplate text, with heavily revised opening section describing the violent union of a male and a female figure.

Plate 4    Page 23. Possibly conceived of as beginning the poem at one time.

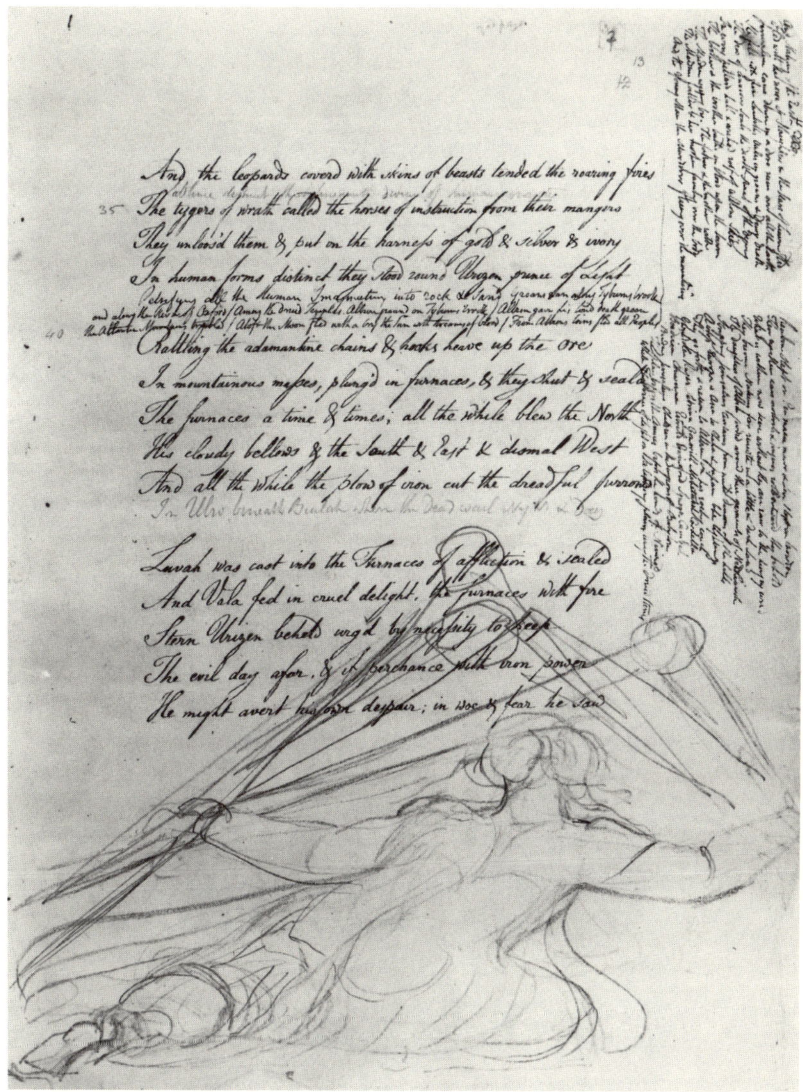

Plate 5   Page 25. The mixture of early copperplate text and later additions in the usual hand is clearly visible here.

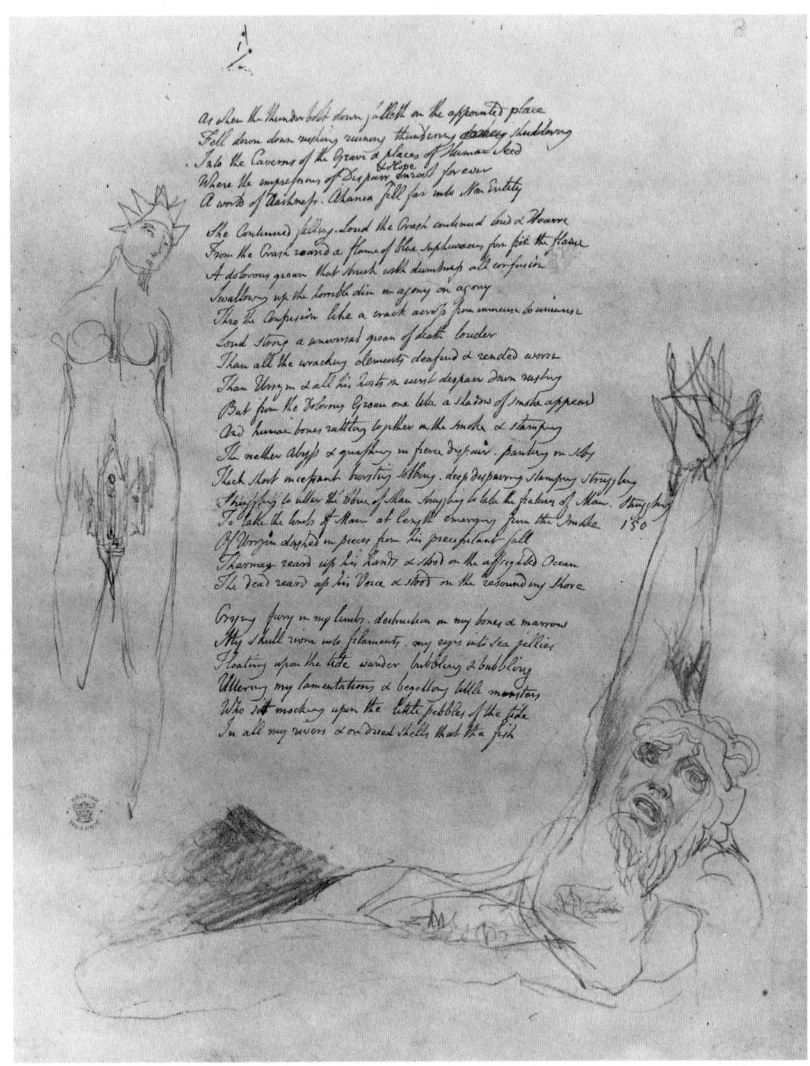

Plate 6   Facing pages 44 and 45. A good example of Blake's usual hand, with sketchy portraits of a female and a male figure on page 44. The male figure is a conscious echo of the figure on page 45, from the *Night Thoughts*

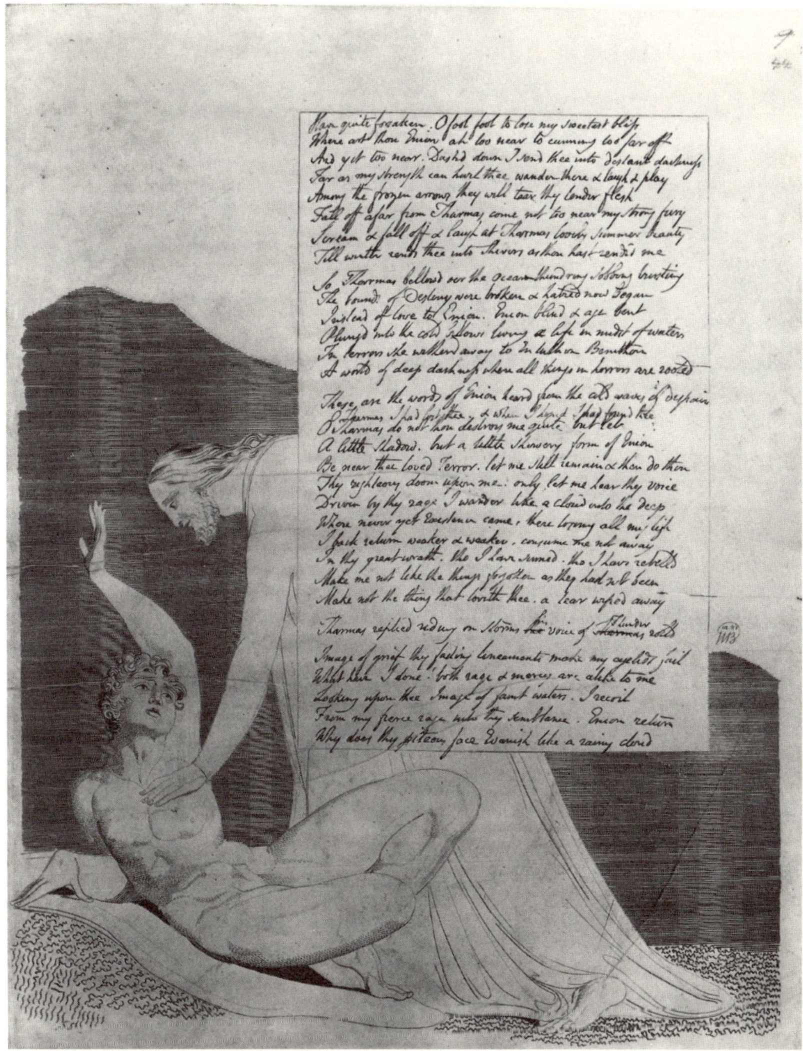

proofs. The sharpness of Blake's engraved figures there contrasts strikingly with the sketchiness of such figures as those on page 44.

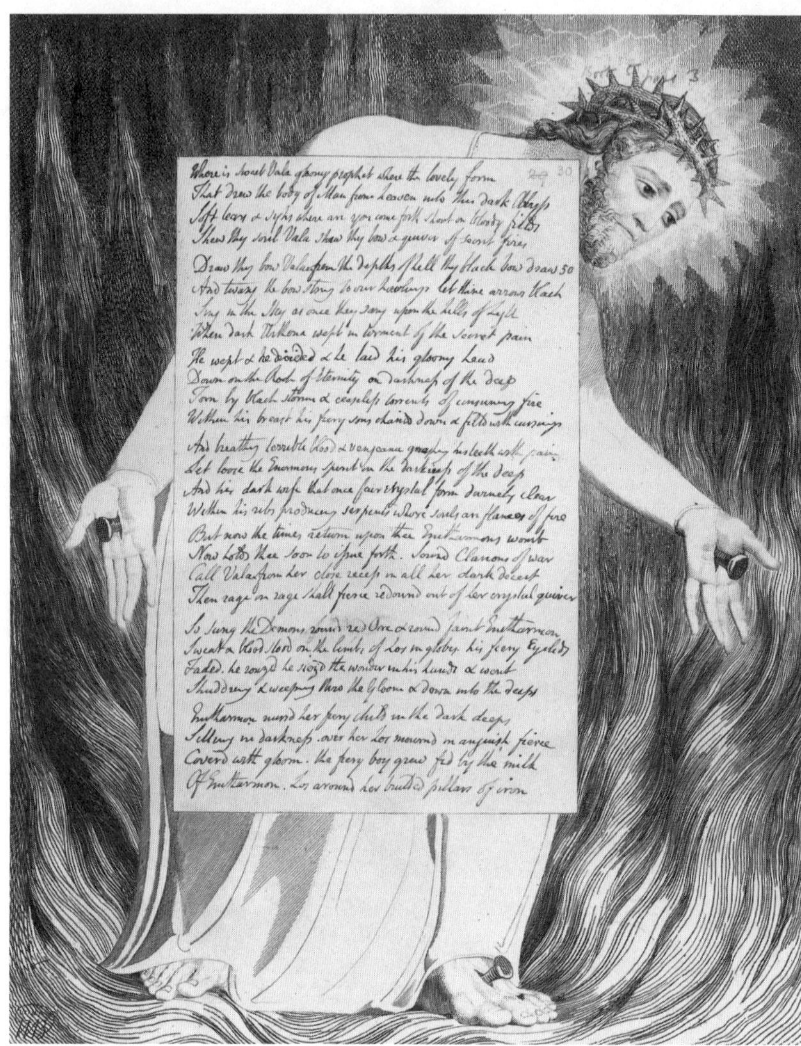

Plate 7    Page 59. An example of the usual hand transcribed on the proofs for Young's *Night Thoughts*.

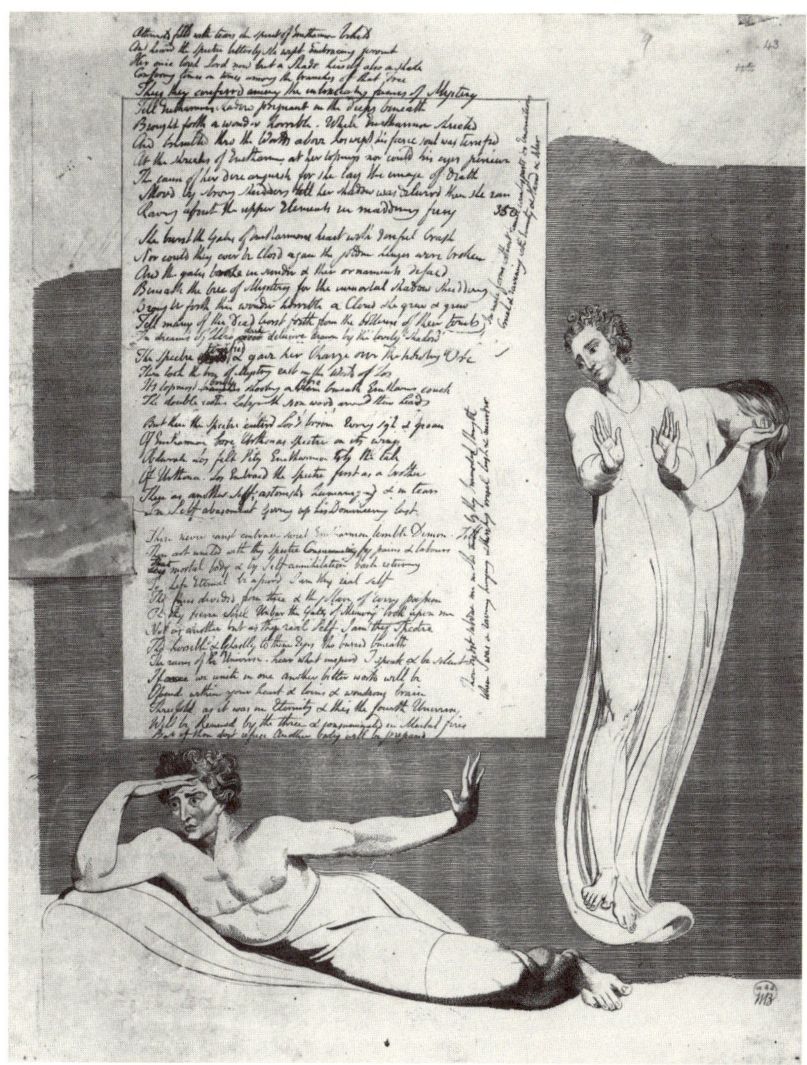

Plate 8   Page 85. The end of Night vii[a], a central crux in which Blake extended the end of the Night several times.

# Introduction:
# Manuscript and Poetics

Since Blake does not mention *Vala* or *The Four Zoas* by name in his correspondence or other prose works, it is difficult to develop a complete argument about the genesis of the poem from external sources.[1] Any critical approach must rely mainly on piecing physical evidence in the manuscript together with internal evidence supplied by the poem itself. Yet even a cursory glance at the often contradictory accounts of the development of *Vala* offered by Bentley, Erdman, and more recently Andrew Lincoln reveals that descriptions based on internal manuscript evidence may be no more definitive than attempts to find external evidence. Erdman reminds us that "only a sorting of fragments and a fragmentary tale of growth may ever be possible; yet at every turn some unexpected chink may offer further access, or we may be halted by some new challenge to bibliographic ingenuity."[2] Despite the fragmentary nature of this tale, a few relatively fixed elements observable in the physical format of the manuscript and some generally agreed-upon theories about the phases of transcription allow us to develop a rudimentary account of Blake's method of composition and revision. My object here is not to offer an exhaustive narrative of the mass of textual minutiae in the manuscript but only to recite the essential, if fragmentary, details that form the ground-plan for my later discussion of Blake's use of narrative experiment to contain his continued revisions to the poem.

## THE MANUSCRIPT:
## ITS FORMAT AND DIVISIONS

The physical format of the manuscript itself, as Bentley has pointed out, falls into three main groupings,[3] and each group of pages corresponds approximately to a different phase in the poem's development.[4] The first group includes the transcription of the first forty-two pages of the manuscript on blank sheets supplied to Blake for his *Night Thoughts* proofs. Bentley has labelled the "elaborate, beautiful, and delightfully clear" handwriting Blake used on these pages the "copperplate hand" (B.196).[5] This "copperplate text" includes a heavily erased version of the First Night, all of the Second and roughly the first two-thirds of the Third.[6] Bentley argues that it was "surely intended as the model to be copied when the poem was engraved" (B.158). Later critics have disputed or modified this assumption, however. Erdman suggests that "the objective of these carefully ruled and beautifully inscribed and 'ambitiously' illustrated pages was not to be the model for something else but to be themselves a unique Illuminated Manuscript."[7] Paul Mann offers the idea that Blake "was either testing the possibility of using the *Night Thoughts* designs directly to frame his own letterpress text, or using those designs as a general model while planning to replace them with new designs; or perhaps at different stages of composition, he considered doing both."[8] Recently, Robert Essick has argued convincingly that Blake originally intended to etch *Vala* in intaglio just as he had done for *The Book of Los* and *The Book of Ahania*. Essick then, following Mann's theory, suggests "that the change from fine scripts to plain might record a change in publishing plans" from intaglio etchings or engraving to "a letterpress text accompanied by intaglio etched and/or engraved designs surrounding selected pages of text." Yet as Essick himself admits, "it is impossible to prove any theory about Blake's production plans for *The Four Zoas*"; we can only hope for "a better understanding of the manuscript and the intentions it never completely reveals."[9]

It appears, then, that whatever Blake's original intentions for this copperplate manuscript, he abandoned or simply changed his mind about them. Thus, the second group of pages was transcribed on proof sheets for Young's *Night Thoughts*. These *Night Thoughts* proof sheets, including pages 43–84 and 111–12, were at one time stitched together by Blake. The text on these pages includes the latter third of Night III, Nights IV, V, and VI, and most of the first of the two Nights VII (known as VII[a]). The script on these pages appears in Blake's "usual hand," the handwriting he used for everyday writing activities in letters and revisions to his manuscripts (B.196; see Plate 7). This writing is cramped and often difficult to read, but with it Blake was able to get from 30 to 38 lines per page, compared with about 16 per page in the copperplate hand (B.158, 162). The hurried writing, relatively few slips or erasures, and the increased line-count suggest a rather rushed transcription, perhaps Blake's attempt to create a fair copy from a revised or messy rough draft. Before additions, the text of this section appears uniform in terms of theme, plot, characterization, image, and tone. Perhaps for these reasons Blake decided to bind these pages (and whatever else may have been lost) together as a completed unit. Bentley has established a date of sometime after the end of May 1802 for the transcription of pages 48ff. on the basis of his discovery, on page 48, of a "faint impression of mirror-printing, made when the still damp leaf of the last page of Hayley's first *Ballad* was pressed against it [page 48] in the process of printing the *Ballad* engraving" (B.162).[10]

The third group is somewhat similar in physical appearance to the second in that it too is written on *Night Thoughts* proof sheets in Blake's usual hand, with about 38 lines per page. Unlike the second group, though, these pages were never stitched together. This section includes pages 85–140, comprising the last page of Night VII[a], another Night VII (denoted VII[b]), Night VIII, and Night IX. Presumably, as revisions were constantly added to the manuscript as the poem evolved, Blake did not wish to take the time to rebind his manuscript in case he found it necessary to add more pages. The text of this transcription seems to follow logically on that of group two; however, Night VIII and portions of Night IX reflect the early impact of Christian imagery on Blake's work. The entrance of this new element into the poem signals a slight change in the direction of Blake's thought, away from exclusive use of his own mythological creations to a direct adaptation of Biblical figures and stories. Although no certain date can be established for Blake's use of Christian imagery in the poem, the letters after around 1802 show a renewed interest in Christianity. The poetry reflects this renewed per-sonal vision by at least 1804, the date on the title-pages of *Milton* and *Jerusalem*. Thus it seems safe to assume that group three was transcribed in the period 1803–05.[11]

I would also add to Bentley's list another grouping composed of a miscellaneous collection of sheets added to the manuscript at various stages late in its development. For the most part these leaves seem to be late additions to the poem. Among these is leaf 21–22, added to the conclusion of Night I. It contains material transferred from Night VIII and was presumably partially stitched into Night I after VIII was written. Leaf 19–20 was also added to the end of Night I. The characters and symbolism on this leaf are drawn largely from *Jerusalem* and therefore seem to date from a later period as well. Of the remaining miscellaneous pages Bentley remarks, "Pages 87–90 also show signs of being a very late addition. It is a different kind of paper; the handwriting is smaller than that usually used; there are no stitching holes; and there is no line numbering or 'End of the Night.' This evidence suggests that it was added after Night VIII was completed" (B.195–6). Moreover, the text on these pages introduces Los's reconciliation with his Spectre and Enitharmon as a central preparation for the Last Judgement, but there is no real preparation for him in this role in the preceding Nights, and he plays only a minor part in the following Nights. Finally, although Bentley leaves them out, I would tend to include pages 111–16 in this grouping, since they were not a part of the first transcription of the present Night VIII, and the symbolism on these pages seems to be of a kind later than that of the rest of Night VIII.[12] Also, like pages 19–22 and 87–90, leaves 113–14 and 115–16 have no stitch marks or line numbering and have smaller than usual handwriting, allowing Blake to get more than his average of 30 to 38 lines per page of text.[13] These complicated textual matters are summarized in Table 1.1.

## THE PHASES OF TRANSCRIPTION

As we trace Blake's progress through these groups of pages, it appears that he began sometime around 1797 to transcribe the first portion of his poem in the fine copperplate hand, but then for some unknown reason changed to his usual hand and the *Night Thoughts* sheets for his remaining drafts after 1802. The copperplate text has a relatively small cast of characters: Los, Luvah, Urizen, Enion, Enitharmon, Vala, and Ahania. There is also an Ancient or Eternal Man and a host of Elemental Spirits. Tharmas, his Spectre, the Spectres of Urthona, the Daughters of Beulah, the Lamb of God, and the host of biblical characters are absent from the initial transcription of these pages. The rather limited cast of characters and the more intensive focus on developing each pair of male and female characters reflect the early stages of Blake's poem: as he continued to transcribe the work, Blake expanded his central group of characters and developed in intricate detail the complicated interrelationship of each figure with all the others. At this point in his

Table 1.1
Format and Divisions of the *Vala* Manuscript

| | *Copperplate text* | *Usual hand on* Night Thoughts *proofs* | |
| | *I* | *II* | *III* |
|---|---|---|---|
| Pages | 1–42 | 43–84 | 85–140 |
| Nights | i–iii[a] | iii[b]–vii[a1] | vii[a2]–ix |
| Stitched | Yes | Yes | No |
| Handwriting | Copperplate (with additions in modified copperplate and usual hand) | Usual hand | Usual hand |
| Lines per page | 16 | 30 (iii–v) 35–8 (vi–vii[a1]) | 35–8 |
| Anomalous leaves | 15–16, 19–20, 21–2 | 56 | 87–8, 89–90, 111–12, 113–14, 115–16, 117–18 |
| Date | ?1797 | 1802 | ?1803–?05 |

transcription, however, Blake was content with a limited set of principal actors and the description of their falls away from a state of unity within the Eternal Man.

Pages 43–84, the second group, seem to represent part of a single draft of the poem that followed upon the transcription of the copperplate text. This draft of the poem may have extended to the end of the present Night IX but probably did not include the present basic version of Night VIII (from 99–110:28). It is possible that Blake transcribed portions of the poem before the entire work was complete, but it appears that he had, at one time, a relatively complete version of *Vala* that was probably pre-Christian in both vehicle and tenor. Much of the action and symbolism on pages 43–84 is drawn either directly or indirectly from the Lambeth books. The binding and creation of Urizen by Los and the birth and binding of Orc are mainly an expansion and elaboration of events in *The Book of Urizen*. The conflict between Urizen and Orc in Night VII[b] (not stitched in with this group) is more or less an extrapolation of *America* and may have been composed in the same draft with pages 43–84. Also, with the exception of Tharmas, Enion, the Spectre of Urthona, Luvah, and Vala, there are no new major characters in the text of pages 43–84 who do not appear in the Lambeth books. Moreover, the narrative of these Nights follows a relatively coherent and consistent development, although it appears that as Blake approached a description of the Apocalypse and the necessary narrative transition to the redemptive process of the Last Judgement, he experienced significant difficulties. Blake's difficulties in large part arise from his introduction of biblical and Christian symbolism, particularly that derived from Revelation, to the latter two Nights of his text. In the wake of such additions we find a second version of Night vii and a heavily revised version of Night viii. The latter introduces several new characters not appearing elsewhere in the poem (except in additions) and a relatively disjointed narrative unlike that of the previous Nights. Night ix contains only the barest hint of the new symbolism in Night viii and thus appears to have been composed and transcribed before Night viii was finished in its present form.[14] From these various and often confusing factors we can speculate further on the steps in Blake's post-Christian additions to the poem.

As I noted above, Night ix, in its restricted use of late symbolism, appears to have been written earlier than Night viii. With its references to the Lamb of God on page 122 and the book of Revelation, however, Night ix may mark all that is left of the initial turn towards the direct inclusion of Christian imagery in the poem. The rather isolated presence of the Christian imagery in Night ix suggests that this symbolism was in its nascent stages when Blake transcribed the Night. As this symbolism developed, Blake concentrated on a revision of the apocalyptic turning-point in his poem in order to prepare for such a biblically influenced ending and to stress the thematic importance of this imagery.

The present Night viii, with its many additions and disjointed narrative, seems to indicate extensive tampering preceding the transcription of pages 99–110. Bentley suggests that Blake wrote an earlier version of Night viii that "may have described a titanic war among the Zoas ... [that] would have resulted in 'Universal Confusion' (with which Night ix begins, page 119), and been resolved, perhaps, in the reunion of the four Zoas in the Eternal Man" (b.163). As Blake added his Christian symbolism to this earlier version of viii, it "probably became exceedingly long and unwieldy, and almost of its own accord broke into two Nights" (b.163). Thus Blake recopied this earlier (hypothetical) version of Night viii into the present Night vii[b] and Night viii (the latter extending over pages 99–110:28 before additions). Andrew Lincoln has developed these assumptions further to show the displacement of elements from this earlier version of Night viii to the retranscribed forms of Nights vii[b] and viii. He argues convincingly that "there are traces of a narrative sequence which may have been dislocated in the process of revision. This sequence probably began with the embrace of Vala and Orc, may have described how Urizen's empire-building culminated in an apocalyptic confrontation with Tharmas and Los and in the collapse of Urizen's web and the stupefaction of all of Man's faculties except Los – who pulled down the heavens."[15] Although no argument can hope to explain all the anomalies in the manuscript, Bentley and Lincoln do offer a reasonable explanation for the existence of two Nights VII, the rather chaotic state of VIII, and how the transition in Blake's thought after 1800 affected the later stages of his manuscript.

## POETICS OF REVISION

Armed with this basic understanding of the physical properties of the manuscript and a general theory of its overall development, we can now construct a set of hypotheses about Blake's methods of revision and subsequent recomposition with a view to exploring the implications of the emerging poetics of the poem. Although we have no external testimony about Blake's methods of composition, there is much internal evidence to suggest that he often composed short passages of a few lines or pages and then attempted to yoke a series of short sections together into a longer narrative.[16] Recently V.A. De Luca has shown how chapter 2 of *Jerusalem* began with a "hypothetical core" sequence of plates to which Blake later added other units that contain an "autonomous coherence both in verbal content and in framing visual design."[17] It is likely that Blake may have composed these autonomous segments at different times and then brought them together within the larger framework of *Jerusalem*. "The work as a whole," argues De Luca, "comes to look like a compilation of brief epic lays devoted to the same cycle of myths, with the inevitable variations, overlaps, and repetitions that such compilations display"[18] and is consistent with Blake's view of the synoptic and synchronic tendencies of all myths.[19] As a result, the layout of the work militates against a linear reading.

Morton Paley's discussion and charting of what he calls the "synchronous" form of *Jerusalem*'s narrative reveals how diligently Blake worked to separate and obscure causal connections between events. The synchronic form, as Paley points out, "is primarily to be read not for its relatively subordinated story line but for the way in which its interrelated parts explain one another."[20] The consistency of this kind of construction in *Jerusalem* lends a peculiar cohesiveness to the work that creates difficulties and misunderstandings in a simple reading of the text from beginning to end but still allows us to call the work a unity, or, from Blake's viewpoint as writer, a work of unified fragments.

In the case of *Vala*, these synoptic and synchronic tendencies are more evident in the process of revision than in the initial transcription. In attempting to fuse smaller, later narratives into the larger earlier one, Blake sometimes introduces potential threats to the coherence of the poem but then incorporates these threats by accentuating discontinuity as a strategy within the framework of synoptic and synchronic narrative. Developed from discrete units, the synoptic narrative, like that constructed from the first three Gospels, enlarges into a set of overlapping visions whose coherence is resolved in synchronic alignment both within the poem and across Blake's other works, often at the expense of diachronic logic and sequence. As the revision progresses, the associative properties of the synchonic emerge in competition with the syntagmatic relations of the diachronic. Ultimately, the synoptic impulse carries the work into a revisionary poetics that seeks to incorporate all forms of what I might call here "micro-narratives" within a larger conceptual whole.

To some extent, the notion of a micro-narrative is similar to De Luca's use of the "epic lays" bound together into a single whole. However, I wish to use the term micro-narrative as a complement to the macro-narrative that comprises the whole poem. In looking at the introduction of later episodic elements, I find that these later micro-narratives are not always wholly consonant with the predominantly diachronic form of the macro-narrative. The later micro-narratives are often of greater density and allusiveness than the surrounding narrative and tend to create ruptures in the existing macro-narrative of *Vala*. Blake capitalizes on these ruptures in sequence and significance by making a virtue of discontinuity. In a strange way the macro-narrative begins to reorganize its formal characteristics around those of the invading micro-narrative rather than the other way around.

The steady addition of these micro-narratives creates pressure within the flow of the original narrative, resulting in ruptures in the sequential orientation of the macro-narrative; the subsequent ruptures reorient the build-up of signification in a vertical rather than horizontal relationship. While the organic reciprocity of micro- and macro-forms could argue for their equal influence, and a strictly ontological process framed in what Derrida has called a "metaphysics of presence" would render the macro the stabilizing centre for the micro-forms, neither is wholly the case in Blake's adaptation of micro-narrative. While there does seem to be some sign of organic connection across the micro- and macro-levels, the connections often seem a result of the fact that both narrative forms emerge from the same mythic structure framed by Blake. In his additions it often seems that the newly added material begins to dominate and realign the already existing macro-narrative in relation to synchronic, associative properties rather than diachronic, syntagmatic ones. While any number of changes and additions might be cited at this point as proof, two in particular – two relatively late additions – will serve effectively as points of departure for a set of hypotheses about Blake's revisionary poetics: the first, a lengthy addition of the text on pages 113–16 to Night VIII; the second, a shorter addition of lines 6–33 on page 25 of Night II.

*Micro-Narrative 1: pages 113–16*

Ostensibly, the text of pages 113–16 offers a detailed working out of the Looms, Forges, Spindles, and Mills associated with Enitharmon, Los, Rahab and Tirzah, and Satan respectively. While these symbolic attributes are not elsewhere associated with the particulars of character and setting represented in the base transcription of *Vala*, they are relevant as part of the synoptic framework of Blake's overall myth as it develops in *Milton* and *Jerusalem*. The Mills of Satan are a crucial backdrop to the Bard's song in *Milton*; the Looms, Forges, and Spindles help to contextualize the work of Enitharmon, Los, and Rahab and Tirzah in *Jerusalem*. Similarly, the panoply of Sons of Los and Enitharmon, the conflict of Satan and Palamabron, the doctrine of States, and the advent of the Seven Eyes of God are all elements grounded more solidly in *Milton* and the background of *Jerusalem* than in the base text or even many of the later additions to *Vala*. Indeed, the text on these pages, although transcribed on *Night Thoughts* proof sheets like those that surround them, does not necessarily appear to have been written expressly for *Vala*; page 113 originally began, "Daughters of Beulah describe Enitharmons Looms & Los's forges," and thus seems to have been intended for another, perhaps more general, context. The entire text of pages 113–15 reads more like an attempt by Blake to consolidate the imagery and character relations in his developing mythology as it grew more complicated. The overly schematic presentation of symbolism in the first half of page 113 and rather mechanical listing of "the Sons of Los & Enitharmon" on page 115 sound like a workbook of Blake's mythology between the writing of *Milton* and *Jerusalem*. References to events in the Bard's Song in *Milton* (115:12–17) and the doctrine of States and Individuals, without any explanation of these events, suggest that

Blake composed these pages after much of *Milton* was written, perhaps in an attempt to summarize important elements of his grand poetic universe within a narrow compass. In adding these pages to *Vala*, he seems to have been relatively unconcerned that the introduction of new and unexplained characters, events, or symbols to his main narrative might result in potentially irreparable damage to the poem; he seems to have been intent only upon a synoptic process of revision and expansion at any cost. Roughly the first third of the entire micro-narrative covered by pages 113–16 is inserted into the core of the song of "the Sons of Eden" (104:5) between two grammatically parallel expressions:

> Now we behold redemption Now we know that life Eternal
> Depends alone upon the Universal hand & not in us
> Is aught but death In individual weakness sorrow & pain   (104:8–10)

and

> We now behold the Ends of Beulah & we now behold
> Where Death Eternal is put off Eternally.   (104:11–12)

The addition of lines 1–39 of page 113 places the Looms, Forges, Spindles, and Mills, the conflict of Los and Palamabron, and the destruction of the "Universal Humanity" (33) by Rahab within the context of redemptive vision. Framed by two portions of the hymn by the Sons of Eden "to the holy Lamb of God" (104:6), the narrative sequence describing the putting off of the Satanic body is enclosed in sequences of vision appealing to the vertical perspective linked to the Incarnation. Through this strategy, Blake encloses the pain of Crucifixion – part of the temporal identity of the Lamb – within the hymn to Incarnation, a hymn that points to the failure of the material to diminish the divinity of the Lamb:

> Assume the dark Satanic body in the Virgins womb
> O Lamb divin it cannot thee annoy O pitying one
> Thy pity is from the foundation of the World & thy Redemption
> <Begun> Already in Eternity.   (104:13–16)

The next two-thirds of the micro-narrative on pages 113–16 would seem to have caused Blake greater difficulties as he brought it into the main narrative of Night VIII. Placed after the identification of Rahab as "Mystery Babylon the Great the Mother of Harlots" (106:6), pages 113–15 occasion additions to the bottom of page 106 and 113, additions recounting the removal of the Lamb of God from the Cross and heightening the juxtaposition of Rahab's error with Los's increasing vision. Partly a nod to the principles of causal sequence, these additions offer only tangential motivation for what follows: Los's statement of self-recognition in response to his sight of the Crucifixion and Rahab's part in it. I cannot help but suspect that Blake included this speech, in which Los says, "I am that shadowy Prophet who six thound years ago / Fell from my station in the Eternal bosom" (113:50–2), as part of an attempt to intensify the sense of Los's visionary powers in accord with the additions at the end of Night VII[a]. Motivated initially, perhaps, by a desire for coherence and a concern to foreground the role of Los, the actual attempts to integrate this large-scale proclamation of prophetic insight have several other effects on the narrative.

When we examine the text of pages 113:40 through 115 and 116 more closely, we begin to suspect that these pages themselves were not necessarily conceived of as a narrative whole. The first eleven lines of page 115 have an independent life in the catalogue of the Sons of Los & Enitharmon. Appearing in both *Milton* and *Jerusalem*, portions of these lines stand as constant points of reference in shifting contexts. The doctrinal lines on States and Individuals (23–7) and the Seven Eyes of God (42–50) also appear in *Milton* and have a certain autonomy from narrative that makes them easily movable units. Like counters in a game, they move from square to square, retaining a basic identity that shifts slightly according to location. Beginning with a few simple gestures towards contextualization, Blake makes cosmetic changes to page 115, changes designed to place its text within the frame of Los's speech at the bottom of page 113. Past tense becomes present; "their" becomes "our," and "Los" becomes "Me," to recontextualize this passage from third-person narrative to first-person proclamation. No longer a simple recitation of genealogy, past conflict, or doctrines about States, Individuals, and the Seven Eyes of God, the passage, now framed within Los's own discourse, validates his assertion that "I am that shadowy Prophet who six thound years ago / Fell from my station in the Eternal bosom" (50–1). His recognition is extratemporal and results in the expression of knowledge beyond the immediate narrative, knowledge that reaches out, not into eternity but into Blake's later (and at this point in his life, developing) texts.

This peculiar form of incestuous intertextuality draws a family of works into a vertical relationship that demands a synchronous approach by Blake's reader. The entire project of heightening Los's significance as the

Prophet of Eternity serves to incorporate the core conflicts in *Jerusalem*, conflicts that place Los at the poem's conceptual centre. The synoptic parallelism in both *Vala* and *Jerusalem* constructed around Los's attempt to keep his eyes fixed on the Divine Vision is bolstered by a narrative of juxtapositions placing Crucifixion and Incarnation, Rahab and Los, in constant tension. Such narrative juxtaposition gives primacy to consistent thematic relationships and synchronic identities, rendering secondary the sequential, causal, and diachronic forces active in the development of character. Thus Los develops through the significance of a series of parallel situations throughout Blake's works rather than as an accrued function of a series of events and experiences in a single narrative.

*Micro-Narrative 2: Page 25:6–33*

Our next passage for discussion – the addition of lines 6–33 to page 25 – illustrates even more boldly the inexorability of the syncretic impulse in the development of the poem and the resulting realignment of the work's characterization and narrative around synchronic principles (see Plate 5). This brief passage, one comprised of only twenty-seven lines, constitutes a particularly late addition to the poem, making full use of the characters, place names, and druidical symbolism typical of the later developments in *Jerusalem*. Representing Blake's most mature and complex stage of thinking, this addition synthesizes many divergent elements in the poet's late thought – the fusion of biblical and British symbolism, the exile of "all Peoples and Nations" (25:11) from Albion's limbs, and the fate of Reuben, Levi, and the Daughters of Albion – but enters *Vala* with no supporting internal or diachronic frame of reference. Indeed, the contrast of early and late styles in *Vala* is perhaps nowhere more evident than in this juxtaposition of micro- and macro-narrative. Set within the copperplate transcription of Urizen's creation of his Golden World, this brief addition stands in stark contrast to the macro-narrative contexts established in the early development of the poem. Not only are the narrative elements at odds with the existing copperplate text, but the process of characterization creates a Urizen distinctly different from that seen in the pre-existing narrative context.

In the earliest portions of the copperplate text Urizen's act of creation does not manifest the extreme malevolence that appears in this and other later additions. Any limitations or negative associations in his "Golden World" seem more a function of the fact that he creates out of "fear & pale dismay" (24:2) and that he struggles to create order from the fallen chaotic "world of Tharmas, where in ceaseless torrents / His billows roll where monsters wander in the foamy paths" (33:6–7). The earliest version of Urizen's creation as an act of mercy, as protection against a world of chaos, predominates in the copperplate text. As Michael Benzel points out, Urizen acts under orders from the Eternal Man and does the best he can in building a world without having access to imagination.[21] Donald Ault concurs in this assessment, demonstrating that one of the main perspectives of Night II is that of "Urizen's creation *as a redemptive act*"; the redemptive vision "expresses (and is bound to) Urizen's consciousness that Albion has given him legitimate power to 'rebuild' the universe from its present crisis state and his certainty that his aesthetic creation is positive and redemptive, despite the anxiety he feels and the suffering he glimpses on the fringes of his awareness."[22] When Urizen is called by the Man, he faces a fallen existence that is nearly non-existence, and his reaction is understandable:

> Pale he beheld futurity; pale he beheld the Abyss
> Where Enion blind & age bent wept in direful hunger craving
> All rav'ning like the hungry worm, & like the silent grave
> Mighty was the draught of Voidness to draw Existence in
>
> Terrific Urizen strode above, in fear & pale dismay
> He saw the indefinite space beneath & his soul shrunk with horror
> His feet upon the verge of Non Existence ...   (23:15–24:4)

Despite this vision of a future of horror in a world of "Non Existence," Urizen rises to his task and creates "the stars of heaven ... like a golden chain / To bind the <B>ody of Man to heaven from falling into the abyss" (33:16–17). Urizen's world is like that perceived by the Bard of Experience in which the "starry floor" and "watry shore" are both the foundations of existence that protect man from further fall until "the break of day" and also the physical boundaries restraining man's spiritual activities.[23] Thus, Urizen's work of creation is described in terms of sublime grandeur achieved through the exercise of rational restraint:

> And the leopards coverd with skins of beasts tended the roaring fires
> The tygers of wrath called the horses of instruction from their mangers
> They unloos'd them & put on the harness of gold & silver & ivory
> In human forms distinct they stood round Urizen prince of Light
> Rattling the adamantine chains & hooks heave up the ore

In mountainous masses, plung'd in furnaces, & they shut & seald
The furnaces a time & times; all the while blew the North
His cloudy bellows & the South & East & dismal West
And all the while the plow of iron cut the dreadful furrows.   (25:1, 3–5, 34–8)

Placed after the fourth line quoted above, the twenty-seven-line addition radically alters the tone, character, and narrative structure of the scene. Gone are the "tygers of wrath" and "the horses of instruction" so reminicent of *The Marriage of Heaven and Hell*; these images are superseded by the expressly anthropomorphic forms of Albion, Jerusalem, Reuben, Levi, and the Daughters of Albion. The change in character with the addition of the new micro-narrative moves the depiction of Urizen away from any sense of pity for him. The new addition picks up on the participle of line 34 and shifts the energetic action of "Rattling" to the reductive constrictions of "Petrifying"; Urizen's work is now defined as "Petrifying all the Human Imagination into rock & sand" (25:6).

Against the newly defined anthropomorphic background Urizen's actions are recast as an objective counterpart of an actively malevolent character. He is still engaged in an act of construction, but the new narrative refocuses his work solely and emphatically as an act of constriction. Where elements of constriction are suggestively placed in the copperplate text, the late addition wrenches them into the foreground. No longer forgotten by the narrative in "the dark sleep of Death" (23:6), the Eternal Man resurges into the foreground of the macro-narrative through this addition. The "loud death groan" peals through the text again as a dissonant counterpoint to the single-minded work of creation. This juxtaposition of apparently purposeful creation against the resulting universal agonies felt by Albion indict Urizen and his creation, eroding any sympathy the reader might initially have had for him.

By creating a point of grammatical indeterminacy at the point of textual rupture, Blake renders the logic of causality unstable. The squinting modifier that begins the insertion – "Petrifying all the Human Imagination into rocks & sand" – attaches both to Urizen's servants and to Albion's groans. The participle looks backwards to Urizen's agents and forward to Albion's groans, connecting both outside of diachronic sequence but within a synchronic set of associations that renders them inextricable. The sheer scope of references to groans extending through Urizen's creation, Albion's body, Tyburn's brook, the Moon, the Sun, and "all Peoples and Nations of the Earth" shifts the entire tone of the macro-narrative, from the desperate urges of necessity's forming an ambiguously constructed Golden World to the universal foreboding in "The dew of anxious souls the death-sweat of the dying / In every pillard hall & arched roof of Albions Skies" (25:15–16). The general change in emphasis seems to move away from the constructed nature of our fallen state to the range and depth of human suffering: our fallenness is not as debilitating as its ongoing effects.

The radical shift in Urizen's character is consonant with tendencies in later Nights but undermines any sense of character development through the middle nights. The later portions of *Vala* or *The Four Zoas* offer a blatantly evil characterization. In Nights VII and VIII Urizen can claim equal malevolence with Vala as prime mover in the cataclysmic war preceding the Last Judgement; indeed, he has been described as "the villain of the epic."[24] Even Blake's latest drafts for the poem reveal a continued emphasis on his malevolence. Blake first wrote out a rough draft of Urizen in confrontation with the Lamb of God before the Synagogue of Satan. The passage initially began "The Lamb of God stood before Urizen opposite" (145:1). When Blake transferred the passage, he changed "Urizen" to "Satan": the line now reads "The Lamb of God stood before Satan opposite" (105:1). Such a change illustrates Blake's late sense of the interchangeability of Urizen and Satan.[25] By this point the more ambivalent characterization of Urizen in the early copperplate text, a characterization in which he is as much constrained as constraining, has been completely undermined.

After the description of Urizen's work as "Petrifying all the Human Imagination into rock & sand," the passage turns away from his work to the externalization and shrinkage of the universe from "Albions loins:"

> Groans ran along Tyburns brook and along the River of Oxford
> Among the druid Temples Albion groand on Tyburns brook
> Albion gave his loud death groan the Atlantic Mountains trembled
> Aloft the Moon fled with a Cry the Sun with streams of blood
> From Albions loins fled all Peoples And Nations of the Earth
> Fled with the noise of Slaughter & the Stars of heaven Fled   (25:7–12).

The passage goes on to describe Jerusalem's fall (25:13–16), the sleep of Reuben and Levi on Penmaenmawr and Snowdon (25:21), the formation into "Nations far remote in a little & dark Land" (25:24), and the "Binding [of] Jerusalems children in the dungeons of Babylon" (25:31) by the daughters of Albion. These events clearly lie outside the scope of *Vala*. Their effect is interesting, however. Essentially, Blake revises the rather abstract Creation myth of the copperplate text into a highly place-specific Fall narrative. The "North / ... the South & East & dismal West" (25:36–7) of the copperplate text are superseded by actions running "along Tyburns brook and along the River of Oxford" (25:7) and the movement of the daughters of Albion "Across Europe & Asia to China & Japan" (25:27). The complicated Fall narrative explains not only the effect of Urizen's actions but also the limitations and the range of the Fall in particular geographical terms. The added text specifically links Urizen's act of creation to a narrowing of the senses (25:22–3) and in turn describes the shape of the geographical dimensions of the fallen world as a function of this narrowed perception (25:24). These associations are an extension of Urizen's activities as presented in the Lambeth works, but the interconnection of narrowing perception with such events and places weaves biblical and British and mythical and realistic elements into a complicated fabric, expanding the range of *Vala* beyond the Lambeth works and beyond the original conception of the poem.

This expanding range is further complicated by the radical multiplication of narrative levels within the added passage. While the copperplate narrative of Night II frames Urizen's work between the command of the Man on the one hand and the sealing of Luvah in "the Furnaces of affliction" (25:40) on the other, the insertion of the micro-narrative on page 25 complicates the relatively simple set of narrative frames. The addition reorients the whole of Urizen's creation within a series of apparently concentric narratives, no one of which seems to have causal priority over any other or to be determinately distinct from any other. Thus the groans of Albion, which from the perspective of the copperplate narrative envelop the world of Urizen's creation, now also emanate from a distinct point within Urizen's world: "Among the druid Temples Albion groand on Tyburns brook" (25:8). Presumably, the Universal Man shrinks as a physical entity to a position smaller than Urizen's world, but his groans, his spiritual torments, pervade and are in a sense larger than Creation. The rest of the narratives seem to function at concentric levels along a continuum between an Albion located at both the circumference and the centre of articulate existence. Jerusalem falls towards this centre at lines 13–14 but seems more widely spread than Albion; she falls "in dire ruin all over this Earth." The generic narrative of fratricide, involving brothers and maidens, fathers and mothers, stands alongside of but within the narrative of Jerusalem in a world of "blood upon the Severn" (17–20).

After these narrative units about Albion, Jerusalem, and a generic fratricide, the sequence shifts to Reuben and Levi. Less a narrative development and more a register of these collapsing states as reflected in perception, this epistemological pause gives way to the narrative of the Daughters of Albion as they move to and from Albion, "Binding Jerusalems children in dungeons of Babylon" (31). The concluding line in this overall addition offers the cold comfort that these narrative events occur "*While* The Prince of Light [is?] on Salisbury among the druid stones" (emphasis mine). My addition of a copula here – [is?] – is necessitated by the absence of any indication of action at this point of union between micro- and macro-narrative. Urizen's inaction seems somehow appropriate within the micro-narrative, however; his apparent motion is futile in defining points of direction in this universe of groans. Moreover, the location of Urizen "among the druid stones" is an attempt to isolate him with the fallen and shrunken body of Albion along Tyburn's brook. The intensive and extensive overlapping of events and characters seems to reject a process of distinguishing neatly among these narratives in favour of synchronic associations. Effectively, it cuts the power of reason off from the work of Urizen. Their simultaneity in time (or perhaps across it, since we have little sense of beginning and end) argues for a synchronic principle of construction and reading, as does the thematic recognition that all these events express the "death-sweat of the dying" as the Human Imagination petrifies at all narrative levels. The effect on the macro-narrative is an alternation of contraction and expansion of narrative densities. Every event, however, becomes subordinate to the intensified associationism of passages like that in lines 6–33. Thus, even the ensuing narrative of Luvah and Vala from the copperplate text will be read as an extension of Albion's death groans. Luvah's "howlings" and Vala's "voice" are now added modulations in the universal spiritual cry of Albion.

### SUMMARY

Overall, Blake's process of revision and recomposition seems part of a sometimes frantic attempt to save all that he wrote, no matter whether it fit the immediate context or not. For example, he seems to have added his new ending to Night vii[a] (85:23- 90:67) without taking account of the fact that this addition would damage the narrative link between Nights vii[a] and vii[b]. Indeed, with its new ending, the narrative of

Night vii[a] seems to lead more directly into Night viii than into vii[b]. It appears that, in an attempt to save Night vii[b], Blake changed the order of the Night around, so that it began at 95:15 and extended to the earlier end of the Night (98:31), which was then followed by the first half of the Night (91:1–95:14). Blake perhaps realized that even a drastic rearrangement of Night vii[b] did not return its original narrative consistency with vii[a]; however, he did not discard it, perhaps in the hope that he could somehow integrate it with the rest of the poem. In another less dramatic instance we see evidence of Blake's desire to save and reintegrate material in his transference of the first lines of Night viii (page 99) to page 8 in Night i and finally to page 21 of *Vala* in an attempt not only to save the passage in question but also to develop this concept throughout his manuscript.[26] To this extent Blake appears intent upon developing these later additions within the earlier portions of his manuscript; in never completing this task, he left behind an apparently confusing array of characters and symbols in unexpected places.

Although my two examples have centred mostly on Blake's method of revision, it is reasonable to assume that he followed a similar pattern in his process of composition. It is clear that he drew large sections from his earlier works to use in *Vala*. For example, he took the story of Los's creation of Urizen from chapters iv[a] and [b] and v of *The Book of Urizen* and adapted it to the Fourth Night of *Vala*. Although drawn from another independent context, the episode itself is carefully prepared for insertion in *Vala* by the story of Urizen's fall into chaos in Night iii and Tharmas's subsequent order to Los to rebuild the fallen universe and Urizen along with it. Many other passages in the present transcription seem to stand on their own and may have been composed in isolation from the rest of the poem. The laments of Enion and Ahania provide an obvious example of such a practice. Moreover, it is entirely possible that episodes such as the "woes / Of Vala & ... of Luvah" (30:54–5) at the furnaces of affliction were composed apart from the description of Urizen's world and then spliced into this other narrative. What these practices suggest is a sort of episodic development of Blake's epic in which he attempted to join various different speeches and narratives into a coherent whole.

As he continued to revise *Vala*, Blake became less concerned with creating smooth transitions between various episodes, perhaps because of lack of time, diligence, or certainty about where these new revisions would take his epic. Thus his additions to the poem began to rest more uneasily in their new context. To some extent these observations contradict attempts by Blake's critics to discuss the poem as a unified work. I do not wish to say, however, that Blake did not attempt to weave his various narrative threads into a seamless garment; he seems to have struggled with the poem for many years to unify earlier with later material. At times the flexibility of the poem seems to stress the sense of coherent design, yet Blake's persistence with his revisions suggests that the expansion of his poetic vision forced him to risk the diachronic coherence of his narrative. By leaning on synchronic principles of juxtaposition and association, Blake found a narrative form, a flexible poetics, that could incorporate all developments in theme, character, and imagery.

No matter how complicated or apparently inconsistent the transfer of passages from one poem to another, from the Lambeth prophecies to *Vala*, from *Vala* to *Milton* and *Jerusalem*, or from *Jerusalem* to *Vala*, Blake seems to have been committed to revising earlier material to fit later and later to fit earlier. Indeed, he seems almost obsessed with a sort of centripetal intratextuality that makes the synchronic dimensions of his overall mythology more clearly defined than the particular narrative of a particular poem. This overall consistency seems designed to shape our reading and understanding of Blake's works in general, since we are virtually forced to interpret individual lines and episodes within the mental framework of this larger mythology. As he reworked his poems, Blake changed his predominant narrative strategy from a continuous to a non-continuous form; a sequential or chronological narrative would then be replaced by a disjunctive or discontinuous narrative unified by thematic wholeness rather than sequences of cause and effect. With a consistently discontinuous narrative, fragments could be inserted into the work to heighten moments of thematic significance without damaging the narrative integrity of the whole.

Metaphor and typology serve as excellent vehicles for this revisionary tendency, since they allow for continued elaboration and expansion yet are still driven by a consistent source of thematic power. Blake's concern with humanity's relationship to divine energy, for instance, is consistent throughout his canon. Whether this energy appears in the abstract form of a poetic genius or in the more concrete form of a Tyger, Orc, Los, or Jesus Christ does little to change the core of meaning in this energy. By invoking and strengthening this thematic consistency through synchronic structures, Blake gains the additional power of history and human experience in his myth without consigning his poems to absolutes of time and space. Finally, the interdependence of texts, the expansion of meaning consistently through a group of poems rather than in a single poem, counterbalances the authority of the single text; it sets the centripetal force of metaphoric reading against a totality of textual possibilities, and is limited only by the individual imagination.

Such strategies, however, make great demands on the reader, creating a hermeneutic circle that expands beyond the relationship of micro- and macro-narrative elements to the intratextual nature of all Blake's works. Apart from the complex rhetorical structures, the main difficulty in reading Blake arises from the sheer scope of the complex metaphoric structure that must be kept in mind while reading the smaller unit. Meaning, at times, seems imposed from without rather than within the text. Yet, at the same time, it is clear that the larger meaning of Blake's canon arises from the component parts of his text and the interdependence of these parts. As he adds particular passages to a poem like *Vala*, Blake changes the larger shape and meaning of the individual poem; as he transfers and modifies passages between poems within a larger symbolic superstructure, he changes the overall shape of this superstructure or myth. Blake seems to see his myth, like the human mind, as an infinitely flexible form. Text and mind are thus seen as interconnected; following Blake's text is like following the sometimes disjunctive movement of mental processes. In Blake's canon, the whole can accommodate itself to the particular no matter how unusual the part may at first seem. Ultimately, then, the reader must learn the mental flexibility of Blake's intratextual poetic form in order to fill out the poetic indeterminacies of Blake's text.

In the pages that follow, my discussion of Blake's revisionary poetics is conditioned by the following hypotheses:

1  Blake's method of composition was piecemeal in construction.
2  His revisions were not controlled by a desire to continue the integrity of *Vala* as he first conceived of it but more in terms of the overall evolving shape of his myth. According to this postulate, the synoptic impulse fed back from later works (*Jerusalem* and *Milton*) to earlier ones (the manuscript of *Vala*).
3  The process of revision has an inexorability that allows later material to flood the original text without concern for a predetermined sense of fixed structures, organic integrity, or determined identity.
4  The horizontal diachronic principles of sequence and syntagmatic relationship are replaced by the vertical synchronic principles of association, discontinuity, and indeterminacy.

# Narrative

# 1 Beginnings and Creation

Without the benefit of a careful consideration of the complexities of the manuscript, critics generally accept the description of Tharmas's fall as a most logical starting-point for the poem, especially given his role as the "parent Power" (4:7). The motifs of love, jealousy, fragmentation, and apostasy coalesce in his story. Moreover, the consequent creation of "the Circle of Destiny" (5:24) explains the origins of time and space, giving a context to the poem's action, and the violent union of the Spectre of Tharmas with Enion brings about the birth of Los and Enitharmon as the inhabitants of this fallen world of destiny. However, the heavily erased text on the first seven pages attests to Blake's uncertainties about the authority of this beginning, and other modifications in the opening three Nights, particularly in their numbering, call the definitiveness of this beginning into question. Besides erasing and rewriting the opening of Night 1 several times, Blake renumbered the headings for the first three Nights, experimenting with many different possibilities for the opening of the work. In all, the manuscript evidence suggests he considered at least three different starting-points for the poem and two for the second Night, and it is not clear he definitively ruled out any or all of these possibilities.

In Appendix A I have provided a transcript of the copperplate text in an attempt to isolate and illustrate the foundations from which Blake developed what we now take to be the first three Nights of *Vala*. In the copperplate text Tharmas is virtually absent, the identities of the battling figures who give birth to Los and Enitharmon obscure, and the overall sense of male-female conflict understated. The indeterminate nature of the poem's beginning as revealed by an examination of the manuscript attests to an irresolvable conflict between the demands of sequence and causality characteristic of narrative on the one hand and the analogous sets of vertical relationships comprising a synchronic poetics on the other. Before turning directly to the manuscript, however, I will consider the demands of narrative and how they impinge on Blake's attempts at beginnings.

### NARRATIVE AND BEGINNING

In Night 1 we see the great importance of narrative to the construction of *Vala*. The union of Tharmas and Enion, the consequent birth of Los and Enitharmon, followed by their nuptial feast and leading to Urizen's descent and attempted containment of Los's apparent will to power, all are events established along a causal or diachronic line of development. The choice of a narrative form is not altogether surprising given Blake's attempts to forge a cosmology through the late Lambeth period in *The Books of Urizen*, *The Book of Ahania* and *The Book of Los*. *Vala* seems to be an attempt to develop this cosmology more fully.

Narrative, with its essential attributes of beginning, middle, and end, offers an obvious containing form for a poem outlining the Fall, the strife of human history, and the Apocalypse. Yet the rudimentary and essential demands of narrative – the need for logic, sequence, and causality – place uncomfortable restrictions on Blake as his poetics becomes more synchronically based. One of the theoretical foundations for his synchronic poetics comes in his attacks on the principles of sequence and causality themselves. In his annotations to Bacon's *Essays*, probably written sometime soon after 1798,[1] Blake writes, "He who says there are Second Causes has already denied a First The Word Cause is a foolish Word" (E.626). Much later, in *Milton* (circa 1804), Blake elaborates:

And every Natural Effect has a Spiritual Cause, and Not
A Natural: for a Natural Cause only seems, it is a Delusion
Of Ulro: & a ratio of the perishing Vegetable Memory.

(26[28]:44–46; E.124)

Natural cause, Blake suggests, is nothing more than a fallen remnant of our understanding of spiritual action. Such an argument is opposed to the notion of a time-bound narrative and literary form controlled by sequential verisimilitude. It also removes authoritarian claims about any single point of origin, for the point of beginning is the moment most burdened with diachronic obsessions.

There is therefore no real reason why the poem should begin with Tharmas's fall or with any other narratively defined moment in particular. While this theory is to Blake's advantage synchronically, it perhaps causes difficulties on a very practical level: all poems must have beginnings, but if causality is rendered meaningless, then every beginning is equally unauthoritative. Indeed, as Leslie Brisman points out in his *Romantic Origins*, citing Michel Foucault, epic mythologies that attempt to depict the genesis of the created universe encounter crucial difficulties in their beginnings:

The essential fictionality of a declared origin is a point summarily articulated by Foucault: "It is always against a background of the already begun that man is able to reflect on what may serve for him as origin. For man, then, origin is by no means the beginning – a sort of dawn of history from which his ulterior acquisitiveness would have accumulated. Origin, for man, is much more the way in which man in general, any man, articulates himself upon the already-begun."[2]

The indeterminacy of the manuscript in defining a preferred beginning draws attention to the fictionality of any declared origin for the narrative of the poem.

Combined with the fictionality of origins in narrative is a scepticism about language, the medium of narrative expression in *Vala*. Blake addresses these impediments of language on the first page of the poem. In an addition to the invocation to the poem he writes of the ineffable core of his central characters: "What are the Natures of those Living Creatures [i.e., the "Four Mighty Ones ... in every Man"] the Heavenly Father only / Knoweth <no> [*Man*] Knoweth [*not*] nor Can know in all Eternity" (3:11–12). The succeeding narrative lays claim to the task of describing mythically the emergence of "substance" from such unknowable and therefore ineffable essence. Blake's very practical problem is to offer a beginning that is both the beginning of a poem and also a departure from the essence of eternity to an existential world of art that is expressed in created forms. Theoretically, Blake's epic, expressed through the fallen forms of temporal and spatial existence, would begin at the first moment that is created rather than eternal and uncreated. At such a moment beginning and creation would be one. But how to express such a moment poetically? The constantly shifting opening of the poem may reflect not only the difficulty of creating a consistent and coherent theogony but also an initial moment that hesitates at expressing both beginning and Creation simultaneously. In terms of breadth of subject, Blake is embarking upon a cosmological epic that aspires to an inclusive depiction of human experience, temporal and eternal; but it seems difficult if not impossible to locate and describe a point of departure adequately defining the parameters of human experience. In scope, he plays out this cosmological epic across divine, human, and demonic realms. While language may prove relatively reliable in the description of much of the human realm, its resources inevitably falter in attempting to express the divine and demonic; moreover, attempts to describe the emergence of these ineffable forces into the world of narratibility are fraught with difficulties. The picture of humanity in an infinite and eternal state is destined either to be merely an amplification of all that humans see as good in the natural world or an abstract and rather formless description of ethereal essences such as those that people Milton's Heaven in *Paradise Lost*.

The Bible, as Blake's central literary model, offers a general theological context that ennables his narrative and a beginning that frustrates it. Essentially, Blake uses the poetic form of the Christian-biblical epic to convey his message about eternal life as well as the reasons for present fallen existence. In Blake's mythology, Man's error in eternity causes his Fall, and the events at this point of departure from eternity determine the shape of his fallen existence. The larger structure of Blake's mythology, as Frye points out, ultimately attempts to present "the gigantic myth which is the vision of this world as God sees it, the outlines of that vision being creation, fall, redemption and apocalypse."[3] Blake's mythology further draws upon the biblical formulation of a typological equivalence between Creation at the beginning of time and Apocalypse or recreation at the end of time. As Bernhard Anderson points out, the biblical scholarship of Hermann Gunkel "expressed this correspondence in his famous formula, *Urzeit gleich Endzeit* ('beginning-time equals end-time')." In the apocalyptic tradition of this formulation, man's life in time is presented "as a historical and even a cosmic drama which moves from the absolute beginning of time (creation) to the absolute end, when history will be completely transfigured and transformed in the New Creation (the New Heaven and the New Earth)."[4] In the epic mythology that Blake sought to develop he is limited initially only by his sense of how the Creation reflects man's present state and, later, by the completed pattern in which Creation is undone by the Apocalypse. In this sense, he is attempting to correct or, perhaps more accurately, to complete the Bible. As Frye points out in commenting on the Bible,

by the time we have reached the end we realize that the Bible, like other epics, has started with the action fairly well advanced, and that the Book of Genesis needs a prelude about a fiery city in which a single divine and human body formed the circumference of the whole of nature. Such a prelude, if we could be sufficiently inspired to compose one, would turn out to be very similar to the conclusion of the existing Book of Revelation. All things have proceeded from a divine Man, the body of Jesus, and will be reabsorbed into him; and the total vision of life must have a circular form.[5]

In *Vala* Blake does not exactly go to "a fiery city in which a single and divine human body formed the circumference of the whole of nature," but the copperplate text of Night 1 appears to have begun as a prelude to Creation. The elemental forms represent the forces of unfallen nature, which present a wedding feast, an apocalyptic banquet, for Los and Enitharmon. Originally, Blake may have conceived of this feast as an antipode to the feast at the end of the poem, where his figures are reunited at the Apocalypse (assuming, of course, that Blake had at least a vague idea of the larger shape of his poem.) Night 11 would then relate the Creation-as-Fall story through Urizen's building of a golden world and his casting out of Ahania, his mate, and a portion of his own being. The succeeding Nights describe the Fall of Man as a series of conflicts between various characters who externalize the disintegrations and fragmentation within the psyche of the Eternal Man.

The Bible provides the most influential model in the construction of *Vala*, but as is customary with Blake, influence also means critique. The Bible, for instance, does not depict a point of origin consonant with Blake's view of the present state of human existence. The biblical account, with its resounding "In the beginning God created the heaven and the earth,"[6] opens with an abruptness that appears to forestall or simply to pass over any question of what went before and what kind of life, if any, human consciousness had in the eternal world before the Creation. Further, the translation of the opening line of Genesis creates a certain confusion about whether it was intended to sanction the theory of creation *ex nihilo* or creation from chaos.[7] The King James and Revised Standard Versions of the Bible support *creatio ex nihilo*, but a purely grammatical translation of the opening verse suggests that "God worked on a pre-existent chaos (In the beginning of God's creation of the heavens and the earth – the earth being chaos and darkness over the deep, and a wind of God hovering over the waters – then God said, 'Let there be light')."[8]

In the traditional Christian interpretation of the first chapters of Genesis, such as that of Augustine, God is said to be complete unto himself and to create the cosmos *ex nihilo*, out of nothing.[9] The central problem with presenting a God who creates *ex nihilo* is that such a being, described as "the ineffable Spirit, eternal, infinite, immutable, and incorruptible locked securely ... within an impenetrable numerical unity,"[10] becomes little more than a cold abstraction of the type Blake detested. This God, whether it be Aristotle's First Principle, the Absolute of the Neoplatonists, or God the Father in *Paradise Lost*, is "wrapped within himself in a sort of 'frozen passivity' or eternal rest."[11] The account of God's ordering of chaos originates mainly from Plato's *Timaeus* and is passed down to the Gnostic and Manichean dualism of early Christianity.[12] Dennis Danielson, in his book on *Milton's Good God: A Study in Literary Theodicy*, points out that "such a view [the idea of creation from chaos] is contrary to the biblical teaching that 'there is but one God, ... of whom are all things' (1 Cor. 8:6), for it supposes that something other than God alone is primordial, that something apart from him existed in the beginning, which limited his creativity."[13] Creation in these terms becomes "primordial opposition of Good and Evil, Light and Darkness, God and Matter,"[14] and was roundly opposed by writers such as Ireneaus and Augustine.

Blake rejects both Creation theories in *A Vision of the Last Judgement*:

Many suppose that before [*Adam*] <the Creation> All was Solitude & Chaos This is the most pernicious Idea that can enter the Mind as it takes away all sublimity from the Bible & Limits All Existence to Creation & to Chaos To the Time & Space fixed by the Corporeal Vegetative Eye & leaves the Man who entertains such an Idea the habitation of Unbelieving Demons Eternity Exists and All things in Eternity Independent of Creation which was an act of Mercy   (91; E.563)

Here Blake simultaneously equates and rejects both the theory of *creatio ex nihilo* (All was Solitude) and creation from chaos (All was ... Chaos). Figures of solitude had been satirized by Blake as early as the *Poetical Sketches*, and he consistently rejects the idea that anything positive can come out of such self-absorbed acts of creation. His objection to the notion of creation from chaos is in its accompanying supposition that matter is coexistent with God "& Limits All Existence to Creation." Matter and the created world, as we have seen, are in Blake's view a part of man's Fall, a kind of incrustation that forms over the spiritual man when he falls from the infinite and eternal world into the corporeal world of time and space. But in identifying "Solitude" and "Chaos," Blake seems also to imply that the God who creates out of nothing exists in a solitude that is itself chaos. Blake's earlier cosmological work, *The Book of Urizen*, encapsulates his objections to this kind of linking of beginnings and Creation. The opening of *Urizen* sets the context for a god of solitude and abstraction:

> Lo, a shadow of horror is risen
> In Eternity! Unknown, unprolific!
> Self-closd, all-repelling: what Demon
> Hath form'd this abominable void
> This soul shudd'ring vacuum? – Some said
> "It is Urizen", But unknown, abstracted
> Brooding secret, the dark power hid   (3:1–7; E.70)

The participle "Brooding" (7) identifies Urizen with Milton's version of the God of Genesis, whose spirit broods on the waters before Creation,[15] and later descriptions of Urizen as "A self-contemplating shadow, / In enormous labours occupied" (BU.3:21–2; E.71) show him to be like the God who, in Blake's symbolism, mistakenly tries to be entirely self-contained and to create a world from this self-centred brooding. More-over, in *The Book of Urizen* Blake equates this state of solitude with that of chaos when he writes that Urizen, "Brooding shut in the deep" (BU.3:25; E.71), becomes a "petrific abominable chaos" (BU.3:26; E.71).[16]

Blake exacerbates the practical difficulties of beginning through repeated modifications to the narrative well after the entire poem was transcribed. The major internal changes and revisions reverberate throughout the work, altering its cast of characters, overall shape, and thematic emphases. By Bentley's computations, for instance, there are "143 symbolic names in *Vala*," and of these "117 names, 82 per cent. of the total, appear only in added passages or in Night VIII" (B.171). With only 26 names, or 18 per cent of the total, providing the character basis of narrative, the effect of the addition of 117 names to the poem after much of it was transcribed cannot be fully documented here. I will comment further on the impact of some of these character changes in the second part of this book; for now it is enough to remark that such drastic changes must have a powerful impact on narrative, particularly on a nearly fully developed diachronic sequence. Internal development, motivation, and relative importance all shift among the various characters. Their ultimate interrelationship will in part be determined by the beginning of the poem, a beginning that is a departure giving rise to and defining their states of departure, separation, and difference.

### BEGINNING THE MANUSCRIPT

Given the problematic nature of beginnings, particularly the definition of an authoritative point of origin and the difficulty of describing transitions from the eternal and ineffable to the temporal and articulate, it is not surprising that, when we turn to the opening pages of Blake's manuscript, we find obvious evidence of his struggle with the initiating events in his poem. Layers of palimpsest entirely obscure the earliest transcription on pages 3 through 7. The headings for what are usually printed as Nights II and III also show evidence of repeated tampering: Night II was twice labelled "Night the First" but never "Night the Second," and the third Night was labelled "Fourth," "Third," and perhaps even "First." Moreover, the opening of the second Night was at one time moved from its generally accepted position on page 23 to the middle of page 9 (see Plate 4). These changes undermine any clear sense of authority for a declared point of origin in Blake's narrative and convey a degree of tentativeness in his representation of a single point of origin for the poem. As a result of these textual indeterminacies, the poem plays out its own anxieties about the unresolved conflict between a diachronic and a synchronic poetics. At the same time that the extensive reworking of and experimentation with the poem's opening Nights attests to the crucial importance of beginnings in establishing the overall contexts of the work, Blake's refusal to cancel out many of the potential arrangements of these defining moments in the manuscript diminish the authority of any beginning. Hence, the manuscript simultaneously seems to endorse the demand for a beginning, a demand consequent upon a diachronic narrative, and the denial of the authority of a single point of origin, a denial emerging from the synchronic poetics Blake grafts on to the poem.

Of three possible beginnings Blake considered, each offers a myth about Creation and the transition from eternity to the world of time and space, and each offers a parody of different visions of godhood. The present beginning of Night I depicts the fall of Tharmas, the "parent Power" (4:7), which brings about the creation of the Circle of Destiny, within which the world of time and space revolves. Urizen's creation of his Golden World in Night II offers an equally appropriate starting-point, since it depicts the creation of forms out of chaos and emerges "like visible out of the invisible" (33:10). Finally, Night III offers a beginning in which Urizen, enthroned and in control of his perfect universe, brings about his own downfall by casting out Ahania; his fall brings into being a world of undefined matter and form from a perfect golden world. Thus, the three nights offer a point of origin synchronous with each other. The difficulty in finding a poetic beginning that expresses a point of origin consonant with the moment of Creation brings into conflict the essential dimensions of diachronic and synchronic narrative poetics. *Vala*, however, retains a large degree of linearity, and Blake seems uncertain how to balance the desire to complete an epic work outlining the movement from Creation to Apocalypse against the denial of physical causality.

While generally accepted as the natural starting-point for the poem, the description of Tharmas's fall in the opening pages of the manuscript is, perhaps surprisingly, one of the most complex and elusive cruxes in the poem. The earliest copperplate text on pages 3–7 is erased, and several layers of revision render each underlying palimpsest irrecoverable despite the best efforts of Bentley and Erdman to uncover them. Most intriguing is that Tharmas, the central figure in this point of origin, is nowhere named in the copperplate text of the first Night, and he appears only once in the first 42 pages. He does not enter the base transcription of the poem as a fully realized character until the second stage in transcription, when Blake changed handwriting styles and the kind of paper he used to transcribe the poem. These factors may suggest that Tharmas was a character not fully developed or radically reconceived (or perhaps not even invented) when the present pages were initially transcribed. Whatever the case, the authority of this character and his actions as a single point of origin in initiating the narrative action seems dubious. By twice labelling the second night "Night the First," Blake seems to indicate his persistent sense that the events on the opening pages of his manuscript lack authority as points of origin for his poem.

At the same time that some portions of the manuscript record Blake's notions of abandoning the opening pages, however, others illustrate attempts to retain and reorganize the narrative around these drastic reworkings. A case in point is the movement of the heading "Night the

Second" from page 23 to page 9. Blake's motive for this change is relatively clear. As he rewrote and expanded the opening story of Tharmas and Enion and that of Los and Enitharmon, he probably wished to redress a growing imbalance in the relative lengths of the nights. The movement of the beginning of the Second Night from page 23 to page 9 isolates the Tharmas-Enion episode, leaving the following Nights to deal respectively with Los and Enitharmon, the subjugation of Luvah and Vala during Urizen's accession to power, and the conflict of Urizen and Ahania. This division of Nights adds a structural clarity to the poem and signals a shift in emphasis from the story of Vala to the story of the Four Zoas. W.H. Stevenson, the only critic to discuss the division of the First Night in detail and the implications of this change, argues:

In the original plot, the first turning-point was the accession of Urizen to power on p. 23; the preceding action was introductory and preparatory. But now the introduction is more complex. The sequence has now three parts – Vala's first corruption of Man; the disintegration of balance among the Zoas; and the emergence of a new creation in which Los and Enitharmon wander. The first of these three parts becomes merely a vague memory, first recalled by Enitharmon (10:9ff.); the second becomes the material of the First Night, and this is found partly on pp. 3–9, partly on 21a-19c. The activities of Los and Enitharmon, leading to the introduction of Urizen to their fallen world (p. 12) is the material of the Second, starting at 9:34. The turning-point is now the change of scene from Eternity to mortality. Where the action in the fallen world begins, the Second Night now begins.[17]

Yet Blake did not follow through with this change. In commenting on the insertion of "Night the Second" after 9:34, Bentley points out that "Blake evidently intended to begin Night II here, but he never confirmed the intention by deleting 'End of the First Night' on p. 18 and p. 19."[18]

Blake seems to have continued his experiments with the order of the Nights in equally tentative ways by giving serious consideration to starting the poem with what is now taken as the second Night. On at least two occasions he titled this Night "First," and, more intriguing, he never titled it second, even though he did place "End of the Second Night" on page 36. He pencilled in a "First" beside the original heading on page 23, perhaps as part of a tentative move to try this possibility, but then struck this out either when he decided that this Night would not be suitable as the first or when he decided to enter a "First" over the original heading. In erasing the original number heading and adding "First,"

Blake may have contemplated rejecting the preceding Night and starting his epic with the second Night. It is possible that he considered beginning *Vala* with the Second Night while reconsidering the appropriateness of the original text on pages 3–7. Perhaps the revisions he required were so significant that he considered discarding the whole Night. It is also possible that, even after he made extensive revisions to these pages, he was still unhappy with the results. Therefore, he changed the title of the Night to "Night the First" and at the same time may have changed the "Then" of the first line to "The"[19] in an attempt to remove or blunt the sense of narrative continuity implied by the adverb.

These opening lines provide a good starting-point for the poem. The Man literally and figuratively articulates his origin in the opening of Night II: "The Man calld Urizen & said. Behold these sickning Spheres / Take thou possession" (23:3,5). As Brisman points out, these lines hasten over the fictionality of a declared point of origin both by implying an "already-begun" in "Behold these sickning Spheres" and by leaping immediately into a fallen world of causality and possessiveness in the Man's cry "Take thou possession."[20] Urizen's rise to power concomitant with the Eternal Man's demise sets the stage for Urizen's subsequent attempts to proclaim himself god over all. Acting as a parody of Genesis, this beginning depicts the act of Creation as articulation, but a verbal act that is motivated by despair, fear, and possessiveness. Beginning with Urizen as a malevolent figure emphasizes his centrality and focuses the reader's attention on his actions throughout the work. Yet this beginning may make the "villain" too central. Blake, we recall, did not settle on either the division of "Night the First" into two parts or starting his epic with the second Night, erasing the "First"s from the second Night and leaving the Second Night unnumbered, except for the notation "End of the Second Night" on page 36.

Further evidence suggests another possible beginning for the poem. Bentley offers a tentative but enticing reading of an erased "First" under the "Third" of "Night the Third" (B.38).[21] If Bentley is right, then it seems that Blake may have considered starting his epic at this point and forgoing the first two Nights. Certainly this Night would also work well as a starting-point, since it does not depend on events in the preceding Nights in the same way that Night II's description of Urizen rising "from the Feast of envy" (23:10) depends on Night I. Night III begins with Urizen bringing about his own fall, followed by his subsequent attempt to rebuild and dominate his ruined world. Blake, however, abandoned this idea and, after trying other possibilities, labelled this Night the

"Third." The throne-room scene depicting an insecure tyrant casting out his feminine counterpart establishes the sexual and political sources of fallen life but perhaps give Urizen a too-prominent role at the ostensible origin of human existence. While his and Ahania's fall leads to a state of chaos and its restructuring (through the agency of Tharmas and Los), it does not generate the same degree of universal anxiety and despair that Blake achieves through the involvement and separation of Tharmas and Enion.

With these beginnings comes an unavoidable conflict between the narrative form of the poem and its emerging content. The epic form depicting "The Death and Judgement of the Ancient Man" defines the poem as a traditional narrative with its "succession of events,"[22] a diachronic structure interconnecting a linear sequence of conflicting elements, a sequence designed to reach a culminating unity. In particular, the choice of the adjective "Ancient," written over the word "Eternal," highlights a temporal framework defining the story of the Man's Death and Judgement. The power of such diachronic forms is that they render intelligible human existence in the context of historical and physical life. *Paradise Lost*, for instance, offers a cyclical structure encompassing divine, demonic, and human life, bringing the whole to a point of completion and significance. Frye's elaborate analysis of the cyclical structure of Milton's epic highlights its intelligibility but also perhaps indicates a deterministic emphasis on structure.[23] Even the formulaic opening of the epic *in medias res* does little to overcome the demands of diachrony. Beginning in the middle of things is, as Edward Said has remarked, "a convention that burdens the beginning with the pretense that it is not one."[24] Ultimately, even this middle must point to another sequentially related beginning and end. The emerging dilemma is that, while the formal elements of narrative allow a structure for discourse, they also in themselves reinforce the very ideological restrictions Blake writes against.

As distinguished from narrative, the content of Blake's poem moves towards an affirmation of the atemporal and negation of the power of natural causality. The opening of the poem emphasizes these factors in its dedication to the "day of intellectual battle" (3:7) and the elaborate psychomachia depicting "the Four Mighty Ones … in every Man" (3:8). The mental space that provides the contexts for the epic is not ruled entirely by physical causality or logical sequence: sequence is only the smallest part of intellectual experience. These themes are increasingly synchronically related in the course of revision as the struggle of each of "the Four Mighty Ones" overlaps with the others. Such synchronic thematics break the chains of physical causality and reinforce the sense of the fictionality of declared origins, even as they frustrate the poetics of narrative form.

Blake's most immediate contemporary influence for the kind of epic he sought to write is Young's *Night Thoughts*, a poem that frees itself, to some extent, from the narrative trammels we find in *Paradise Lost*. While not exactly a synchronic form, as the preface points out, Young's *Night Thoughts* attempts to break from a "long Narration" and make "the Morality arising from it … the Bulk of the Poem." Moreover, the work is framed by the world of dreams, of Night Thoughts, a context not sharply defined by natural logic and cause. Reshaped by the world of dream, causality intervenes only as a process of mental association, of "intellectual battle." At the opening of Young's poem we find a point of origin described as a moment of awakening to conscious misery and psychological conflict:

> I wake, emerging from a sea of Dreams
> Tumultuous; where my wreck'd, desponding Thought
> From wave to wave of *fancy'd* Misery,
> At random drove, her helm of Reason lost;
> Tho' now restor'd, tis only Change of pain,
> A bitter change; severer for severe:
> The *Day* too short for my Distress! and *Night*
> Even in the *Zenith* of her dark Domain,
> Is Sun-shine, to the colour of my Fate.   (9–17)

This opening may reflect to some degree the situation in all three of Blake's potential beginnings. The "sea of Dreams" points forward to Tharmas's watery chaos in Night i; the struggle to wake reflects the Man's situation in Night ii, with the "wreck'd, desponding Thought" analogous to Urizen's "fear & pale dismay" (24:2) at being commanded to make order from chaos; and the restored thought, which sees only "Change of pain," describes the state of Urizen in Night iii, a "King of trouble" (38:4), fearing the future in which he must serve the "boy … born of the dark Ocean" (38:2). The ensuing collapse of his world in Night iii ensures that Night is "the colour of … [Urizen's] Fate." Yet Blake's poem is not directly modelled on Young's. It avoids the meditative emphasis on "Morality" and the movement towards abstraction attendant on the extensive use of direct personifications. The indeterminacy over the specific cause or occasion for creation, transition, and false self-deification, however, acknowledges the ever-present desire for points of origin at the same time as it disrupts the truth-value invested in such specific moments. We are not determined by the specific events, characters, or faculties involved in beginning and creation, but by the synchronous mental pattern that defines beginning and creation as departures from Eternity or from intellectual wholeness. The manuscript's refusal to offer a determinate beginning results in an indeterminacy that is not just a property of the text but instead is a record of the poet's acts of composition and creation.

# 2 Experiments in Structure

Perhaps one of the most complex and hotly debated cruxes in the entire *Vala* manuscript appears at the moment of its own narrative crisis; Nights vii[a] and vii[b] and Night viii recount the consolidation of error in Blake's universe, leading into the poem's apocalyptic conclusion in Night ix. The existence of two Nights vii at this crucial moment has troubled scholars intensely since the first editorial work on the poem began; the complex narrative of Night viii, with its use of Christian image patterns not present in the base text of the rest of the poem and its several pages of added text containing material clearly adapted from *Milton* and *Jerusalem*, has also occasioned general recognition that it is part of a different phase of composition. The basic disruptions in the entire sequence from the end of vii[a] up through the beginning of ix come about through the introduction of two new elements at the point of Apocalypse: first, the addition of extensive and detailed Christian symbolism revolving around the conflict between the Lamb of God and the Synagogue of Satan in Night viii; and second, the expanded role of Los, Enitharmon, and the Spectre of Urthona at the end of vii[a] as precursors and architects of the Apocalypse. All this has been observed before; what has not been widely discussed in current scholarship, however, is the way in which the incorporation of new characters and the expanding roles of existing ones bring with them thematic shifts that in turn have a significant effect on modes of narrative representation.

Essentially, the revision of the apocalyptic crisis can be understood in terms of three interrelated phases. The earliest shows Orc, Urizen, and the Shadowy Female in a struggle for temporal domination of the physical universe. Their battle reflects the deterioration of the cycles of history through revolution and tyranny to a fixed state ruled over by a principle of nature – the Shadowy Female. The "stony stupor" she inspires is broken by Los's tearing down of the sun and moon. This action causes the physical universe to collapse, awaking the Eternal Man. All these materials seem well worked out by Blake at the time he transcribes the work. He simply continues the existing narrative of the emerging struggles of Urizen against Los, Tharmas, and the Spectre of Urthona as it develops up through Night vii[a]; the relatively new complicating factor of the Shadowy Female's appearance seems a logical extension of this conflict and something easily developed, her appearance in vii[a] being modelled on that depicted in the Preludium to *America*. It is mainly this narrative thread that drives the diachronic structure of the narrative through vii[a], [b], and viii.

Blake, perhaps dissatisfied by the lack of hopeful and conscious direction in this rather dark vision of history, then turns to a more directly Christian vision of the Apocalypse. In this second phase of development, the Lamb of God and Satan now become the male protagonists, to some extent replacing Los and Urizen; the historical cycle of tyranny and revolt is now replaced by the cycle of death and resurrection. Rahab takes the place of the Shadowy Female as the domineering form of nature; after trying out alternative versions of her fate, Blake finally decides on one depicting her self-destruction. The third phase directly takes into account the second but centres on the conflict between Los and the Spectre of Urthona. Their conflict is that of the poet-prophet working within the restrictions of rationality to create a visionary world from the fallen one. The female form who initially opposes this visionary transformation is Enitharmon. Unlike the Shadowy Female, she is not defeated by the Apocalypse, and unlike Rahab, she does not bring about her own immolation; instead, after seeing a vision of the Lamb of God, she joins Los and his Spectre in an artistic transformation of the fallen universe. I stress that this is a process of evolution because these three narratives are not clearly distinct stages in the manuscript's development. Each stage grows out of the previous one in a complementary way; as he revises each stage, Blake attempts to blend the different characters and narratives within a single framework. Each set of characters exists as a synoptic extension of the others, and motivation based on action and reaction among them becomes secondary to the synchronic alignment of their experiences.

The progression through these three character groupings and their attendant thematic concerns necessitates a gradual revision of the basic structures of narrative. From the predominantly diachronic intensification of conflict among Blake's own creations – Los, Urizen, and the Shadowy Female – to an interlacing of the Lamb of God, Satan, and Rahab and finally to the expanding micro narrative of Los, his Spectre, and Enitharmon, the forms of apocalyptic representation shift significantly. The first phase is depicted in the form of an inexorable teleology that releases humanity from the fallen world through spatial and temporal processes. The problem is that this teleology is overdetermined by the mundane structures. The awakening of the Eternal Man in Night ix seems an arbitrary completion to the struggles within time, leaving them meaningless. Phases two and three offer stories of Christ and Los acting as vertical ruptures in sequential teleology. Such thematic incongruities necessitate a shift in narrative poetics, a shift that undermines the gathering of meaning along a diachronic route and replaces this process of signification with vertical synchronous associations. This marked change increasingly diminishes the sequential drive of narrative and emphasizes the ascendency of vertical intersections by divinity and imagination.

Such intersections may not be new to Blake's thinking, but increasingly they begin to restructure narrative, beginning at this point of Apocalypse. Such restructuring eventually reverberates through the rest of the poem. At its simplest the changing poetic works through narrative juxtapositions and interlaced structures, as we see in Night viii. At its more complex, the micro-narrative of Los's reconciliation with Enitharmon and the Spectre at the end of vii[a] introduces a completion of the poem's teleology at the total expense of the need for further diachronic development.

## EMERGING JUXTAPOSITIONS: NIGHT VIII

Night viii exhibits a narrative complexity exceeding that of any other night in the poem, a complexity that is clearly evident in Donald Ault's detailed attempt to map out the narrative patterns of the Night. He isolates no fewer than seven "series of discrete segments," and, summing up the combined form of these segments, he argues that "Night viii employs a narrative alternation between vastly different discontinuous scenes of action (without the aid of continuous mediating transitions) while simultaneously employing near repetitions of whole lines, indicating that if the same events recur, they do so with constantly altered meaning, and that the overall structure infolds, encloses, and embeds at the same time it alternates and progresses."[1] Seen in the light of the complexities of the manuscript itself, rather than as part of a typographical edition, these "discrete segments," "narrative alternation[s]," and "discontinuous scenes of action" attest to the incorporation of a diverse range of narrative materials assembled in various overlapping stages of revision. An examination of the manuscript tends to show that many of these complexities arise from the extensive revisions made to the Night.

Given its Christian symbolism of a type not found elsewhere in the base text of the poem (not even in Night IX), Night VIII appears to be the last one transcribed (or at least the last composed). Its disproportionate size in comparison with many of the other Nights also implies a problematic construction. Moreover, the possibility that it is a retranscription of an earlier draft expanded until it split into Night VII[b] and the base text of the present Night VIII suggests that the final turn towards Apocalypse cost Blake considerable reworking of earlier plans, a reworking that was facilitated by gradual narrative restructuring. Apparent in the base text of Night VIII – the text of Night VIII before any revisions – is a three-part structure: the first contains a relatively straightforward narrative of Urizen's war against the World of Los, which culminates in his entrapment in his own Web of Religion under the power of the Shadowy Female; the central section outlines the descent, judgement, crucifixion, and burial of the Lamb of God; and finally, the Urizen narrative resumes at 106:18[2] with the description of his transformation into a stony serpent and the fall of "All things" under the influence of the Shadowy Female. The narrative of the first and third sections surges forward, directed mainly by an obvious causal connection between events. Still, we see evidence of a more complicated pattern underlying this plot-motivated action in the alternating scenes depicting Urizen's and Los's activities in the war.

The structure of the first part of the Night might be divided as follows:

| | |
|---|---|
| 99:1–14 | Council of God establishes Limits of Contraction and Opacity |
| 99:15–27; 100:1–25 | Redemptive action of Los and Enitharmon inspired by Divine Vision |

| | |
|---|---|
| 101:1–4 | Urizen's terror and confusion when he sees Lamb of God |
| 101:5–25 | Orc as serpent in Urizen's Constellations |
| 101:26–9; 100:26–34; 101:30–2 | Urizen's battle against World of Los continues |
| 101:33–7 | Satan emerges from war |
| 101:38–48; 102:1–13 | Los builds Golgonooza as defence against war and humanizes Spectres in war |
| 102:14–22 | Urizen escalates attack |
| 102:2–33; 103:1–20 | Urizen in temple and confrontation with Shadowy Female |
| 103:21–31 | Urizen subdued by Shadowy Female in own Web of Religion |

As this outline reveals, the first portion of the Night is based on a simple interlace structure that juxtaposes the destructive action of Urizen to the redemptive action of Los and Enitharmon. Blake uses this juxtaposition to emphasize parallels between the positive and negative agencies represented in the work. For example, immediately after we hear that Los and Enitharmon humanize the "bestial droves" (101b:47) by singing "lulling cadences" (101b:45) to relieve the battle-weary in Urizen's war, we are told how Urizen gives "life and sense" not to his troops but "To all his engines of deceit" (102:4–15). For his troops he forms

> harsh instruments of sound
> To grate the soul into destruction or to inflame with fury
> The spirits of life to pervert all faculties of sense
> Into their own destruction ... (102:18–21)

Significance in the narrative is thus developed as much through symbolic juxtaposition as through narrative connection. The addition of page 113, which sets "Enitharmons Looms & Los's Forges" against "the Spindles of Tirzah and Rahab and the Mills of Satan & Beelzeboul" (113a:1–2), may reflect Blake's conscious use of this same strategy in *Vala*. This addition also has the effect of demonstrating the polarization of forces that is most pronounced at the point of the Lamb's incarnation.

The third section of the Night demonstrates a surprising degree of continity with section one, in terms of both narrative structure and a diachronic sequence of events:

| | |
|---|---|
| 106:18–48; 107:1–20 | Urizen's fall under the dominance of Vala (he takes on a serpent form) |
| 107:21–38 | Tharmas and Urthona affected along with Los: Tharmas and Urthona transfer their power to Los |
| 108:1–36; 109:1–35; 110: 1–28 | Laments of Ahania and Enion |
|   108:9–36; 109:1–12 | Ahania |
|   109:14–35; 110:1–28 | Enion |
| 110:29–32 | Los and Enitharmon place body of Lamb in Sepulchre |
| 110:33; 111:1–24 | Rahab's final triumph |

Here there are no radical discontinuities, no synchronic fragments, and a limited use of new characters. Only the radical alternation of antagonists shapes the narrative: Los and Enitharmon on the one hand, Urizen and the Shadowy Female on the other. The strength of these continuities and the powerful coherence of this diachronic narrative suggest that this may have constituted an earlier version of the Night. Despite its careful finish, the counterpoint developed here does seem somewhat rigid and threatens to resolve into a militaristic dialectic rather than an interplay of contraries. Moreover, this entire battle seems weighted largely in favour of Urizen and the Shadowy Female; at the very least there is only a limited sense of the full role of a divine creative, protecting, and guiding agency.

The middle section of the Night – a section outlining the Lamb of God's descent and crucifixion – seems designed to right the imbalance. While juxtaposed to the action of battle, this middle section demonstrates most vividly a new kind of narrative form towards which Blake was striving. This portion of the Night appears to be structured as follows:

| | |
|---|---|
| 103:32–9; 104:1–4 | Formation of Jerusalem and Incarnation of Lamb |
|   104:5–10; 113:1–37; 104:11–18 | Song of Sons of Eden and "Enitharmons Looms & Los's Forges" vs "The Spindles of Tirzah & Rahab and the Mills of Satan" |
| 104:19–30 | War takes hermaphroditic form with Vala hidden in bosom of Satan |
| 104:31–8; 105:1–4 | Descent of Lamb |

| | |
|---|---|
| 105:5–7 | Judgement of Lamb |
| 105:8–27 | Formation of Rahab from fruit of Urizen's tree of Mystery |
| 105:28–54 | Song of Females and Amalek in praise of Rahab's creation |
| 105:54–6; 106:1–6 | Crucifixion |
| 106:7–13 | [Rahab's] <Jerusalem's> reaction |
| 106:14–16 | Los removes body to Sepulchre |
| 113:38–42 | Rahab cuts off Mantle of Luvah from Lamb |
| 113:43–53; 115:1–51; 116:1–2 | Los confronts Rahab as Prophet of Eternity |
| 116:3–6; 106:17 | Rahab retreats to Urizen |

The fairly straightforward chronological narrative of the Lamb's first appearance "within Jerusalems Veil" (104:2), his incarnation, descent, judgement, crucifixion, and burial is interrupted or, perhaps more accurately, punctuated by thematically significant events that bear little causal relation ship to the plot. For example, the transition from the judgement to the crucifixion of the Lamb is interrupted by Blake's addition of the story of Rahab-Tirzah's creation from the fruit of Urizen's tree of Mystery. This event does not move the narrative forward in the sense that it explains how the judgement of the Synagogue of Satan turned against the Lamb, but it does show the female evil worshipped by the Synagogue of Satan and lurking behind it.

As the draft of this passage on page 145 reveals, Blake also added the Song of Tirzah to his original depiction of the judgement scene. Again, this passage does not contribute to the development of the chronological narrative, but it strengthens the symbolic or thematic narrative by establishing a parallel for the birth of Rahab within the bosom of Satan with the formation of Jerusalem and appearance of the Lamb "within Jerusalems Veil." Both events are celebrated with a song that shapes our apprehension of the figure involved. Moreover, the moment that each of these events occurs in the narrative is not determined by an obvious development in the plot but by a thematically or symbolically significant connection. For example, the descent of the Lamb and the Song of the Sons of Eden occur when Urizen's religion has completely paralysed Urizen himself, its own high priest, and a truly divine revelation is needed to counteract the coming epiphany of the Shadowy Female. The birth of Rahab and the song praising her religion of torture are not caused directly by the judgement of the Lamb but are an epiphany of the religion that subsumes Christianity into a new form of natural religion. The epiphany of Rahab thus provides a demonic antitype, a religion of death, arising from Christ's crucifixion and set in opposition to the religion arising from Christ's resurrection.

In terms of the larger structure of Night VIII, this middle section has the virtue of interrupting the oppositional structures of the Urizen-Los wars. The point of intersection – the moment of the Shadowy Female's entrapment of Urizen – marks the decisive moment in the triumph of maternal nature. Through a narrative mimesis, the descent of the Lamb acts as a vertical marker, a synchronic disjunction, that ruptures the teleology of a diachronic narrative of war as it moves to its temporal climax and spatial completion. With the Shadowy Female's triumph, categories of time and space – the defining dimensions of narrative – become fixed into a narrative of death, an obliteration of the spiritual. The vertical rupture brought to this narrative of death through the intervention of the Lamb of God offers an alternative focus, redirecting attention from the foregrounded cataclysms of sequential development to the apocalyptics of synchronic perception. Sight, vision, and beholding mark the appearance of the Lamb in the narrative and act as figures of expanded perception, in contradistinction to the auditory confusion of the Los-Urizen battle:

> Troop by troop the beastial droves rend one another sounding loud
> The instruments of sound & troop by troop in human forms they urge
> The dire confusion till the battle faints those that remain
> Return in pangs & horrible convulsions to their beastial state
> For the monsters of the Elements lions or Tygers or Wolves
> Sound loud the howling musing <Inspird by Los & Enitharmon>
> Sounding loud   (101:47–102:5)

While the disruptions occasioned by this change mark a breakthrough in narrative strategy, they do not come without some threats to a poem nearly completely transcribed. Grafting a new set of characters to an existing narrative at the point of its climax makes extraordinary demands on the coherence of the existing narrative. To some extent the incorporation of divine interventions into the already transcribed poem is facilitated by the unpredictable nature of spiritual agencies from the perspectives of mortal observers. The apparent capriciousness makes plausibility only a minor concern in poetic construction. Yet Blake may also have felt uneasy about the almost mechanical opposition that is played out impersonally between the Lamb and Satan. Erdman points out that the later Christian revisions to *Vala* give it "a providential and even predestinarian emphasis." Blake's Christ, continues Erdman, appears "as a *deus ex machina*, a 'Finger of God' who sets the limits beyond which tyranny (Satan) cannot go and man (Adam) cannot be further enslaved (F.Z.iv.56:17–26). In this view, the French Revolution appears to have been a predestinated pageant rather than a drama of human conflict."[3]

In attempting to graft Christian imagery and thought on to his poem, Blake appears to have asserted the same kind of predestinarianism he objected to in his annotations to Swedenborg's *Divine Providence*.[4] Donald Ault points out that "Blake forces us to experience the Lamb of God and Satan totally from the outside: they appear and disappear enigmatically throughout Night VIII." He adds that, "though they are in some ways the most important 'characters' in Night VIII, we have no sense of their motives: they seem, even more than other characters, to be complexes of relationships, with no real interiors."[5] The impersonal quality of the Lamb-Satan conflict sits uneasily in the work of a poet obsessed by humanity. In addition, the redemptive power of the Lamb exists wholly apart from the wilful initiation of the Last Judgement by the Eternal Man. Lincoln points out that Blake was willing "to use Christian symbolism in a direct way, but the providential awakening mentioned here [Night IX] seems quite irrelevant to the awakening actually described, and seems to deny the importance of Man's struggle to reassert his will."[6] At this relatively early stage in his adoption of Christian symbolism, Blake seems to have been somewhat at the mercy of the images in his external source, the book of Revelation, and had not fully assimilated its biblical images to his already established personal mythology. With the addition of the Los, Enitharmon, and Spectre of Urthona passage to the end of Night VII[a], Blake's narrative poetics undergoes further revision.

## BREAKING THE BONDS OF NARRATIVE SEQUENCE: NIGHT VII(A) AND NIGHT VII(B)

The existence of two versions of Night VII creates an editorial and critical crux in *Vala* that may never be entirely resolved, yet some recent debates throw interesting light on the implications of our sense of a developing narrative, structure, and coherence. Initial debates about the two

Nights VII raged over which came first[7] or how to arrange the two Nights;[8] however, in the fall 1978 issue of *Blake: An Illustrated Quarterly*, John Kilgore, Andrew Lincoln, Mark Lefebvre, and David Erdman[9] raised the stakes in debating the editorial fate of Night VII[b] in relation to the *Vala* manuscript as a whole and Night VII[a] in particular. As a result of this exchange, Erdman made the bold move of incorporating VII[b] into the final pages of VII[a] in his 1982 revised edition of Blake's works.

It is perhaps unfortunate that this debate has shaped the poem into something we have no manuscript evidence for, but Erdman's reasons for choosing this path are instructive. While I can agree with Erdman's statement that "the relegating of VII[b] to a postscript or the printing of VII[a] and VII[b] in tandem" – as has occurred in previous editions – may not respond adequately "to the manuscript or to the reader's appreciation of an inclusive yet coherent narrative or thematic sequence or structure,"[10] the embedding of one Night in another with no manuscript authority can only obscure the problem of the separate state of the two Nights VII for future readers. Donald Ault, also troubled by this new arrangement, points out, "Erdman's willingness to entertain these possibilities (with little encouragement from Blake) reflects his deep concern for what he repeatedly calls 'fit' between the two Nights – an odd concern, it might seem, in a poet who refused to accept even the 'fit' between world and mind."[11]

Blake left explicit instructions about the rearrangement of VII[b] and the insertion of pages 113–16 in Night VIII, for instance, but the insertion of VII[b] in VII[a] seems to contradict the overall direction of Blake's revisions to the poem. Many of the revisions in Nights VII[a] and VII[b] began as minor disruptions occasioned by subtle character and plot shifts, but I hope to show that, increasingly, they moved the poem away from a diachronic concern with narrative sequence towards a synchronic principle of juxtaposition or discontinuity.

In commenting on the vexed relationship between the two versions of Night VII, Frye situates the cause of this apparent anomaly at the feet of a plausible instigator – the Spectre of Urthona. Frye writes, "The conception of the Spectre of Urthona seems to have broken on Blake quite suddenly when he was proceeding to a simpler climax, and occasioned the rewriting of Night VII, if not of the next two Nights as well. Eventually it burst the whole Zoa scheme altogether, and was one of the chief reasons for abandoning the poem."[12] I think Frye is right here, but perhaps not for reasons the manuscript ostensibly supports. The

Spectre was an invention developed as early as the transcription of Night IV, and so the "conception" of the figure alone was not enough to cause Blake to abandon the poem entirely; still, the potential significance of this figure was not exploited by Blake until after the poem was fully transcribed and is a result of a multitude of shifts in the poem that disrupt an earlier "conception" of the poem's narrative. Indeed, the emergence of the Spectre seems not to "burst the whole Zoa scheme altogether" but instead to enable a radical form of representing it. Ultimately it is not really the "conception of the Spectre of Urthona" but the re-evaluation of him in relation to the revised roles of Los and Enitharmon that has such a radical effect on the poem's design. In particular, the connection of the Spectre, Los, and Enitharmon as central to the redemptive movement of the text is a late but overwhelming notion, one that overpowers the bulk of the base transcription of the poem.[13] Indeed, except for Night VII[a], there are no moments of prophetic awareness, divine vision, or humanizing tendencies leading to an apocalypse.

Signs of this change, this transformation of Los to a central role of redeemer, appear in a host of additions to the poem. When Blake added pages 113–16, he did so by using a completion of the Rahab story as a bridge to introduce the later material on these pages; however, this extra material had more to do with Los than Rahab and reflects a shift in Blake's attention away from an expansion and completion of Rahab's role to a fuller depiction of Los. Los's assertion on page 113, "I am that shadowy Prophet who six thound years ago / Fell from my station in the Eternal bosom" (113:50–1), indicates his self-conscious awareness of his eternal identity and temporal profession. The text of page 115, with its catalogue of Los's descendants, then, establishes him as the beginning of a significant prophetic line and tradition. Also, his insight into "The Difference between States & Individuals of those States" (115:24) and the Providential division of history into Seven Eyes of God (115:42–50) demonstrates that he is a purveyor of Divine Vision and understanding. Moreover, the placement of 113:40–116:6 immediately after the crucifixion of the Lamb and Rahab's epiphany as "the Temple & the Synagogue of Satan & Mystery" (113:42) locates the source of his prophetic vision in the Christian tradition of self-sacrifice and juxtaposes his realization of himself as a true prophet against the deceptive appearances of Rahab as the source of error in the Synagogue of Satan. We should note here that Blake's attempts to expand Los's new role in the poem come about mainly through large-scale additions to the poem that introduce material from his later works, containing characters and ideas not directly prepared for in the base transcription of *Vala*.

The only portion of the base text adding this redemptive tone to Los and Enitharmon's action (without the Spectre) comes at the opening of Night VIII. In the base text of Night VIII, Los and Enitharmon are given a more significant position in the poem through their perception of the Divine Vision (99:20–3) and their creation of Jerusalem in the form of "a Vast family wondrous in beauty & love / ... a Universal female form created / From those who were dead in Ulro" (103:37–9). Los and Enitharmon work together in Night VIII creating Jerusalem in Golgonooza, with Los receiving the dead as they descend from the war of Urizen and Tharmas, and Enitharmon weaving "Bodies of Vegetation" (100:4) as a protection for these Spectres. The general co-operation between Los and Enitharmon marks a new development in *Vala*; it stands in stark contrast to the jealousy and strife that characterize their other appearances in the poem. Indeed, Los's redemptive posture in Night VIII creates an apparent inconsistency with his warlike appearances in Night VII[b], where he rears

his mighty [*forehead*] \<stature\> on Earth stood his feet. Above
The moon his furious forehead circled with black bursting thunders
His naked limbs glittring upon the dark blue sky his knees
Bathed in bloody clouds. his loins in fires of war where spears
And swords rage where the Eagles cry & Vultures laugh saying
Now comes the night of Carnage now the flesh of Kings & Princes
Pamperd in palaces [*of*] \<for\> our food the blood of Captains nurturd
With lust & murder for our drink the drunken Raven Shall wander
All night among the slain & mock the wounded that groan in the field.

(96:20–8)

The emphasis on "blood" and "Carnage" as Los prepares to oppose Urizen in Night VII[b] clearly seems to be part of an earlier narrative in *Vala*. In Night VIII the revised narrative emphasizes a spiritual rather than physical opposition to Urizen's war. As part of an attempt to create dramatic development within Los in preparation for his new role in Night VIII, Blake turned back to the end of Night VII[a] and Los's confrontation with Enitharmon and the Spectre of Urthona. Through a renewed use of the Spectre – a character absent from Night VIII and its revisions – Blake attempts to depict dramatically the internal development of Los that makes him worthy of the Divine Vision prior to Night VIII and the Last Judgement in Night IX. The additions lead to a disruption of the earlier diachronic narrative strategies, but a potential rebirth in a new poetics.

Evidence from the manuscript itself indicates that the narrative connection between the two Nights VII was – at the point of its transcription on the *Night Thoughts* proof sheets – largely determined by logical sequence and narrative "fit." Bentley, in arguing that Night VII[b] followed VII[a] in terms of transcription, first outlined in detail the definite narrative links between the earliest ending of Night VII[a] (85:22) and the earliest beginning of VII[b] (91:1ff; B.162–3). Night VII[a] ends:

> She burst the Gates of Enitharmons heart with direful Crash
> Nor could they ever be Closd again the golden hinges were broken
> And the gates [*burst*] <broke> in sunder & their ornaments defacd
> Beneath the tree of Mystery for the immortal shadow shuddering
> Brought forth this wonder horrible a Cloud she grew & grew
> Till many of the dead burst forth from the bottoms of their tombs
>
> The Spectre [*smild*] <terrified> & gave her Charge over the howling Orc.
> (85:13–18,22)

Night VII[b] begins:

> Now in the Caverns of the Grave & Places of human seed
> The nameless shadowy Vortex stood before the face of Orc
> The Shadow reard her dismal head over the flaming youth
> With sighs & howling & deep sobs that he might lose his rage
> And with it lose himself in meekness she embracd his fire ...   (91:1–5)

Blake made three separate additions to the end of Night VII[a], each more disruptive than the last, producing a serious rupture in this narrative sequence, a rupture that increasingly precluded any attempts at maintaining sequential "fit." He seems to have gone so far as to rearrange Night VII[b], perhaps as an attempt to regain some sort of fit, but his lack of instructions about how VII[b] was ultimately to be positioned in relation to VII[a] suggests either a sense of defeat on his part or, more likely, a growing disregard for notions of fit.

### Addition 1

In his first revision to the end of Night VII[a], Blake erased the "End of the Seventh Night" after line 85:22, modified the earlier final line, added lines 23–31, and again wrote "The End of the Seventh Night" at the bottom of the page (see Plate 8). The change takes place beginning with a revision of the Spectre's response to a parodic apocalypse orchestrated by the Shadowy Female, an apocalypse in which the "dead burst forth" (85:18) from the bottom of the graves. Blake first wrote "The Spectre smild" as he gave the Shadowy Female "Charge over the howling Orc" (85:22). Later, "smild" was replaced by "terrified," and Blake began to emphasize the dichotomy between the horrific influence of Urizen's tree of Mystery and the potentially redemptive power of the Spectre of Urthona. The addition reads in full:

> Then took the tree of Mystery root in the World of Los
> Its topmost [*branches*] <boughs> shooting a [*stem*] <fibre> beneath Enithar-
>    mons couch
> The double rooted Labyrinth soon wavd around their heads
>
> But then the Spectre enterd Los's bosom Every sigh & groan
> Of Enitharmon bore Urthonas Spectre on its wings
> Obdurate Los felt Pity Enitharmon told the tale
> Of Urthona. Los Embracd the Spectre first as a brother
> Then as another Self; astonishd humanizing & in tears
> In Self abasement Giving up his Domineering lust.   (85:23–31)

Beginning with "Then," the addition offers at least a tentative sense of sequential unity and also uses a second "then" to strengthen logical continuity and juxtaposition. However, the second "then" (actually a "But then") offers an event not fully prepared for by earlier developments. Indeed, the second half of the addition functions in terms of the juxtapositional logic we have seen in Night VIII. The effects of the tree of Mystery are set in opposition to the reconciliation of Los and the Spectre.

The tension between redemption and fall is also set in relief by an addition just preceding the originally transcribed ending of VII[a]:

> In male forms without female counterparts or Emanations
> Cruel & ravening with Enmity & Hatred & War
> In dreams of Ulro [*sweet*] <dark> delusive drawn by the lovely shadow
>
>                                           (85:19–21)

The redemptive counterpoint blunts the earlier continuities with Night VII[b] but gains a dynamic sense of juxtaposition. The narrative of redemption begins here with Enitharmon's telling of the "Tale of Urthona" and Los's embrace of the Spectre, events that seem fairly logical as an afterthought, but not prepared for by the preceding narrative. This addition establishes the idea of self-annihilation that became so important to Blake during the writing of *Milton* and *Jerusalem*, suggesting perhaps a comparison of Los with the Lamb through his act of self-sacrifice, a comparison that Blake would later elaborate upon. While the disruption caused by this change might not be termed radical, it does introduce a minor schism between the neat fit of Night vii[a] and vii[b] as they originally join at and reinforce the growing dominance of the tree of Mystery and the growing rule of the Shadowy Female. At its simplest, this change introduces a slight alienation of the Shadowy Female's dominance, an emerging state of self-sacrifice on the part of Los, the Spectre, and Enitharmon, and a reassertion of the Shadowy Female's triumph over Orc.

### Addition 2

In a continued expansion of the dramatic conflict of Los with the Spectre and Enitharmon, Blake again erased his finis for the Night and added a lengthy conclusion, including the text of 85:32–47, page 86, and the added leaves 87–8 and 89–90. All indicators, both editorial and critical, suggest that the second set of additions is extremely late in the overall life of the manuscript, probably following the transcription of even Night viii.[14] The text on these pages develops Los's conflict with his Spectre, and although the transcription is late, the characterization of the Spectre appears less malevolent and more ambivalent than the bat-winged, devouring spectre in *Jerusalem*. As part of the new ending to Night vii[a] on page 85, the Spectre suggests to Los:

> If [*once*] we unite in one another better world will be
> Opend within your heart & loins & wondrous brain
> Threefold as it was in Eternity & this the fourth Universe
> Will be Renewd by the three & consummated in Mental fires.   (85:43–6)

If Los follows this suggestion out, argues the Spectre, his labour will become part of a divine mission to return man "to Life Eternal" (85:35).

As Los attempts to persuade Enitharmon to co-operate with him and the Spectre, he becomes conveyor of and mediator for the Divine Vision; he tells her, "Turn inwardly thine Eyes & there behold the Lamb of

God / Clothd in Luvahs robes of blood descending to redeem" (87:44–5). He also appeals to her through the Christian doctrines of forgiveness and self-sacrifice:

> O Enitharmon
> Couldst thou but cease from terror & trembling & affright
> When I appear before thee in forgiveness of [*former injuries*] <ancient injuries>
> Why shouldst thou remember & be afraid. I surely have died in pain
> Often enough[*t*] to convince thy jealousy & fear & terror.   (87:46–50)

Finally, when Los has convinced Enitharmon to join with him and the Spectre in the process of generation, their work becomes one of self-sacrifice and externalizes the Christian doctrine of forgiveness. As they create "Counterparts" or "Female forms" (90:56) to comfort "The Spectrous dead" (90:42) from Urizen's wars,

> … Los loved them & refusd to Sacrifice their infant limbs
> And Enitharmons smiles & tears prevaild over self protection
> They rather chose to meet Eternal death than to destroy
> The offspring of their Care & Pity.   (90:51–4)

Here Blake presents the first fully developed act of complete and intentional self-sacrifice for another in the poem, and for a time, Night vii[a] ended here.

Significantly, Los's self-sacrifice on pages 85–90 is combined with his reintegration with the fragmented Urthona: through the drama played out among Los, his Spectre, and Enitharmon, Blake demonstrates that imaginative co-operation followed by self-sacrifice leads to the reintegration of the individual in a personal Last Judgement that precedes and indeed brings about the final Apocalypse. I do not wish to oversimplify Blake's meaning, but it is worth pointing out that acts of willing co-operation and especially self-sacrifice of this kind mark a significant change in a poem obsessed with wilful selfishness and escalating antagonisms. Certainly, there is co-operation in the Ninth Night, but it is enforced by the Eternal Man and only follows the Last Judgement. Moreover, although the Lamb sacrifices himself in Night viii, this act seems more a part of a providential plan than a personal sacrifice. The dramatic depiction of Los, Enitharmon, and the Spectre's sacrifice shows the mental struggle necessary to make such a sacrifice. No matter how forward-looking these changes appear in terms of the growth of Blake's mythology, however, no matter how much they bolster a synoptic connection particularly with the later works, they created significant structural problems within *Vala*.

As Blake began to reinterpret Los's role in the poem and the nature of his relationship to Enitharmon and the Spectre, the structure of the poem began to shift and the place of the subsequent Nights, especially vii[b], came into question. The revisions to vii[a] rendered vii[b], if not superfluous, at least inconsistent with the rest of the narrative development from vii[a] to viii. After the elaborate reconciliation of Los with his Spectre and Enitharmon in the new ending of vii[a], Night vii[b] continues without the Spectre and with renewed but unmotivated tension between Los and Enitharmon.

The reversal of Night vii[b] illustrates the process of revision towards a more disrupted text. We may never know exactly when or why Blake reversed the order of Night vii[b]; however, a strong possibility is that as he began to add to the end of vii[a], he realized that the earlier narrative continuity between the earliest end of vii[a] and the beginning of vii[b] became a wholly insufficient reason to keep Night vii[b] in the poem. Therefore, he experimented with the strategy of dividing Night vii[b] after 95:14 and reversing the order of the two halves. This action resulted in a complete replacement of narrative continuity by narrative juxtaposition.

The division and rearrangement of Night vii[b] seems consciously designed to reinforce the idea of juxtaposition since the reworking of the original order creates a structure parallel to that of Night vii[a]. "Nights viia and viib," writes Ault, "function as alternate routes of realization of the same events" and allow Blake "to explore the implications of alternative fictional possibilities."[15] Each Night begins with Urizen in a mood of triumph, followed by the vision of an opposing figure. Night vii[a] opens with Urizen chasing off Tharmas and the Spectre of Urthona and continues with his confrontation with the rebellious Orc. Night vii[b] opens with Urizen's triumphant proclamation, "The time of Prophecy is now revolvd & all / This Universal Ornament is mine" (95:18–19), and his establishment of a Universal Empire. This scene is followed by the appearance of Los and Tharmas, plotting to undermine Urizen's rule. Each Night concludes with a bursting forth of the dead from the bottoms of their tombs (cf 85:18 and 95:11).

Yet the addition of the new endings to vii[a] leaves us with the sense that Blake did not feel bound by mathematically exact parallel structures.

Such exactness takes imagination out of life and art. It was condemned by Blake as "Grecian ... Mathematical Form," which is "Eternal [only] in the Reasoning Memory" and therefore subject to decay and distortion; against this form Blake championed a Gothic or "Living Form [which] is Eternal Existence" (E.270). In the continued additions to VII[a] Blake develops his text in terms of Gothic Living Form, nurturing the seed of an idea unconstrained by the limitations of rigid consistency in form.[16] He repeatedly broadens the apocalyptic implications of the union of Los, Enitharmon, and the Spectre of Urthona until Night VII[a] seems not only to render Night VII[b] almost superfluous but also to undermine the apparent climax of the poem in Night VIII.

The absence of a finis line and "End of the Seventh Night" for Night VII[a] may suggest its continued open-endedness in Blake's mind.[17] We probably will never know what Blake might have done to rectify the problem – if indeed this was as troubling to him as it has been to his readers – yet the development of the new endings to VII[a] illustrates vividly the way Blake's writing process would transcend all expectations of a sequentially developing narrative. The two Nights VII seem to defy expectation of a finite text in favour of an indeterminate text. This crux thereby multiplies rather than limits potential meaning. The existence of two Nights VII may ultimately have struck Blake as no more inconsistent than the two versions of creation in Genesis. Both are part of a consistent vision. Conflating or embedding Night VII[b] in VII[a] seems only to obscure the evidence of imaginative development for the convenience of reading and interpretation.

This type of revision seems conscious on Blake's part and may be influenced by juxtapositional structures in the Bible. Tannenbaum has, of course, described several possible biblical analogies. Jerome McGann, in an investigation of the textual complexities of the *Book of Urizen*, finds possible sources for textual anomalies such as the two fourth chapters in *Urizen* in a different source: Alexander Geddes' "Fragment Hypothesis" of the Bible. Under this hypothesis the Bible is understood as "a heterogeneous collection of various materials gathered together at different times by different editors and redactors." The apparently "disorderly text" of Blake's *Book of Urizen*, argues McGann, represents a deliberate act on Blake's part, an attempt to "make *Urizen* a parody of Genesis carried out along lines opened up by the new biblical criticism and by the radical priest Alexander Geddes in particular."[18] Although not a direct parody of the Bible, *Vala* imitates the broad structural pattern of Creation, Fall, Crucifixion, Apocalypse, and Last Judgement that characterizes the biblical myth. The disruptive tendency of Blake's revisions enlarges the scope of this imitation and also bring it closer to the kind of heterogeneous textuality found in the Bible.

Equally as problematic as the role of vii[b] in relation to vii[a] is material contained in Night ix. Indeed, the opening of ix seems to undercut the later developments in the Los-Enitharmon-Spectre narrative in vii[a] and viii. For example, the union of the Spectre of Urthona and the "Spectre" of Enitharmon[19] at the beginning of Night ix (117:24–118:6) may have served as an earlier "attempt to resolve the problem of Urthona's disintegration"[20] in the pre-Christian narrative. At some point Blake seems to have concluded their story in the added opening to Night the Ninth, where

> The Spectre of Enitharmon let loose in the troubled deep
> Waild Shrill in the confusion & the Spectre of Urthona
> Recievd her in the darkning South their bodies lost they stood
> Trembling & weak a faint embrace a fierce desire as when
> Two shadows mingle on a wall they wail & shadowy tears
> Fell down & shadowy forms of joy mixd with despair & grief
> Their bodies buried in the ruins of the Universe
> Mingled with the confusion. Who shall call them from the Grave.
>
> (117:24–118:6)

The emphasis on shadows and confusion conveys the futility of their union, and the statement that "Their bodies ... / Mingled with the confusion" demonstrates that they are just another part of the conflagration of the Universe. The final question, "Who shall call them from the Grave," also demonstrates the general powerlessness of Spectre and Shadow in the Last Judgement. Although this passage offers a reasonable conclusion to the story of the Spectre and Shadow as outlined in the first stage of vii[a]'s development (before any additions), it seems anticlimactic in light of the subsequent revisions. Blake's failure to amend passages such as these in accord with additions like those to the end of vii[a] results in a shift of the main climax of the action from Night ix to the new endings of Night vii[a].

The overall thematic effect of pages 85–90, however, is to shift attention from the broad focus on the struggle of universal forces in the Eternal Man to the internal redemption of an individual part of that Man. Los, Enitharmon, and the Spectre together represent different aspects of the fallen fragmented Urthona. Their struggle represents the attempt of the individual to achieve a personal apocalypse in preparation for the universal Last Judgement of Mankind. The product of the individual's personal apocalypse, his perception of eternity, is art, and through the added story of Los on pages 85–90 Blake demonstrates the importance of the poet-prophet and his art as a vehicle for the universal recreation of the present heaven and earth in preparation for the one to come. In the Lambeth books Blake, buoyed by hopes founded on the initial successes of the French Revolution that tyranny might be overcome, adopted a prophetic view of history in the belief that the appearance of the kingdom of God was imminent, and with the development of the Los story at the end of VII[a] he appears to have returned to his earlier concerns with the role of the prophet.

Yet, as Paley points out, "After the failure of the French Revolution and the consolidation of Napoleonic tyranny, Blake turned ... from a Prophetic to an apocalyptic model of history. As nothing was now to be hoped for from revolutionary energy, Orc became merely an encumbrance to be disposed of at the Last Judgement."[21] Therefore, Blake turned to an apocalyptic dualism of sorts, played out in a confrontation between the Lamb of God and Satan. Their confrontation raises the central conflict above the world of human failings, and the death and resurrection of the Lamb offers a logical transition from the fallen world to the regenerative action depicted in Night IX. The addition of figures such as the Lamb and Satan helps to clarify the identities of the forces involved in the Apocalypse, but these characters are largely external to the action and to Blake's personalized mythology. The overall action strays into a story of abstract spiritual life and death warring against one another while Rahab-Tirzah, a principle of physical generation, torments a totally victimized humanity. With the development of Rahab's character and her moral struggle between pride and repentance, Blake narrows his dramatic focus to the changes within one character that the Crucifixion and Last Judgement bring about. Yet her struggle is essentially limited to only one page in Night VIII (page 111), and she hardly figures as a central protagonist in the rest of the work.

The story of Los and Enitharmon returns a human and prophetic interest to *Vala*. Through them Blake depicts a human couple attempting to build spiritual life out of the spiritual death of the physical universe. The central tool of their recreation is art. Conflict is displaced from the external war, which finally manifests itself in the form of Satan, to the psychological struggle of Los and his own Spectre. Their struggle is an internal one of self-discipline that takes on a cosmic significance when they act in unison. Together, they open "new heavens & a new Earth beneath & within / Threefold within the brain within the heart within the loins / A Threefold Atmosphere Sublime continuous from [*Urizens*][22] <Urthonas> world" (87:9–11). Together, as part of a prophetic tradition, they guide the movement towards Apocalypse, or at least retain the Divine Vision in a fallen world and maintain the possibility of redemption. Also, Los's acceptance of his Spectre represents an acknowledgment and acceptance of personal error[23] rather than a polarization of truth and error such as that demonstrated through the confrontation of the Lamb and Satan.[24] The focal point for redemption shifts away from the rage of Orc and the torture of the Lamb to the maintaining of the Divine Vision by Los, "that Shadowy Prophet who … / Fell from … [his] station in the Eternal bosom" (113:50–1). Thus Blake returns a note of hope for the recreation of flashes of the Divine in the fallen world of history.

The concerns reflected by Los, Enitharmon, and the Spectre of Los, however, are those particularly of *Jerusalem*, where Blake stresses the significance of the "Human form divine" (EG.[f]66; E.522) and the gospel of the forgiveness of sin. Although these concerns are not wholly incompatible with *Vala*, their explicit appearance only in the story of Los and Enitharmon and the Spectre on pages 85–90 of Night VII[a] implies a reworking of their appearances throughout the poem and particularly in the final Night, where the Spectre appears only briefly and Los initiates the Last Judgement through "prophetic impatience" or "an act of desperation"[25] rather than enlightenment. Although the struggle between Los and his Spectre is crucial to *Jerusalem*, where it serves as a dramatic centre for the action of the poem, the added weight of their constant mental strife, compressed into a few pages of the *Vala* manuscript, seems just another strain on an already weakened frame. While it is not altogether clear, as Frye argues, that the Spectre of Urthona "burst the whole Zoas scheme altogether, and was one of the chief reasons for abandoning the poem,"[26] the changes made to the end of Night VII[a] introduce events into the text not prepared for by a diachronic narrative.

The yoking of prophecy, Apocalypse, and self-sacrifice in a mental arena rather than an external cosmic space demands some rethinking of narrative structures that depict them. Representation is no longer a matter of spatial and temporal sequence, a diachronic expansion of events, but instead an attempt to convey the experience of a simultaneous moment of apprehension. This moment cuts across the deterministic structures of time and space, reorienting them in terms of individual recognition. As a result, two plot structures play off against and energize each other. The external plot developing across the larger categories of time and space seems arbitrarily deterministic and, most importantly, beyond the control (and perhaps the interests) of individual humans. The additions to vii[a] increasingly highlight a counterpointed narrative that cuts across the cosmic plot and reorients it within the framework of individual mental acts. The diachronic form of narrative setting up the initial framework of the poem will inevitably experience some stress and strain under this epiphanic or synchronically rich event. Yet Blake delivered one final blow to this earlier narrative experience.

### Addition 3

In the third and final development in the life of vii[a] Blake went on to make one final addition to the poem, lines 59–68 on page 90.[27] These lines tell how Los draws Urizen's "[*Spectre*] <Shadow> away / From out the ranks of war separating him in sunder / Leaving his Spectrous form which could not be drawn away" (90:59–61). The effect of these lines is to demonstrate Los's forgiveness of even his worst enemy and his triumph over his own hate. Blake achieves this effect, however, at great cost to the diachronic narrative consistency with the rest of the poem. The peaceful union of Los and Urizen obviates the need for the war between them in Nights vii[b] and viii. Moreover, although one could argue that the "Spectrous form" of Urizen carries on the war, this isolation of Urizen's Spectre from his human form in Night vii[a] renders his transformation into the Spectrous form of the stony serpent in Night viii redundant. Also, Los's separation of Urizen's human form from his Spectrous form makes the Eternal Man's destruction of Urizen's dragon form in Night ix equally redundant. Last but not least, the addition introduces a whole new series of characters – Thiriel, Rintrah, and Palamabron, for example – who do not play a significant role in the base text of the poem. The net effect, then, of this addition is to undercut much of the narrative action that follows. Yet Blake seems committed to developing Los's positive characterization as redeemer and prophet capable of extreme acts of self-sacrifice that make him worthy of receiving the Divine Vision, even at the possible expense of significant portions of *Vala*.

Ultimately, the expansion of vii[a] brought changes necessitating a narrative framework more complex than diachronic development or simple juxtapositional structures could allow. Instead, the radical realignment of events around the personal and imminent experience of self-sacrifice begins to emerge. Textual modifications to Night VIII in the form of added lines (99:32–3, 101:38–46) or pages (113–16) attempt to add continuity to the notion of self-recognition born of self-sacrifice; such additions thrust the vertically aligned concerns of prophecy and Apocalypse to the forefront of the poem. In this new context, narrative significance emerges through the revised form of Los's vertical consciousness as Prophet of Eternity, particularly as this consciousness has coherent connection with the presence of a host of later additions – the Daughters of Beulah, the Council of God, and the Seven Eyes of God – whose orientation is to constant concerns of the spiritual rather than the fitfully developing battles of the physical.

I should point out at this juncture that I am not convinced Blake resolves these conflicts of narrative representation fully in *Vala*. Blake's move towards a synchronic narrative, a narrative of the kind found in *Jerusalem*, for instance, is incomplete. The host of later Christian additions helps to create an impression of a move in this direction since they create alignment of symbols with those appearing in Night VIII and of narrative disruptions like those found in the additions to Night VII[a]. The force of these changes alerts the reader to a vertical dimension of significance overriding a horizontal development of meaning. Blake's apparent shifts in attention from one set of characters to another and one portion of the manuscript to another did not last long enough for him to complete fully any one stage of revision. Yet the central mythic concerns of his poem remain relatively consistent despite the growing cast of different characters. The apocalyptic hopes that Blake had depicted through Orc in the Lambeth books and then through the Eternal Man in *Vala* were eventually realized through the sacrificial figure of the Lamb of God after the Christian revision of the poem. As Blake's myth evolved further, his development of the Lamb as a symbol of redemption gave way to a fuller depiction of Los and his externalized psychological struggle with Spectre and Emanation. Similarly, the depiction of the masculine errors of exclusive rationality, warlike aggression, empire building, and repressive morality that were Urizen's particular domain in the pre-Christian narrative of *Vala* became vividly embodied in Satan and his Synagogue with the advent of Christian symbolism.

When Blake re-evaluated Los's character, he slowly developed the Spectre of Urthona as a representation of this masculine error.[28] Finally, the feminine errors of elusiveness, delusive beauty, and manipulative control that first appear in the Shadowy Female in *Vala* are, after the

Christianization of the poem, developed in Rahab. But yet again, with Blake's re-evaluation of Los, he was able to depict the individual's struggle with these errors through Los's conflict and reintegration with Enitharmon in VII[a]. Although Blake did not add the redemptive thread of the Los-Spectre-Enitharmon narrative to other parts of *Vala*, he did attempt to add particular redemptive themes and images throughout the poem with various other characters; not until *Jerusalem* would he fully develop the synchronic narrative structures capable of exploiting these many characters and interests.

# Character

# 3 Recasting the Copperplate

The observation that Blake's characters tend towards flat symbolic types rather than rounded lifelike characters has often been accepted as a weakness in his method; simple realism, however, was never Blake's aim. A close examination of the way he revised the attitudes and attributes of his characters shows that he was keenly interested in developing them as types depicting "the Physiognomies or L[i]neaments of Universal Human Life beyond which Nature never steps" (E.570). Character, as he argues in his prospectus to the engraving of Chaucer's Canterbury pilgrims, has a constancy to it that art tries to bring into relief:

The Characters of Chaucers Pilgrims are the Characters that compose all Ages & Nations, as one Age falls another rises. different to Mortal Sight but to Immortals only the same, for we see the same Characters repeated again & again in Animals in Vegetables in Minerals & in Men. Nothing new occurs in Identical Existence ∴ Accident ever varies Substance can never suffer change nor decay. (E.569)

What seems an obvious attribute of character in the early portions of *Vala* – that is, an obsession with "The torments of Love & Jealousy" – is a theme not entirely obvious in the copperplate transcription of pages 1–42, the earliest transcribed portion of the present manuscript. Indeed, as the title-page reveals, this subtitle – "The torments of Love & Jealousy" – is a late, perhaps a very late addition to the poem. Indicators such as handwriting style and writing instruments (a pencil instead of pen and ink) suggest that the addition of the subtitle occurred simultaneously with the change of the title of the poem from *Vala* to *The Four Zoas* and the identification of "Albion" as "the [*Eternal*] <Ancient> Man." The earlier subtitle, "The Death and Judgement of the Eternal Man," offers a very different thematic basis for character construction. Rooted as it is in a teleological structure leading from death to judgement and presumably to redemption, the earlier subtitle suggests a continuity of developments along a diachronic sequence. Within this model, character could be constructed in terms of expanding psychological development, moving from revelation to revelation as something like a series of mental reconfigurations leading to a recognition and rejection of error. However, the insertion of a new subtitle shaping the text in term of "torments of Love & Jealousy" foregrounds the emotional turmoil specifically within the members of the Eternal Man, diverting attention to some degree from his teleological development from Death to Judgement.

The shift from teleology to states of torment emerges in the methods and modes of characterization in the earlier portions of the text as each of the Zoas and his respective Emanation becomes embroiled in personal internal strife; any sense of others or an other is blotted out by a solipsism that negates external concerns, awareness, or internal development. A fragmentary narrative becomes easier to construct within this poetics of character. As Blake revises the copperplate text, he makes changes that draw Los, Luvah, Urizen, Tharmas, and their respective mates further into the conflicts and occasioned by torments of love and jealousy. To this end he relies on a surprising flexibility in characterization, reshaping his figures in terms of analogical relationships among themselves. Each set of characters – Los and Enitharmon, Luvah and Vala, Urizen and Ahania, Tharmas and Enion – is increasingly shaped by "Love and Jealousy"; each contains remnants of eternity within the turmoil of fallen experience. In complementing the overlaying principles of synchronic narrative, the characters are revised to highlight their analogical, typical identities as variations on the theme of tormented sexuality. In essence, we begin to read the same character struggles repeated with subtle alterations, each incorporating a mixture of cynicism and antagonism with remnants of a divine origin.

## LOS AND ENITHARMON

Of the four narrative threads present in the opening pages, the Los-Enitharmon story offers the most tantalizing evidence of its own

development: the copperplate text is easily discernible and the revisions
– often substantial – appear largely in the form of additions rather than
erasures. In a process of accretion extending from the earliest stages of
transcription to fairly late revision, we can trace extensive modifications
to the text designed to foreground the torments of love and jealousy.
Starting with a detailed description of a natural paradise, complete with
elemental gods and a relatively unconflicted relationship between Los
and Enitharmon, Blake turns his attention towards an extrapolation of
the latent antagonism evidenced ever so slightly in the copperplate text.
The growing emphasis on their jealous relationship, along with an
increasingly antagonistic attitude to others in the narrative, is symptom-
atic of the overall changes to this portion of the manuscript. Making
each couple a sometimes exaggerated illustration of some aspect of the
love-and-jealousy motif that defines the Eternal Man emphasizes the
vertical rather than horizontal connection between their story and the
surrounding ones.

Unlike the latest version of *Vala*, where the relationship between Los
and Enitharmon is defined almost entirely through their jealous argu-
ments and recriminations against one another, the earliest version of *Vala*
focuses on the glory and fecundity of the natural world into which they
are born and on their power to control this paradise. In a passage placed
immediately after the birth of Los and Enitharmon as "two little Infants
… [on] the desolate wind," Blake describes the emergence of a nurturing,
vital, and benevolent natural world:

> The barked Oak, the long limbd Beech; the Ches'nut tree; the Pine.
> The Pear tree mild, the frowning Walnut, the sharp Crab, & Apple sweet,
> The rough bark opens; twittering peep forth little beaks & wings
> The Nightingale, the Goldfinch, Robin, Lark, Linnet & Thrush
> The Goat leap'd from the craggy [*Rock*] ‹cliff›, the Sheep awoke from the
>    mould
> Upon its green stalk rose the Corn, waving innumerable
> Infolding the bright Infants from the desolating winds.   (8:14–20)[1]

This extended description of nature is of a kind not found elsewhere in
*Vala*. The sheer number of different trees and birds mentioned conveys
a sense of natural richness and abundance. Further, the green stalks of
corn "waving innumerable" (8:19) emphasize the fecundity of this world
in contrast with the rocky one from which it springs. The nurturing
quality of the various trees that offer shelter for young birds, the vitality
of the leaping goat, and the protective attributes of the corn stalks

present a benevolent picture of the natural world that is characteristic of certain parts of *Milton* but seems atypical of this earlier stage of Blake's writing.

Later in the First Night, just before the nuptial feast of Los and Enitharmon, Blake offers a view of sublime nature conjoined with simple rural life:

> [*The*] <But> purple night [*the*] <and> crimson morning & the golden day
>     <descending>
> <Thro'> the clear changing atmosphere display'd green fields among
> The varying clouds, like paradises stretch'd in the expanse
> With towns & villages and temples, tents sheep-folds and pastures
> Where dwell the children of the elemental worlds in harmony.   (13:11–15)

The "harmony" of this pastoral vision arises not simply from a peaceful coexistence among the "children of the elemental worlds" but also from the interplay of sky and earth in the description of the breaks between the clouds as "green fields" or "paradises stretch'd in the expanse." At the feast itself, the "Elemental Gods" of this world are described as "Bright Souls of vegetative life, budding and blossoming" (13:24), who

> Stretch their immortal hands to smite the gold & silver Wires
> And with immortal Voice soft warbling fill all Earth & Heaven.
> With doubling Voices & <loud> Horns wound round sounding
> Cavernous dwellers fill'd the enormous Revelry, Responsing,
> And Spirits of Flaming fire on high, govern'd the mighty Song.   (14:1–5)

Los and Enitharmon – the "two little Infants" – are placed at the centre of this emerging world and "enormous Revelry," and retain the godlike ability to control this elemental paradise, an ability that belies their status as "two little Infants" and reminds us of their divine lineage:

> His head beamd light & in his vigorous voice was prophecy
> He could controll the times & seasons, & the days & years
> She could controll the spaces, regions, desart, flood & forest.   (9:26–8)

Even after Los and Enitharmon are drawn down into Urizen's "Golden World," a world we later find is created from the remnants of Luvah and Vala, they are not depicted as petty or fallen beings but like the Immortals of *The Book of Urizen*:[2]

> ... Los & Enitharmon walkd forth on the dewy Earth
> Contracting or expanding their all flexible senses
> At will to murmur in the flowers small as the honey bee
> At will to stretch across the heavens & step from star to star
> Or standing on the Earth erect, or on the stormy waves
> Driving the storms before them or delighting in the sunny beams
> While round their heads the Elemental Gods kept harmony.   (34:9–15)

Yet the overt idealism in the copperplate description of the elemental paradise is implicitly qualified by its context in the narrative and the subtle dissatisfaction hinted at between Los and Enitharmon.

The surrounding scenes, although more textually enigmatic, seem to suggest that all is not well in the elemental paradise. First, of course, is the proximity of the horrific union of Woman and Serpent on page 7 (see Plate 3). Much of this union is written in a complex palimpsest of additions, but the five lines introducing the "two little Infants" survive from the copperplate stage and set a chilling introduction to the birth of the elemental world:

> Mingling his [*horrible*] <terrible> brightness with her tender limbs; then high
>     she soar'd
> <Shrieking> Above the ocean; a bright wonder [*that* [*Beulah*] <Nature>
>     *shudderd at*]
> Half Woman & half [*Spirit*] <Spectre> all his lovely changing colours mix
> With her fair crystal clearness; in her lips & cheeks his poisons rose
> In blushes like the morning, and his scaly armour softening
> A monster lovely in the heavens or wandering on the earth
> With [*Serpent*] <Spectre> voice incessant wailing, in incessant thirst
> Beauty all blushing with desire mocking her fell despair.   (7:21–8)

This union precedes the description of oak, beech, nightingales, and goats, offering a striking tonal contrast to the idyllic natural vision that follows. Such contrasts are bound to colour our perception of this apparently ideal natural world. It is clear that the rape scene produces the "two little Infants," and Blake seems to suggest through narrative proximity rather than direct causal statement that the pastoral paradise is also a product of this union. Thus he produces a subtly ironic commentary on his paradise through narrative indirection. Then, as his description develops during the marriage feast, he adds a foreboding and elegiac tone to this paradise. As Urizen descends, his "Indignant muttering" (12:7) suggests discontent elsewhere, presumably a result of his conflict with Luvah. Soon after Urizen's descent Blake offers an elegiac statement about the impending loss of this paradisal state:

> Not long in harmony they dwell, their life is drawn away
> And wintry woes succeed: successive driven into the Void
> Where Enion craves.   (13:16–18)

Finally, the feast is followed by Enion's lament, a lament carefully structured into the copperplate transcription at the end of both Nights I and II, which reinforces the elegiac quality of the entire Night.

Los and Enitharmon exist in tense juxtaposition to this pastoral world. Like Blake's Thel, they are not part of the harmony of nature. Although they control the "times" and "spaces" of the elements, they still seem prisoners of them. Their restrained condition is apparent, not in the extent of their powers but in the moderate antagonism they feel towards each other and to other forms of life they encounter. An underlying sexual tension defines their relationship, yet this tension emerges in the copperplate text only in a brief comment during the nuptial scene:

> Alternate Love & Hate his breast; hers Scorn & Jealousy
> In embryon passions. they kiss'd not nor embrac'd for shame & fear.   (9:24–5)

This comment seems almost out of place when set against their godlike power over nature. Yet the latent antagonism suggests that restraint, frustration, and repression are not alien to a physical paradise.

These antagonisms are also present in Los and Enitharmon's relationship to their parent Enion. Unfortunately, the extensive revision of lines describing their relationship to the parent figures on page 7 renders Blake's earliest version of this narrative difficult to reconstruct. The first description of the "two little Infants" appears to be part of the copperplate description but may be an early addition in Blake's modified copperplate hand. It shows how

> Ingrate they wanderd scorning her <drawing> her [*life; ingrate*] <Spectrous
>     Life>
> Repelling her away [*from them*] <& away> by a dread repulsive power
> Into Non Entity revolving round in dark despair.   (9:4–6)

The immediate earliest context of these lines is partially obscured by the fact that they are preceded by three erased copperplate lines on the top of page 9 and two more at the bottom of page 8. In addition, this passage may be followed by another erased copperplate line. Moreover, the status of at least the third line as part of the original copperplate transcription may be questioned. The line itself appears somewhat cramped, and the *n*'s of "Non Entity" appear to be in a slightly different writing style from those in the "nine" of the following line. It is possible that this line was an interlinear one placed between the preceding one – "Repelling her away [*from them*] by a dread repulsive power" – and the following erased copperplate line. Yet interestingly, we see signs that Los and Enitharmon seem to work co-operatively against Enion.

Another copperplate passage depicting Los and Enitharmon's discontent with parent figures occurs in Enitharmon's "<Song> of Vala" and contains the same latent aggression directed more against external sources than each other:

> To make us happy [*how they*] <let them> weary their immortal powers
> While we draw in their sweet delights <while we return them scorn
> On scorn to feed our discontent> for if we grateful prove
> They will withhold sweet love, whose food is thorns & bitter roots.   (10:5–8)

First, the identity of the "they" (10:5, 8) to whom Enitharmon refers is relatively uncertain. Later additions to the poem make it clear that "they" are Tharmas and Enion, but neither is included in a clear relationship to Los and Enitharmon in the copperplate text. Tharmas is mentioned once, and Enion appears only as a brooding (8:12) or lamenting figure (17:1–18:8; 34:95–36:13). Neither figure appears to "weary … [his or her] immortal powers" for the benefit of Los or Enitharmon. It may be that the speech refers to some event lost in the erasures on the first six and a half pages, but it is worth stressing that Blake either had not fully worked out the nature of Los and Enitharmon's relationship with the immortals from whom they were born or else he was not satisfied with the connection between progenitors and offspring. A change in either of these factors (particularly the latter) may have caused some of the extensive revisions in the first six and a half pages. However, even if we accept this assumption, it seems that Enion became at the very least a surrogate mother at a relatively early stage of revision. Still, the essence of co-operation lies here, and the strategies of "Love & Hate … Scorn & Jealousy" are instruments of self- preservation, uniting Los and Enitharmon in an ambiguous paradise.

In what appears to be one of the earliest changes to the manuscript, Blake develops the antagonism of Los and Enitharmon, not to each other but to Enion, from whom they draw life and vitality. Blake's aim here seems to be to reinforce narrative continuity and the biological connection between Los and Enitharmon and Enion. To this end he erased five copperplate lines on page 8 and carefully entered the following in the modified copperplate hand:

> The first state weeping they began & helpless as a wave
> Beaten along its sightless way growing enormous in its motion to
> Its utmost goal, till strength from Enion like summer shining
> Raised the bright boy & girl with glories from their heads out beaming
> Drawing forth drooping mothers pity drooping mothers sorrow.   (8:3–7)

The care and neatness with which Blake added these lines and those above possibly suggest that he had not made many of the numerous additions yet to come and was still concerned with the appearance of the manuscript page. Further, Enitharmon and Los as "the bright boy & girl with glories from their heads out beaming" (8:6) seem to pre-date the negative characterization developed later, when, for example, the adjective "bright," referring to Los and Enitharmon, is changed to "fierce" (8:6; 9:36) or "Dark" (10:2). This addition may also pre-date the deletion of the tree and bird passage of 8:14–20. There the description of Los and Enitharmon as "bright Infants" remains unchanged, but the entire passage is cancelled. Presumably, the fact that Blake did not change "bright" to "fierce," "Dark," or another adjective with similar connotations argues that the cancellation of the tree passage follows the addition quoted above but pre-dates much of the internal strife between Los and Enitharmon.

Although we cannot always know for certain whether text preceded design or vice versa, the drawings on pages 8 and 9 seem tied to the copperplate text concerning Los and Enitharmon and a mother figure, probably Enion. Although the identification of figures in Blake's drawings is often treacherous, the activities of these figures seem thoroughly compatible with the adjacent text. Thus, it is reasonable to accept Bentley's supposition that the figures on page 8 "seem to represent Enion with the 'two little Infants' Los and Enitharmon as 'They sulk upon her breast.'"[3] The design on page 9 in turn represents the next stage in their relationship as Enion appears bent over or stumbling as she follows the two children. This visual motif is linked closely to these additions describing Los and Enitharmon's antagonism towards Enion, and both seem relatively early. These ideas and designs were probably a part of the earliest states of the manuscript. One factor that seems consistent in the early revisions is that they stress how Los and Enitharmon work together to oppose their parents. Early in the revision of the copperplate text, Blake emphasizes that Los and Enitharmon demonstrate more antagonism towards the mother figure than towards each other.

Another set of additions that might be early since they show Los and Enitharmon working with rather than against one another appears in descriptions of their attitude to Urizen and Ahania. In the copperplate text Los and Enitharmon joy to see the woes of Luvah and Vala and the labour of Urizen, presumably since the "Golden World" created by Urizen from the suffering of Luvah and Vala is largely for their benefit. However, after the lines telling how Los and Enitharmon were "drawn down by their desires" (34:1) into this world, Blake adds in his careful modified copperplate hand, over two pencil erasures, the statement that they seek

> To plant divisions in the Soul of Urizen & Ahania
> To conduct the Voice of Enion to Ahanias midnight pillow.   (34:3–4)

Moreover, on page 32 Blake adds two lines describing the same malevolent activity in a stanza break. After the earliest copperplate lines,

> And Los & Enitharmon joyd, they drank in tenfold joy
> From all the sorrow of Luvah & the labour of Urizen   (32:3–4)

Blake adds, in a more cramped version of the modified copperplate hand,

> And Enitharmon joyd Plotting to rend the secret cloud
> To plant divisions in the Soul of Urizen & Ahania.   (32:5–6)

Like the additions that chronicle an increasing antagonism between Los and Enitharmon and Enion, those that set the pair against Urizen and Ahania show Los and Enitharmon basically co-operating in their venture; they are added to the manuscript in Blake's careful hand and do not greatly disrupt the already existing narrative. Indeed, they seem part of an effort to interweave a causal connection between events in Los and Enitharmon's narrative with those in the stories of Urizen and Ahania and Luvah and Vala.[4] However, the addition on page 32 emphasizes Enitharmon's role in disrupting Urizen and Ahania's relationship and also points in the direction of the additions that emphasize strife between Los and Enitharmon in particular and feminine evil in general.

Evidence of an even more significant revision of character appears in Enitharmon's "<Song> of Vala." The latest version of Enitharmon's recitation of the "<Song> of Vala" has been generally acknowledged by most critics "as a challenge of the Female Will,"[5] told by Enitharmon to make Los jealous of her supposed affair with the Eternal Man.[6] In keeping with the earlier sense of co-operation between Los and Enitharmon, the earliest copperplate version of the Song depicts Enitharmon as merely a reporter of Vala's seduction – if indeed it is a seduction[7] – of the Man while Luvah steals "the Horses of Light" (10:13). The sense that she explicitly sets out to torment Los with this tale is not readily apparent in the copperplate transcription. In describing the Man's awakening after the seduction, Enitharmon reports that he speaks to Vala rather than to her (as in the later version): according to Erdman's reconstructed first reading of this passage, Enitharmon reports that the Man asks,

> Why is the light of Vala darken'd in her dewy morn
> Why is the silence of Vala lightning & her smile a whirlwind
> Uttering this darkness in my halls? in the pillars of my Holy-ones
> Why dost thou weep O Vala? ...   (10:17–20)

But when Blake revised this passage, he substituted "Enitharmon" for "Vala" in the first two lines and added more sinister qualities to Enitharmon's "silence" in the second line by calling it first "a Cloud" and then changing this to "a terror" in the latest version (E.825). Also, in the fourth line quoted above Blake changed the "O" of "O Vala" to "as." Thus Enitharmon is compared to Vala by the Man: "Why dost thou weep as Vala?"

The only other statements that include Enitharmon in the "visions of Vala" are also additions over erasures. In the lines

> <For> in the visions of Vala <I walked with the mighty Fallen One
> I heard his voice> among the branches, & among sweet flowers   (10:15–16)

Bentley (12) and Erdman (825) point out that Enitharmon's statement "I walked with the mighty Fallen One / I heard his voice" is over an erasure. As a result of these changes, Enitharmon's motives for recounting the "<Song> of Vala" shift from mere reporting of past events to an attempt to manipulate Los through deceit and jealousy. This type of change brings about a series of additions to the following lines and pages.

As Enitharmon's motivation for telling the tale shifts, Los's response to Enitharmon changes as well. The earliest version of Los's response is difficult to reconstruct because of the numerous erasures of the copperplate text on page 11, but his "foul indignation hid in smiles" (11:4) seems directed more at the events reported by Enitharmon than at Enitharmon herself. He sees someone, presumably the Eternal Man,

> Seeking to comfort Vala, but she will not be comforted
> She rises from his throne and seeks the shadows of her garden
> Weeping for Luvah [erasure]
> Sickning lies the Eternal Man his head sick his heart faint
> I see, invisible descend into the Gardens of Vala
> Luvah walking on the winds [erasure].   (11:7–10,21–2)

Los's response in this earliest version merely adds further detail to the events reported by Enitharmon in the earliest version of her "<Song> of Vala." Moreover, his answer seems uncoloured by any sense that Enitharmon seeks to manipulate him into a jealous or angry reply. But just as Blake's revisions make Enitharmon more guileful and manipulative, they also show Los to be more defiant and malevolent. His "foul indignation hid in smiles" now becomes a reproach to Enitharmon as he warns her, "I die not Enitharmon tho thou singst thy Song of death / Nor shalt thou me torment" (11:5–6), and says that the fall of the Eternal Man is a "Mighty atchievement of your power!" (11:11) He also holds her responsible for Luvah's demise, "lost in the bloody beams of your false morning" (11:9).

As Los and Enitharmon are further incorporated into the action of the song of Vala, they become more obvious reflections of the action surrounding the Man's fall. Their violence, their antagonism, is now seen as a spiritual (not physical) effect of eternal causes. Viewed in this way, their narrative begins to rely on a vertical or synchronous mode of signification. Instead of being observers existing in a horizontal or diachronic relationship to events, they now function on a metaphoric level of narrative, reinterpreting their own experience as a replay of events with the same tenor but a different vehicle from those in eternity. Thus, Enitharmon becomes Vala; Los becomes Luvah. Their personal strife is measured against both characters' relationship to the Eternal Man. Urizen enters the narrative as a fallen version of the Man. He enters into a relationship with Enitharmon as the Man did with Vala and rejects Los as the Man rejected Luvah.

Even as this synchronic overlapping of characters takes place and would seem to simplify the text, a degree of indeterminacy arises from the retelling of the characters' interconnections in eternity. While their motives and analogical situations emerge more clearly with the revisions, the informational content of the "<Song> of Vala" diminishes. As Blake revises the counter-narratives given by Enitharmon and Los, the truth-value of each is called into question. For the reader attempting to reconstruct a coherent account about just what happened with the Man, Vala, and the others in Eternity, the confusions are only partly begun in the copperplate text, but are radically entrenched by the revisions. The relatively straightforward account of Vala and the Man is complicated by counter-narratives by Enitharmon and Los; these are in turn compromised by the motives and consequent lack of reliability of the speakers. Continued searches for verification of these narratives lead the reader into encounters with other versions of the Fall, versions that may rule out certain details (the presence of Enitharmon in the seduction, for instance) but never the prime textual experience of verbal indeterminacy.

A series of other additions probably made around the same time as the additions to the Song of Death elaborate the antagonism between Los and Enitharmon. They also reinforce the connections between the Man-Vala-Luvah story and the Urizen-Enitharmon-Los story. The additions outline how "Scorn and Indignation rose upon Enitharmon" (11:28) as she warns Los, "Threaten not me O visionary thine the punishment" (11:32). Her subsequent invocation to Urizen to descend and protect her (11:31) and the description of his descent and challenge to Los (12:5–30) seem to be additions that also elaborate on the developing story of strife between Los and Enitharmon. The passages including Urizen explain more clearly his presence at the marriage feast and consequently entwine his story more thoroughly with that of Los and Enitharmon. Initially, the copperplate lines only explain Urizen's descent as somehow related to the bowing of the Man's head:

The <Wandering> Man bow'd his <faint> head and Urizen descended
Indignant muttering low thunders.   (12:5,7)

Perhaps Blake described the reasons for Urizen's descent or his "Indignant muttering" state more fully in the two copperplate lines that originally followed this passage, but in the present state of the copperplate text it is difficult to tell for certain. What emerges from the later additions, however, is an emphasis on Urizen's presence as necessary to protect Enitharmon from Los's aggression.

Los's violent reaction to Enitharmon seems related to this series of additions, although it is hard to say exactly when Blake added the description of his blow and repentance for it. Los's striking of Enitharmon is clearly a part of the additions that mark the decline of their relationship and appears related to the drawing at the bottom of page 12. In his *Vala* facsimile Bentley describes it as "a very rough pencil sketch of a man and a woman. The woman, with her hands lifted as in horror or pain toward the man, has half fallen. The man is in a duelling stance, but has no sword. Between them is a circle, perhaps for a head …" (B.15). "The design," adds Bentley in his 1978 Oxford edition of Blake, "probably represents p. 11, l. 3: 'Los smote her [Enitharmon] upon the Earth.'"[8] It is tempting to speculate that the "circle, perhaps for a head" between Los and Enitharmon was to be that of Urizen. He capitalizes most directly on their strife. The additions to page 12 that set him at odds with Los seem tied directly to Blake's development of a general lack of trust between Los and Enitharmon. Urizen plants further seeds of division between the pair in the addition where we are told,

> a brooded
> Smile broke from Urizen for Enitharmon brightend more & more
> Sullen he lowerd on Enitharmon but he smild on Los.   (12:10–12)

The lines depicting Los's repentance are more problematic. The description of Los's repentance on page 12 was added in two stages. First, Blake neatly wrote,

> Los now repented that he had smitten Enitharmon he felt love
> Arise in all his Veins he threw his arms around her loins   (12:40–1)

in a stanza break between earlier copperplate lines. He later added two more lines to the description of Los's repentance. The final version of these added lines reads,

> Los saw the wound of his blow he saw he pitid he wept
> Los now repented that he had smitten Enitharmon he felt love
> Arise in all his Veins he threw his arms around her loins
> To heal the wound of his smiting.   (12:39–42)

The first line was squeezed in above the earlier addition and the fourth was written in the right margin after the third. Both the first and fourth lines were probably added at the same time, since they are both written in the same "orange-brown crayon" (B.15). The content of these two lines seems contextually related to the new ending Blake gave to Night VII[a]. The apparently genuine pity attributed to Los in these lines seems akin to that he feels towards Enitharmon immediately after mingling with the Spectre of Urthona in the second conclusion given to Night VII[a]:

> But then the Spectre enterd Los's bosom Every sigh & groan
> Of Enitharmon bore Urthonas Spectre on its wings
> Obdurate Los felt Pity Enitharmon told the tale
> Of Urthona. Los embracd the Spectre first as a brother
> Then as another Self.   (85:26–30)

This new ending for Night VII[a] marks a turning point in Los's character, for it begins a reintegration of Los, his Spectre and eventually Enitharmon. Los's "Obdurate" nature, his jealousy and anger, are here mitigated by "Pity." It is tempting to argue that this addition is a relatively late one on this page, since it corresponds to a more positive characterization of Los that is consistent with the later added ending to Night VII[a] but is inconsistent with the other additions to *Vala*.[9] Los's repentance appears inconsistent with his appearance in an addition to Night II, for example, where he is still very much at odds with Enitharmon. In the earliest text of Night V, Los still acts out of fear and jealousy in binding Orc and building Golgonooza.[10] Even in Night VII[b] Los is more a war god than a figure capable of repentance. His insecurity and jealousy in the later Nights seem inconsistent with his penitence in Night I. Yet while it seems possible that Blake wished to prepare for this change by adding lines about Los's pity towards Enitharmon in Night I, he may also have been attempting to develop Los into a more complex mixture of pity and revenge. Such a mixture allows for a credible combination of unfallen and fallen qualities in Los and prepares us for his redemptive role in the revisions to Night VII[a]. Moreover, the struggle of desirable and undesirable attributes anticipates the externalized conflict presented between Los and his Spectre and Enitharmon. It also mirrors the intricate responses of the Man to Luvah and Vala during and after the seduction scene. As a result, Blake achieves a more coherent narrative relying increasingly on synchronic signification.

## LUVAH AND VALA

While Luvah and Vala play an important role in initiating the action of the poem, they have very little to do with the development of plot in the copperplate text on pages 1–42.[11] Not surprisingly, then, there are only minor modifications to their already limited role in the action of the poem. As with the Los and Enitharmon narrative, some of the revisions tend to accentuate "The torments of Love & Jealousy," but Blake also moderates these kinds of additions. Luvah and Vala, by most accounts in the poem, seem to be the initiators and principal agents in the fall; to intensify the sense of error attached to them might lead to an all-too-easy vilification of them and reduction of the indeterminacies Blake seems intent on constructing in the background Fall narrative. Although Luvah's imprisonment in the "Furnaces of affliction" in Night II (25:40) during Urizen's creation may be seen as part of an allegory of the Man's repression of desire in an attempt to reassert his reason over the chaos his passion has released, the story behind the poem hints that Luvah's state is partly retribution for acts of theft and aggression in eternity. Vala's suffering also seems contingent upon some vaguely remembered act in eternity, but this past transgression is related to the reader only through the third-party argument between Los and Enitharmon. Thus, on the one hand, Blake's modifications of Luvah's and Vala's brief narrative appearances tend to emphasize the vindictiveness of feeling between themselves and the Eternal Man. On the other, Blake also adds a redemptive thread to their story in an attempt to generate an interplay of judgement and sympathy from their narrative. The resulting narrative involves a manipulation of the reader's emotional response to Luvah's and Vala's roles in the work and a discourse that conveys only fragmented and apparently contradictory episodes from their story.

In the copperplate text the only untouched material that emerges from the exchange between Los and Enitharmon suggests rather than defines the events that brought about the Fall:

The Eternal Man takes his repose: Urizen sleeps in the porch
Luvah and Vala woke & flew up from the Human Heart
Into the Brain; from thence upon the Pillow Vala slumber'd.
And Luvah siez'd the Horses of Light, & rose into the Chariot of Day.

(10:10–13)

The other major Fall narrative in the copperplate text – that told by Ahania – also brands Luvah as usurper. Ahania asks Urizen, "Why didst thou listen to the voice of Luvah that dread morn / To give the immortal steeds of light to his deceitful hands" (39:4–5). If taken at face value, Ahania's charge could inspire a judgemental feeling against Luvah, yet her stance towards Urizen is no less disinterested than Enitharmon's towards Los. In the background to these accounts lies a story of theft or usurpation that Blake later develops, in Night vii[a] and on pages 21–2, into a full-scale celestial war. As Jackie DiSalvo points out, the completed form of "Blake's myth [of the Fall] … adopts a Miltonic conflation of the war in heaven story with the Greek war of the Titans, the Homeric age of conquests, and Nimrod's abrogation to himself of 'Dominion undeserv'd'";[12] however, the earliest form of this myth seems only a bare outline of what it was later to become. It is relatively clear from the lines above that Blake is casting Luvah in the role of Phaeton to Urizen's Apollo and seems to be presenting the classical myth in terms of a conflict of desire against reason as described in *The Marriage of Heaven and Hell*.[13] The subsequent narrative of Night ii, where Luvah, imprisoned and lamenting in the "Furnaces of affliction," is little more than a shadow of desire, seems to bear out this interpretation. Certainly, in his imprisoned state he bears little resemblance to the Luvah who attacks the Eternal Man and brings about the Fall. And although there is an act of theft or usurpation here that seems to border on a sort of rebellion, the fate of the Man is unclear.

Los's response to Enitharmon's "<Song> of Vala" describes the aftermath of Luvah's actions, but his speech has been revised to place Luvah in an even more sinister role. In the earliest copperplate text Los simply sees "invisible descend into the Gardens of Vala / Luvah walking on the winds" (ii:21–2). The sense of an act of violence and even a full-scale war only appears in a careful addition over the original copperplate. In Blake's revised text Los states, "I see the invisible knife / I see the shower of blood: I see the swords & spears of futurity" (ii:21–2). This addition suggests that Luvah may have attacked the Eternal Man with a knife, an event not referred to in Ahania's version of the Fall in Night iii,[14] although "the shower of blood" alluded to by the Spectre of Urthona in Night vii[a] might be an allusion to this act of violence when he describes how he fell "with cries of blood issuing downward in the veins …" (84:18).

Vala's role in this action is also unclear. The most consistent explanation of her role in the Fall is that she seduced the Eternal Man while Urizen slept and that Luvah was then able to steal the now unguarded

Horses of Light; but it is not clear that Blake had fully worked out such a straightforward myth when he first transcribed the copperplate text of Night 1. We are told that "from thence upon the Pillow Vala slumber'd" (10:12); then she rises, seeks her gardens, and weeps for Luvah. It is generally assumed, based on additions to the text, that when Vala sleeps "upon the Pillow" she actually seduces the Man; however, the degree of malevolence in Vala's actions is difficult to ascertain from the copperplate text. Apparently, she and Luvah act in collusion as they both "[*woke*] <wake> & fly up from the Human Heart / Into the Brain" (10:11), but the motives for their action are not entirely clear. Their story may simply depict the passions' overthrow of the Man's reason, followed by a fall into mental chaos. The expulsion of Luvah, followed by the instating of Urizen as monarch then ensues.

The early story of revolution may have reflected remnants of Blake's initial optimism about the French Revolution in the early 1790s. Luvah and Vala's revolt awakes the Man from a slumber of reason, a sleep not unlike that of Louis in Blake's *The French Revolution*. Blake's earlier poem depicted the King of France, a metaphor for the feudal everyman, awakened "from slumbers of five thousand years" (FR.1:8; E.286) by the revolution. It is conceivable that Blake saw the Man's awakening initially as a positive experience, followed by the universal restrictions of form under Urizen's command. In this case the uprising of the passions, of Luvah and Vala, or the Man's passions, might be interpreted as a positive explosion of physical and sexual vitality like that symbolized by Orc in the Lambeth books. In this interpretation of Luvah's and Vala's actions the pair are not wholly controlled by "The torments of Love & Jealousy." The malevolent elements of their revolt may have been added by Blake as he revised his poem to include these torments in accord with his later pessimism about the French Revolution.

The tendency, then, in Blake's modifications of the copperplate text is to place Luvah in the role of aggressor acting in an obviously violent and usurping manner against the Man. Vala's activities, as seducer and perhaps accomplice in attempts to overthrow the Man, are also suspect. These roles of usurper and seducer encourage the reader to direct his or her judgement against Luvah and Vala for crimes in eternity. On the one hand, Blake's repeated modification of the Fall narratives makes such judgements precarious because it emphasizes that each judgement is based on the past and involves the individual in the use of erroneous judgement. For example, leaf 21–2 contains a rather late version of the Fall narrative in which Luvah and Urizen share responsibility for the

Fall, and both seem engaged in a mutual doublecross. On the other hand, suspicions about these characters are allowed to remain. Blake seems purposely to evoke this dual response by undermining any certain reconstitution of a fixed sequence of events from the narrative discourse. The past in *Vala* yields none of the absolutes necessary to the reconstruction of a single story defining the temporal and causal relationship of events leading to the Fall.

Blake modifies the text on the level of narrative discourse by evoking a response of sympathy rather than judgement for Luvah and Vala. When the reader first meets them, Luvah and Vala are presented as images of passive victimization, a victimization apparently resulting from their transgressions in eternity, which brought about the Fall. In Night 11 they are trapped in a relationship of mutual torment and submission to the tyrant Urizen: Luvah becomes the raw material for Urizen's rebuilding of the Man's ruined universe; Vala is also enslaved in Urizen's universe. Her lament, recalling that of the Israelites under the Pharaoh in Egypt, is almost as striking as those of Enion:

> We are made to turn the wheel for water
> To carry the heavy basket on our scorched shoulders, to sift
> The sand & ashes, & to mix the clay with tears & repentance
> The times are now returnd upon us, we have given ourselves
> To scorn and now are scorned by the slaves of our enemies
> Our beauty is coverd over with clay & ashes, & our backs
> Furrowd with whips, & our flesh bruised with the heavy basket
> Forgive us O thou piteous one whom we have offended, forgive
> The weak remaining shadow of Vala that returns in sorrow to thee.
>
> (31:6–8, 11–16)

In this enslaved state, they cannot be a comfort to each other:

> Thus she lamented day & night, compelld to labour & sorrow
> Luvah in vain her lamentations heard; in vain his love
> Brought him in various forms before her still she knew him not
> Still she despisd him, calling on his name & knowing him not
> Still hating still professing love, still labouring in the smoke.
>
> (31:17–19, 32:1–2)

Such imagery seems designed to evoke the reader's sympathy or, at the very least, to moderate the severity of judgement against Luvah and Vala.

Urizen seems increasingly reprehensible in his constriction of these characters.[15]

When Blake eventually came to make Christian additions to the whole poem, he further qualified a judgemental response to Luvah in particular. The few Christian revisions bring about a radical re-evaluation of Luvah's role, now seen as essential to the redemptive scheme of the poem. At least by the time he transcribed Night VIII, Blake had begun to associate the Lamb of God with Luvah. In the base text of Night VIII the Lamb is described as descending "thro the twelve portions of Luvah / Bearing his sorrows and reci[ev]ing all his cruel wounds" (105:56–7). Presumably, at this time Blake began to make further isolated changes indicating that the Lamb acts through Luvah's form. A brief addition to Night II adds

> O Lamb
> Of God clothed in Luvahs garments little knowest thou
> Of death Eternal that we all go to Eternal Death
> To our Primeval Chaos in fortuitous concourse of incoherent
> Discordant principles of Love & Hate I suffer affliction.   (27:9–13)

Earlier in the poem we also read

> [*The shades of*] <But> Luvah & Vala standing in the bloody sky
> On high remaind alone forsaken in fierce jealousy
> They stood above the heavens forsaken desolate suspended in blood
> Descend they could not. nor from Each other avert their eyes
> Eternity appeard above them as One Man infolded
> In Luvah[s] robes of blood & bearing all his afflictions
> As the sun shines down on the misty earth such was the Vision.   (13:4–10)

And finally, in Night V Blake adds more information on Luvah and the Lamb, connecting them with the Council of God:

> The Council of God on high watching over the Body
> Of Man clothd in Luvahs robes of blood saw & wept
> Descending over Beulahs mild moon coverd regions
> The daughters of Beulah saw the Divine Vision they were comforted
> And as a Double female form Loveliness & perfection of beauty
> They bowd the head & worshippd & with mild voice spoke these words.
> (55:26–31)

Blake offers a rationale for this redemptive approach to Luvah:

For the Divine Lamb Even Jesus who is the Divine Vision
Permitted all lest Man should fall into Eternal Death
For when Luvah sunk down himself put on the robes of blood
Lest the state calld Luvah should cease & the Divine Vision
Walked in the robes of blood till he who slept should awake.   (33:11–15)

Behind this rationale lies another modification of Blake's political views concerning the Revolution in France. In the 1790s Blake's enthusiasm for the French Revolution is reflected in the vitality and energy contained in Orc. He transferred this revolutionary energy to Luvah in the period after Napoleon's rise to consul inspired doubts about the genuineness of this revolution. As a result, Blake was left with a positively charged character, Orc, in a negatively charged historical situation. As P.M.S. Dawson suggests, by around 1800 the conflict of Urizen (England) and the eternal form of Orc, Luvah (France), could no longer be portrayed as "a clear confrontation of good and evil";[16] Blake now sees both figures as mixed. Thus he manages to redeem the energies of Luvah through the redemptive powers of the Lamb. Connecting Luvah and the Lamb through the doctrine of states, Blake was able "to account for the fate of Energy [after the decline of the French Revolution] and still leave open the possibility of regeneration."[17] In terms of narrative structure these last four additions seem part of a concerted effort on Blake's part to emphasize the interplay of sympathy and judgement as necessary to the understanding of Luvah and Vala's role in the story. Luvah is judged to be in error for his part in bringing about the Fall; he suffers accordingly throughout time. Yet Divine mercy, guided by human sympathy, assumes the form of Luvah and intervenes "Lest the state calld Luvah should cease."

It is significant that Blake introduces this note of sympathy through insertions that disrupt the poem's narrative sequence. While such insertions disrupt the continuity of the poem's discourse, taken together they tend to throw the thematic unity of the work into relief. By drawing together the redemptive passages about Luvah and setting them in juxtaposition with the condemnatory passages alluding to Luvah's role in the Fall, the reader attains a composite vision of Luvah's role in the work. In this sense Blake uses a disjunctive discourse to emphasize the coherence and unity of his work. The main strength of the disjunctive discourse in *Vala* is that it does not cohere into a simple story with privileged status. Such a story would exert control on the discourse from outside the narrative and predetermine the reader's response. The narrative itself remains coherent but in a way different from the kind of coherence generated by a sequential, continuous narrative. Blake's discourse has the same type of consistency and coherence as any myth synchretically produced.[18] Unlike Greek or biblical myths, the accretions are all the product of one man and span only a decade or so in time; however, the effect is the same. As with syncretically produced narratives, the authenticity and authority of the text becomes a function of the palimpsest narrative as long as all additions are in keeping with a controlling ideology or thematic purpose.

In the case of *Vala*, all additions and revisions cohere around a single mythic core; at the risk of oversimplifying, I would suggest that these additions crystallize around a myth about the shifting equilibrium involved in a struggle for power over the self and others. Thus, as one figure rises in power, through a cataclysmic struggle or emotional manipulation, another falls, until at the end of the poem a right balance is established among the four faculties within the mind of the Eternal Man. Luvah's narrative lies at the centre of this mythic core. It tends, as Ault points out, to give a voice to the frustrations implicit in the other narratives.[19] Thus, through emphasizing a discontinuous and ambiguous discourse, Blake forces the reader to allow for the most polysemous reading, a reading that makes the Luvah-Vala story compatible with the stories of the other Zoas and their mates. In the Luvah-Vala narrative the result is a constant interplay between sympathy and judgement, both in the act of reading and in the act of interpretation. The interplay of these emotions enacts within the reader the continuous action of contrary responses that reflects the struggle of emotions in the poem.

## URIZEN AND AHANIA

In the third thread of Blake's epic, the story of Urizen and Ahania, we again see a development similar to that of the other narratives towards a more openly malevolent portrayal of the central figures. In this narrative, however, we have an additional complication in the extensive description of Urizen's creation, which receives a similar change towards the harshly satiric and cynical. It is not entirely clear whether Blake began to add cynical touches first to the Urizen-Ahania relationship and then to Urizen's creation or vice versa, but the interconnection of these two developments is clear. From the start Blake is certain that Urizen's creation is as much a reflection of himself as of his relationship with Ahania.

The development of Urizen's character in the copperplate text, however, involves a change in early trends in Blake's symbolism. In Urizen, Blake has a character fairly well developed during the Lambeth period. His appearances in *America* and the books of *Urizen*, *Los*, and *Ahania* remain quite consistent in depicting Urizen as an evil figure constricting and limiting all human and natural forms around him. The later portions of *Vala* or *The Four Zoas* seem to continue this blatantly evil characterization. In Nights VII and VIII, he can claim equal malevolence with Vala as prime mover in the cataclysmic war preceding the Last Judgement. Blake's late drafts reveal a continued development of the malevolent Urizen. The poet first wrote out a rough draft of Urizen confronting the Lamb of God before the Synagogue of Satan. The passage itself initially began, "The Lamb of God stood before Urizen opposite" (145:1). When Blake transferred the passage, he changed "Urizen" to "Satan": the line now reads "The Lamb of God stood before Satan opposite" (105:1). Such a change illustrates Blake's late sense of the interchangeability of Urizen and Satan.[20] Yet the early copperplate text of *Vala* reveals a more ambivalent characterization of Urizen, one in which he is as much constrained as constraining. As I pointed out in my discussion of the micro-narrative on page 25, the copperplate text establishes Urizen's creation as a necessary response to the Fallen Man's imperative to "Go forth in my might" and "Take thou possession" of the "sickening spheres" that constitute the fallen universe. Faced with the chaos of "indefinite space" and "the verge of Non Existence," his response is governed by fear rather than malevolence. While the act of creation described in the copperplate text is no doubt flawed, it has more of the sublime than the demonic in its depiction.

In his act of creation Urizen is aided by a sublime work-force of leopards, tygers, horses, lions, and eagles who "In human forms distinct … stood round Urizen prince of Light" (25:5). Blake depicts the work of creation in metaphors of metal-working and weaving, the two major industries in England, but set on a titanic scale. "Mountainous masses" of ore (25:35) are melted in the "Furnaces of affliction" (25:40) and

in the forge

Roar the bright masses, thund'ring beat the hammers, many a globe
Is form'd & thrown down thund'ring into the deeps of Non Entity
Heated red hot they hizzing rend their way down many a league

Till resting. each his center finds; suspended there they stand
Casting their sparkles dire abroad into the dismal deep.   (28:25–30)

Blake emphasizes the sheer scope of this endeavour in order to create a sense of awe and wonder at Urizen's work. He still seems to be a titanic figure of unfallen majesty and ability. Urizen's work is admirable in that it brings order out of a chaos that borders on non-existence, but this positive view is equally balanced against the restriction or exclusion of forces that threaten his rational ordering of chaos.

Merely as a matter of course, Urizen's active agents trap and condense free-moving spiritual forms into restricted ones to make "The wondrous work flow forth like visible out of the invisible" (33:10). We are told that "the strong wing'd Eagles // … the Spirits of strongest wing enlighten the dark deep" (29:8, 14) as part of this creative effort; however, their activity of spreading "out from Sun to Sun / The vehicles of light" (29:11–12) is counterpointed by the entrapment and reduction of spiritual essences. While the Eagles "enlighten the dark deep,"

The threads are spun & the cords twisted & drawn out; then the weak
Begin their work; & many a net is netted; many a net
Spread & many a Spirit caught, innumerable the nets
Innumerable the gins & traps; & many a soothing flute
Is form'd & many a corded lyre, outspread over the immense
In cruel delight they trap the listeners, & in cruel delight
Bind them, [*together*] <condensing> the strong energies into little compass
Some became seed of every plant that shall be planted; some
The bulbous roots, thrown up together into barns & garners.   (29:15–30:7)

While it is true that the Spirits, perhaps identifiable with the Elemental Gods at the nuptial feast in Night 1, are trapped by these nets "In cruel delight," Blake also emphasizes that those trapped are formed into seeds and roots later planted in the fabric of the created cosmos. Here spiritual forces are reduced to a natural or physical existence, but their suffering seems required in order to produce generative elements that sustain creation and growth. The action of necessity now seems to control all creation. Ultimately, it appears that Urizen's creation, working as it does with the materials of chaos and built from fear of the future,[21] in part depends on some suffering to make it secure.

Moreover, there seems a progressive decline in the greatness of Urizen's creation. The act of limitation is the work of "the weak" as opposed to the "Spirits of strongest wing": each power in Urizen's creation seems weaker than the former, and thus each created product is more flawed than the last. In the succeeding stages of creation this pattern continues. The "Builders" who "The wondrous scaffold reard all round the infinite" (30:8–9) are not described as spirits, nor do they create anything substantially new. They act only according to the physical dimensions of the plan held by "the Architect divine" (i.e., Urizen), and merely set "the hewn stone / ... in beds of mortar." In their work, however, they are aided by

> Multitudes without number [who] work incessant: the hewn stone
> Is placd in beds of mortar mingled with the ashes of Vala
> Severe the labour, female slaves the mortar trod oppressed.   (30:12–14)

The agents of Urizen's creation are no longer free-flying spirits; they are female slaves. In revision the many implicit condemnations of Urizen already present in the copperplate text are emphasized almost to the complete detriment of any positive elements in his character or universe.[22]

It is unclear which revisions came first to the Urizen story, but they generally seem to spring from Blake's attribution to Urizen of an obsession with kingship, and godhood as an extension of this obsession. The revisions in *Vala* to Urizen's character change him from the creator figure of the copperplate text who creates merely by necessity to the malevolent deity found in the Lambeth books and the later Nights of *Vala* or *The Four Zoas*, a figure who is obsessed with ruling the cosmos according to his own laws. In an addition to the feast of Los and Enitharmon, Urizen asserts as he descends, "Now I am God from Eternity to Eternity" (12:8), and demands obedience from Los (12:25). In return, Urizen promises to give Los command of Luvah, Vala, and all his "starry hosts" "if," as Urizen says, "thou wilt obey my awful Law" (12:13–17). He makes a similar proclamation to Ahania in an addition to the bottom of page 42, the last copperplate-hand page;

> Am I not God ... Who is Equal to me
> Do I not stretch the heavens abroad or fold them up like a garment.
>
> (42:21–2)

His proclamation is made in answer to Ahania's story of the Fall, which he sees as a challenge to his authority. This addition is similar to the revised version of Los's response to Enitharmon's "<Song> of Vala" discussed earlier. Both male figures respond defensively and violently to stories about the Fall. The female in each case is seen as a seductress similar to Vala, and the males feel threatened by the possibility that each is involved with another Vala-like emanation.[23]

The similarity in tone, motivation, and symbol between the additions made to the Los-Enitharmon story and those made to the Urizen-Ahania story suggests that the revisions were either roughly contemporaneous with or at least connected to each other. In any event, the two longest additions to Night II seem to be of a similar symbolic import and are all part of one stage of revision. The additions to the Los-Enitharmon story (34:16–94) show Los pathetically chasing after a manipulative Enitharmon, while the addition to page 30 (lines 15–52) depicts the "Golden hall" where Ahania waits totally controlled by Urizen:

> when he smild she brightend
> Like a bright Cloud in harvest, but when Urizen frownd She wept
> In mists over his carved throne & when he turnd his back
> Upon his Golden hall & sought the Labyrinthine porches
> Of his wide heaven Trembling, cold in paling fears she sat
> A Shadow of Despair.   (30:24–9)

Essentially, Los is shown to be similarly trapped by love when he complains about Enitharmon's absences while "the God Enrapturd ... infolds" (34:23) her:

> therefore fade I [says Los] thus dissolvd in rapturd trance
> Thou canst repose on clouds of secrecy while oer my limbs
> Cold dews & hoary frost creeps tho I lie on banks of summer
> Among the beauties of the World Cold & repining Los
> Still dies for Enitharmon nor a spirit springs from my dead corse
> Then I am dead till thou revivest me with thy sweet song.   (34:31–6)

Basically, the expansion of strife and jealousy throughout all the relationships in *Vala* seems to result from the kind of change revealed in Blake's addition of the subtitle "The torments of Love & Jealousy." We have already seen some of the effects that the theme of love and jealousy had on the Los-Enitharmon story, so I would now like to focus on the changes brought to the Urizen-Ahania story.

Ahania's first appearance in the copperplate-hand transcription of the text is at the beginning of the present Night III, where she relates "The vision of Ahania" (39:15) about the Fall of the Eternal Man. The early transcription of this scene shows it to be the original breaking-point between Urizen and Ahania, when Urizen accuses Ahania of becoming like Vala and setting "herself up to give her laws to the active masculine virtue" (43:8). In this interaction, the rift between Urizen and Ahania appears to be their own fault and does not appear to depend at all on the subversiveness of Los and Enitharmon. Further, there is no clear sense of any stress between the two figures before this point in the copperplate transcription.[24] The added direct addresses, however, by Ahania to Urizen – "(I heard him: frown not Urizen: but listen to my Vision)" (41:18) and "O Urizen why art thou pale at the visions of Ahania / Listen to her who loves thee lest we also are driven away" (42:7–8) – add a sense of dramatic tension between the two figures, perhaps a greater sense of desperation in Ahania's voice, that signals previous troubles. The additions of the description of Ahania in Urizen's "Golden hall" intensifies the sense of a prior inner strife between the two that does not appear in the copperplate text. Also, the plotting by Los and Enitharmon to destroy Urizen and Ahania's relationship adds the presence of an external divisive force. The effect of these changes, though, resonates beyond the immediate story of Urizen and Ahania's relationship and undermines the stability of Urizen's "Golden World."

When Ahania first approaches Urizen at the beginning of the present Third Night, she points out that "Thou sitst in harmony for God hath set thee over all" (after 37:9; see E. 830) and reinforces the sense that Urizen's world, although limited, is a world of harmony and proportion. However, Blake struck out this line and made a series of other changes that undermine any positive value in Urizen's creation. For example, the poet replaced the line quoted above with "Why wilt thou look upon futurity darkning present joy" (37:10). In this change, he shifts emphasis away from the positive associations of reason's work of harmony and proportion and towards Urizen's anxiety in the establishment of himself as sole authority in his world. Attempting to present himself as sole authority, Urizen wishes to prove false the prophecy that a "Prophetic Boy / Must grow up to command his Prince & all my Kingly power" (38:6–7). Thus, after Ahania's vision of the Fall of the Eternal Man, which Urizen sees as a threat to his own authority, Blake gives Urizen added lines that constitute a proclamation of omnipotence born of fear and uncertainty of the future: "Am I not God said Urizen. Who is Equal to me / Do I not stretch the heavens abroad or fold them up like a garment" (42:21–2). Urizen's anxiety and uncertainty are also brought out in additions such as Luvah's comment, "And Urizen who was Faith & Certainty is changed to Doubt" (27:15), and the revision of "The[n] he contemplated the past in his bright sphere" (34:6) to "Repining he contemplated ..." Moreover, the sons of Urizen, merely extensions of Urizen himself, are given a despairing quality in their work. "Then went the Planters forth to plant" (32:16) becomes "Sorrowing went the Planters forth," and the motion of Urizen's universe, which at first went forth in "songs & joy," later moves with "sorrow & care" (32:8, 33:18). Finally, in a relatively late pencil addition, the action of the planters and sowers is located at the lowest level of existence in Blake's universe, "In Ulro beneath Beulah where the Dead wail Night & Day" (25:39).

One other intriguing set of emendations, which make a rather oblique contribution to the darkening depiction of Urizen's universe, are the consistent attempts to change the circular imagery of orbs and arches in Urizen's world to the angular imagery of squares, rectangles, and triangles. When Urizen and his sons work on Tharmas's world of chaos, described as "the deeps of Non Entity" (28:27), they do so in imagery that is a direct echo of the circumscription of chaos with the "golden Compasses" from "God's eternal store" in *Paradise Lost* (VII.225–34): "measurd out in ordered spaces the sons of Urizen / With compasses divide the deep" (28:31–2) and establish a world of order and design as protection from the chaos that lies without. This action recalls the frontispiece of *Europe*, which depicts Urizen circumscribing the deep with his compasses, and Blake continued the use of this image in his illustrations of *Night Thoughts* as a model or diagram "of the shape of human experience" in the fallen world.[25] In *Vala* Blake depicts Urizen's world as a series of circular forms. The stars, for example, in Urizen's golden halls "Circled in infinite orb immoveable, within its arches all" (32:12), and the "Lions of Urizen" (28:25) beat the molten metals of Luvah into "many a globe" (28:26), throw them into the deeps until they find a "center" (28:29), "weigh the massy Globes, and then fix them in their awful stations" (29:2). In part, this imagery derives from *Paradise Lost*, where Uriel explains how the "Ethereal quintessence of Heav'n"

Flew upward, spirited with various forms,
That roll'd orbicular, and turn'd to Stars.   (III.716–19)

Informing this use, Milton's imagery is drawn from the model of the Ptolemaic system, which, as Heninger points out, "was based upon the principle of sphericity, upon a belief that the sphere is the standard form in the universal structure – in Aristotle's phrase, 'the primary shape in nature.'"[26] Plato also saw the circle as "the most perfect of all figures, and the most similar to" the creator.[27] The circle came to represent God, and, as George Harper notes, "The endless round in space parallels or symbolizes the infinity of eternity."[28] These associations with divinity, singleness of being, perfection, and infinity are components of Urizen's claim, "Am I not God … Who is Equal to me / Do I not stretch the heavens abroad or fold them up like a garment" (42:21–2). Yet, in the process of revision Blake sought to qualify Urizen's power, to undercut his pretensions to godhood and universal power. Hence the poet changes from a spherical image of perfection to one containing finite lines and angles. Globes become pyramids (28:26) or cubes (29:2, 33:4), and he adds details such as "Quadrangular the building rose the heavens squared by a line. / Trigons & cubes divide the elements in finite bonds" (30:10–11). At times some of the shifts seemed designed with a sense of comic relief in mind.[29] For instance, Blake changed a line describing the motion of the heavens from "Circled in infinite orb immoveable, within its arches all" to "Cubed in window square immoveable, within its walls & cielings" (32:12). Also, instead of having the Lions of Urizen throw "many a globe / … thund'ring into the deeps of Non Entity" (28:26–7) until "each his center finds" (28:29), Blake has them throw "many a pyramid" (28:26) into the "basement" (28:29) of the deeps.[30]

In a lengthy addition to page 33 (lines 19–36), Blake describes the mathematical motion of the stars "along their orderd ways / In right lined paths outmeasurd by proportions of <number> weight & measure" (33:22–3), which recalls the proverb "Bring out number weight & measure in a year of dearth" in *The Marriage of Heaven and Hell* (7:14).[31] Blake then connects this angular motion to the waxing and waning of the seasons of the natural cycle. The emphasis in this description of nature is on the "wasted strength" (33:28) and "wearied course" (33:30) of the seasons in decline. The sense of limitation and entrapment clearly appears in Blake's change of the word "fructifying" to "hard subdued" in the final line, describing the overall motion of this mathematical, angular universe (33:36).

Decay and limitation are more clearly central to this picture of the natural world than to the "Sultry paradise" of Los and Enitharmon. Blake's revisions seem designed to make Urizen's act of creation increasingly fallen. The use of angular as opposed to circular imagery to symbolize such a universe, where seasonal decline predominates, is similar to the symbolism of the Neoplatonists. Proclus, for instance, argues, "If you make a division into the heavens, and the universal regions of generation, you must assign to the heavens a circular form; but to generation, that of a right line."[32] Finally, the description of the heavens' motions appears to become a satire on the nightmare of Platonic order as depicted in the *Timaeus*:[33]

> Others triangular [*their*] <right angled> course maintain. others obtuse
> Acute <Scalene>; in simple paths. but others move
> In intricate ways biquadrate. Trapeziums Rombs Rhomboids
> Paralellograms. triple & quadruple. polygonic
> In their amazing <hard subdued> course in the vast deep.    (33:32–6)

The extent of such changes in this and other passages reveals Blake's persistence with this motif, especially as a satiric commentary on the world of Platonic forms. Throughout, his vision of angular forms is used to emphasize overtly the sense of limitation and entrapment, especially as these forms are connected to the opacity and measure of matter. Certainly these forms look forward to the negative associations of mathematical forms in *Milton*, *Jerusalem*, and Blake's comments on Homer, but more immediately, such changes reflect the development of imagery associated with Urizen's "Golden hall," a place where block forms are used to contain Ahania, the source of Urizen's emotional life.

Perhaps the final addition to the symbolism of Urizen's world is that of the "Mundane Shell" (24:8, 32:15). The Concordance records only two uses of the expression in *Vala*, while it occurs 19 times in *Milton*[34] and 14 times in *Jerusalem*. These facts attest to the lateness of the image. It is likely that this particular image was imported from these later poems, although Blake may have known the general concepts implied by the image much earlier.[35] The rather tentative nature of these additions in pencil also shows that the Mundane Shell was not an integral part of *Vala*. However, it continues the general trend of the symbolism in Urizen's world in almost exclusively emphasizing the fallen, material nature of his creation. Early in Blake criticism, Milton Percival pointed out that "As the epithet 'mundane' suggests the temporal, the word 'shell' suggests the corporeal, for Plato had used it with this significance in the *Phaedrus*, when he wrote that 'we are imprisoned in the body like an oyster in its shell.'"[36] As an imperfect sphere, the Mundane Shell replaces the circle imagery Blake removed from Urizen's creation but does not continue the idea of perfection. The use of the egg image establishes the associations of Urizen's world with the fallen process of creation and generation, from which humanity must be born in order to enter the unfallen life in eternity.

### THARMAS AND ENION

Thus far, the practice of isolating the earliest copperplate text from later additions has proven relatively reliable in outlining the development of the Los-Enitharmon, Urizen-Ahania, and, to some lesser extent, the Luvah-Vala stories. When we turn to the Tharmas-Enion narrative, however, this practice becomes more limited in its effectiveness. The source or sources of their division no longer remain in the copperplate text. The latest text on pages 3 through 7, which depicts the conflict between Tharmas and Enion, is written over at least one and sometimes two or more layers of erased text. Bentley and Erdman have both attempted to recover fragments of the earliest copperplate text with mixed results: their efforts yield readings that are largely conjectural and therefore offer a precarious starting-point for any critical discussion. Further, it must be remembered that it is not always possible to distinguish accurately among different layers of erased script. As a result, we cannot trace each stage in the development or even be certain that the original story resembled the later ones in character or situation. The extensive revisions suggest that the Tharmas character gradually evolved even as Blake transcribed his manuscript and that the significance of the character developed and in some cases shifted as he wrote and revised the first pages of *Vala*. In Tharmas's shifting characterization we again see a process of revision in which Blake added increasingly sardonic elements of love and jealousy to the narrative. In addition, the development of Tharmas seems tied to the stress created within *Vala* as it moves from a linear to non-linear narrative.

Blake seems to have invented Tharmas and Enion while writing *Vala*, since they do not appear in his earlier works.[37] It is not altogether certain, however, that Tharmas, in particular, played a significant role in Blake's plan of the poem even at the time he began to transcribe it. Pages 4–6, those in which the narrative first introduces Tharmas and Enion, are a mass of erasures and rewritings in which different layers of text may be seen but not easily distinguished from one another. The earliest text, the transcription in Blake's copperplate hand, is almost entirely obscured.

Indeed, the extent of these erasures suggests a radical departure by Blake from his original text on these pages. As the existence of two Nights VII indicates, Blake was loath to discard any text if he thought he could salvage anything from it. Thus, it seems possible that the revised text differs radically in tone, image, or perhaps even character from the original transcription. Such a complete change in the story could help to explain why such radical revisions were brought to these opening pages.

Margoliouth, the only critic to speculate at length on this problem, argues

There is evidence that Vala originally played a larger part in Night 1 ... How Vala came into the lost eighty or so lines of the beginning of ... [the earliest erased text of *Vala*] I cannot even conjecture, but somehow she must be identifiable with the Woman-Serpent which Enion becomes at the moment of her mating ... [7] The Woman-Serpent in the text there, in the drawing below and in the drawing on ... [13], must be identifiable with the Woman-Serpent (Woman-Dragon) of the drawing on ... [26], which represents Vala as described by Luvah.[38]

The exact nature of this earlier story remains, and may always remain, in question. It does seem likely, though, that the top layer of text was written considerably later than the rest of the copperplate text and perhaps even later than pages 43–84 of the *Night Thoughts* proof sheets. The surface text contains references to characters and ideas such as Jerusalem, the Daughters of Beulah, and sin and atonement not present in the basic transcription of pages 43–84. This text also contains passages used in *Jerusalem*, and thus it seems likely that the surface layer of pages 4–6 is a relatively late addition to the manuscript.

The only surviving copperplate appearances of Tharmas occur in two brief instances where he is little more than a name associated with watery existence. In Night 1 Los alludes to the "cold expanse where watry Tharmas mourns" (11:27); in Night 11 Blake writes that the windows in the "golden Building" (32:10) raised by Urizen and his sons

Lookd out into the world of Tharmas, where in ceaseless torrents
His billows roll where monsters wander in the foamy paths.  (33:6–7)

Tharmas seems merely a ruler over a watery chaos set in contrast to Urizen's ordered world. His world, with its "ceaseless torrents" and "monsters [that] wander in the foamy paths," seems to be an imminent threat to that of Urizen. Tharmas thus appears to be a sea god, like Poseidon, set in opposition to a Zeus-like sky god.[39] The juxtaposition of Tharmas's chaotic world against Urizen's world of light and order seems to say more about Urizen than Tharmas. It is designed to emphasize the precarious nature of Urizen's endeavours and remind the reader that Urizen has not conquered the chaos of matter on which his world is built, only circumscribed a portion of it. Blake may also have intended, however, that the brief appearance of Tharmas's world of "ceaseless torrents" would adumbrate the world of disorder that follows the collapse of Urizen's world of order.

In her first copperplate appearance Enion is described as brooding "oer the rocks, the rough rocks" (8:12) of the barren world Los and Enitharmon are born into. Her brooding causes "the rough rocks" to "vegetate" and give rise to the forms of nature that protect "the bright Infants from the desolating winds" (8:20) of a hostile world. Her laments emphasize her role as a nurturing earth-mother figure; unfortunately, Enion is forced to substitute tares for crops, pestilence and famine for nourishment, hypocrisy for truth in fallen nature:

> I am made to sow thistle for wheat; the nettle for a nourishing dainty
> I have planted a false oath in the earth, it has brought forth a poison tree
> …
> I have taught the thief a secret path into the house of the just
> I have taught pale artifice to spread his nets upon the morning
> My heavens are brass my earth is iron my moon a clod of clay
> My sun a pestilence burning at noon & a vapour of death in night.
>
> (35:1–2,7–10)

Her laments serve mainly to punctuate the endings of Nights I and II, casting a sense of desolation over the marriage feast of Night I and Urizen's newly planted "Golden World" (32:8) in Night II. Beyond these laments, however, her identity in the poem seems somewhat limited.

Evidence in the manuscript suggests that Blake's development, or redevelopment, of the Tharmas-Enion story on pages 3–7 took place in three fairly distinct phases. The passages involved in these phases are summarized in Table 3.1. Blake began by transferring a portion of his text on page 7 to page 5 (see Plates 2 and 3). Under a series of erasures on page 7, Erdman conjecturally reconstructs the following lines, apparently describing Tharmas:

Table 3.1
Phases of Blake's development of the Tharmas-Enion story

| Phase 1 | Phase 2 | Phase 3 |
|---|---|---|
| Text describing conflict of Tharmas and Enion moved from 7 to 5 | The language of love and jealousy | The language of sin and repentance |
| | Includes 4:7–11, 16–19, 5:6–12, 14, 16–19, 23–28, 46–55, 57 6:5–27, 32–37 | Includes 4:12–15, <16–17>, 27–41 5:13, 15, 20–22 6:27–31 |

? Weeping, then bending from his Clouds he stoopd his innocent head

? And stretching out his holy hand in the vast Deep sublime

? Turnd round the circle of Destiny with tears & bitter sighs

And said Return O Wanderer when the day of clouds is o'er

So saying he ... ?fell ... into the restless sea

Round rolld ?the ... globe self balanc'd.    (E.821–2)

Erdman then points out that "all six [lines] were apparently moved to p 5 for the modified copperplate addition there of lines 9–14 and 25" (E.822). Andrew Lincoln has noted that the Tharmas figure described in these lines is called "innocent," in contrast with the jealous, malevolent figure in the chronologically later text of pages 4–6. The evil tendencies of Tharmas, then, would only emerge after the "innocent" Tharmas falls into the sea.[40] Lincoln's argument demonstrates that Blake had two different ideas of Tharmas and that much of the revision on pages 5–7 was an attempt to reconcile the two figures.[41] On the one hand we have Tharmas, the victim, bending his "innocent head" from the Clouds, turning the "circle of Destiny" and falling into the sea where he is woven into a spectrous form by Enion; on the other we have the proud, malicious, Spectre-like Tharmas who asserts his will over Enion and finally rapes her. Lincoln's argument is compelling; in part, however, it rests upon the idea that the earliest text on these opening pages always referred to the union of Tharmas and Enion. While this is possible, it is not necessarily the case. The text reconstructed by Erdman does not name the male or female figures, and not until this passage is moved to page 5 are their identities firmly established as Enion and Tharmas. Furthermore, from my own examination of the manuscript in the British Museum, I have found that it is not always possible to tell which erased text is the earliest copperplate one.

However, once Blake had decided to transfer his text from page 7 to page 5, for whatever reason and at whatever stage of composition, he began to rework the intervening pages in two fairly distinct phases. Phase 2 includes lines 4:7–11 and 16–19; 5:6–12, 14, 16–19, 23–8, 46–55, and 57; and 6:5–27 and 32–7. Several factors suggest that these lines represent a single phase of rewriting: they seem to be centred over the erased text; they appear in the same writing style; and they are consistent in tone, image, and narrative setting.[42] The emphasis on fear, terror, jealousy, hatred, and delusive beauty characterizes these passages as much later than the copperplate transcription of Night 1, with its rather muted statements of dissatisfaction. I suspect that this stage of revision is concurrent with or follows the revision of the Los-Enitharmon and Urizen-Ahania stories in Nights 1 and 11. An almost cynical emphasis on love and jealousy as motive forces in male-female relationships and a tendency to place the female in the more sinister role seem characteristic of the revision in both stories. As we have seen, references to love and jealousy are far less pronounced in the basic copperplate text; for the most part Blake's later revisions to the Los-Enitharmon, Luvah-Vala, and Urizen-Ahania stories tend to magnify these elements only suggested in the early transcription of *Vala*. The manuscript evidence suggests a similar development in the Tharmas-Enion narrative. It is probable that the passages in the Tharmas-Enion conflict were added as a unit while Blake worked on the rest of the poem, heightening "The torments of Love & Jealousy," and were intended to introduce Tharmas and Enion more fully earlier in the narrative in preparation for Tharmas's appearances in the text after page 43.

The structure of phase 2 in the Tharmas-Enion narrative seems fairly simple. Tharmas laments the loss of his Emanations and calls for Enion to "come forth" (4:8). She appears and proclaims that "All love is lost Terror succeeds & Hatred instead of Love / And stern demands of Right & Duty instead of Liberty" (4:19–20). Then, in an attempt to shield herself from his terrifying appearance, she begins to weave a "tabernacle of delight" (5:7) for herself, which, upon its completion, becomes "the circle of Destiny" (5:11). Tharmas subsequently emerges from Enion's loom in the form of a Spectre and, after glorying in his own beauty, terrorizes and finally rapes Enion. The relative lateness of this text is suggested by the fact that words like "Emanation" are not found elsewhere in *Vala*, nor is the term "Spectre" applied to Tharmas in the narrative of the following Nights. Moreover, the weaving imagery used as a specifically feminine evil activity only appears in arguably late portions of *Vala* and thus would add to the evidence that this text on pages 5–6 is relatively late.[43]

The third phase of development in this narrative incorporates the addition and revision of what are now lines 4:12–15, 16–17, and 27–41, 5:13, 15, and 20–2, and 6:27–31. Apparently all added at the time of Blake's work on *Jerusalem*, they seem significantly later than the preceding phase of rewriting. Phase 3 introduces the ideas of sin and repentance common in *Jerusalem* but found only in the added pages 86–90 of *Vala*. Moreover, this language of sin and repentance is further allied with feminine delusiveness and weaving imagery – Enion states, "I thought to weave a Covering [*from*] <for> my Sins from wrath of Tharmas" (6:38) – as it is in *Milton* and *Jerusalem*.[44] Blake also revised specific lines in his earlier text to include these new ideas of sin and repentance. "Jealous Despair" becomes "Silent Contrition" in 4:10, and the "Seas of Trouble & rocks of sorrow" become "Seas of <Doubt> & rocks of <Repentance>" in 5:51. Further, he changed "false woven bliss" to "Repentance & Contrition" in 5:28. Blake now sets the sexual tension between Female Will and Spectre in a religious context to show the concurrent debasement of human sexuality and religion. By elaborating such confrontation and tension in the opening scene, he establishes the tone and focus of attention for the rest of the work. Moreover, the overtly Christian framework supplied in phase 3 is in keeping with the extensive revision of Night VIII to include Satan, the Lamb of God, and other figures from Revelation. The Christianization of the Tharmas-Enion narrative affords Blake an opportunity to present a more universal confrontation of truth and error in a personalized arena.

Additional changes, however, take place throughout the development of phases 2 and 3. In particular, the source of Tharmas and Enion's strife shifts at least three times, and as it shifts, so does the characterization of Tharmas and Enion. In the first stage strife exists solely between Tharmas and Enion, with no third party involved. Moreover, Tharmas is clearly the oppressor of Enion. Tharmas, in the earliest surviving reading of lines 10–11 on page 4, states, "I have hidden thee Enion in Jealous Despair / I will build thee a Labyrinth where we may remain for ever alone." These lines begin a story of Tharmas's jealousy and possessiveness that prepares for his later appearance as the domineering Spectre with Enion as his victim. Enion's response, after their initial argument, is to weave "A tabernacle of delight" (5:7) that entraps Tharmas, but there is no suggestion that she weaves it for Enitharmon or Jerusalem, as later revisions show.

While modifying phase 2 of pages 4 through 7, Blake complicates the Tharmas-Enion conflict by the addition of Enitharmon as a source of strife. Enitharmon's presence in the story provides an external object for the story of jealousy. As a result, blame for strife in the Tharmas-Enion relationship shifts to Enion. Blake revises Tharmas's opening speech to read

> I have hidden <Enitharmon> in Jealous Despair O Pity Me
> I will build thee a Labyrinth <also O pity me O Enion>
> <Why hast thou taken Enitharmon from my inmost Soul
> Let her Lay secret in the Soft recess of darkness & silence
> It is not Love I bear to Enitharmon It is Pity
> She hath taken refuge in my bosom & I cannot cast her out>.   (4:10–15)

In revision Blake brings out the pitying quality that Tharmas is generally noted for but that was virtually non-existent in phase 2. The cry for pity, even the wrong kind of pity, tends to make Tharmas a little more sympathetic; at the same time, Enion's jealousy of Enitharmon may now qualify our sympathy for her.

The myth, as told here, is elaborated in one of the last additions to Night 1 and indeed the entire poem. On page 22, thought by Bentley to be added sometime after 1804 and the transcription of Night VIII (B.170), Blake tells of Urthona's experience of the fall and how

> dividing from his aking bosom fled
> A portion of his life shrieking upon the wind she fled
> And Tharmas took her in pitying Then Enion in jealous fear
> Murderd her & hid her in her bosom embalming her for fear
> She should arise again to life Embalmd in Enions bosom
> Enitharmon remains a corse such thing was never known
> <In Eden that one died a death never to be revivd>.   (22:20–6)

Blake had used the idea of the love triangle as early as *The Visions of the Daughters of Albion*, but this mythic mode of expressing it was part of a later development. In particular, the interchangeable nature of the female Emanation, fleeing from one Zoa to seek refuge with another, is a later development very important to *Milton* and *Jerusalem*. Before the composition of *Vala*, Blake had written of Enitharmon splitting from Los's side or of Ahania "Cast out from thy [Urizen's] lovely bosom" (BA.5:40; E.90), but he had not yet fully developed the idea that Emanations could leave one male figure's bosom and enter another. Not until *Jerusalem* does he present the most highly developed explication of the Emanative function:

> When in Eternity Man converses with Man they enter
> Into each others Bosom (which are Universes of delight)
> In mutual interchange. and first their Emanations meet
> Surrounded by their Children. if they embrace & comingle
> The Human Four-fold Forms mingle also in thunders of Intellect
> But if the Emanations mingle not; with storms & agitations
> Of earthquakes & consuming fires they roll apart in fear
> For Man cannot unite with Man but by their Emanations
> Which stand both Male & Female at the Gates of each Humanity.
>
> (J.88:3–11; E.246)

In the Lambeth books, after leaving the male source, the female Emanation either becomes highly assertive over the male, as Enitharmon ultimately does, or, like Ahania, becomes "a faint shadow wandring / … / As the moon anguishd circles the earth" (BA.2:38, 40; E.85). There is never any mention of one Emanation fleeing into the bosom of a male figure who is not her place of origin (e.g., Enitharmon entering Urizen's bosom or Ahania fleeing to Los).

As Blake revises the story of Tharmas and Enion, he connects the source of their strife to a breakdown in the free movement of Emanations. At the end of Tharmas's opening speech, Blake adds, "The Men have received their death wounds & their Emanations are fled / To me for refuge & I cannot turn them out for Pitys Sake" (4:16–17).[45] Blake anticipates (or repeats?) his own idea developed in *Jerusalem* that Jerusalem herself is an Emanation comprised of the Emanations of all men, just as Albion is the composite form of the human imagination. Thus the "Emanations" that flee to Tharmas for refuge are symbolized by the figure of Jerusalem, who hides in Tharmas's bosom. We see here that Tharmas has begun to take on a fairly significant role as the repository of the creative emanative power of humanity that survives the Fall. Unfortunately, Tharmas's secretive and deceptive protection of these Emanations demonstrates that his attitudes to the emanative process are perverted by the Fall. By hiding these Emanations, he begins separating himself from his own Emanation and falls further into the chaos of fallen existence.

Yet the idea that Tharmas acts as a repository for man's redemptive Emanations suggests that Blake saw him as an increasingly important figure or quality to be tapped in the process of undoing the effects of the Fall. The Circle of Destiny is composed, at least in part, from the fibres of his being, and although it may be a constraining force of Destiny, it helps to put a limit to the chaos existing at the beginning of the poem. Moreover, when Tharmas re-emerges from the chaos resulting from the collapse of Urizen's world in Night IV, he is instrumental in initiating the reconstruction of the collapsed universe. Ultimately, Tharmas, along with the Spectre of Urthona, infuses power into Los, which enables him to tear down the sun and moon, bringing about the Last Judgement (107:32–5). These features point to Tharmas's growing importance in the poem as the "Parent power," as a kind of encompassing form, central to the substructure of the poem's mythology. Blake was later able to exploit them in the revisions to the first Night, making Tharmas a figure containing the seeds of destruction and recreation. These changes seem designed to make him an increasingly more central figure.

In the basic development of female-male relationships, however, many elements of the Enion-Tharmas story as Blake revises it in pages 3–7 resemble the interactions in the notebook poem "My Spectre around me night & day" and in "The Mental Traveller" of the 1800–04 period.[46] In "My Spectre around me" the Spectre, like Tharmas, complains that his Emanation, like Enion, murders his sweet Loves and seems to have the power of life or death over them and him; he pleads

> When wilt thou return & view
> My loves & them to life renew
> When wilt thou return & live
> When wilt thou pity as I forgive.   (29–32; E.476)

The note of lament for the absent loved one who causes such pain is also typical of Tharmas's complaints. Further, the counter-accusations of sin by Tharmas (6:29–31) and Enion (4:27–41) are paralleled in what appears to be a postscript to "My Spectre around me":

> Oer my Sins Thou sit & moan
> Hast thou no Sins of thy own
> Oer my Sins thou sit & weep
> And lull thy own Sins fast asleep.   (1–4; E.477)

In addition, Enion resembles the "Woman Old" of "The Mental Traveller" – a poem written in the same period as "My Spectre" that describes a similar relationship – who binds her love and

> Her fingers number every Nerve
> Just as a Miser counts his gold
> She lives upon his shrieks & cries
> And She grows young as he grows old.   (17–20; E.484)

Enion torments Tharmas in similar terms:

> In [*dismal*] <gnawing> pain drawn out by her lovd fingers every nerve
> She counted. every vein & lacteal threading them among
> Her woof of terror. Terrified & drinking tears of woe
> Shuddring she wove nine days & nights Sleepless her food was tears
> …
> A Frowning Continent appeard Where Enion in the desert
> Terrified in her own Creation viewing her woven shadow
> Sat in a sweet intoxication of false woven bliss.   (5:16–19, 26–8)

Only the added note of terror differentiates the picture of Enion from that of the "Woman Old"; yet the "sweet intoxication" of her actions seems to mitigate Enion's terror. Thus it appears that the changing face of Tharmas-Enion story is linked to a widespread development in Blake's presentation of the male-female conflict in terms of what he would ultimately depict between the Spectre and Female Will.

Although his latest revisions were not thoroughly consistent, Blake eventually replaced "Enitharmon" with "Jerusalem" in Tharmas's opening speech. It seems probable that he made this change around the time he added the language of Sin and Repentance to his text. The concurrence of these additions is by no means certain; however, Blake cannot have overlooked their thematic congruency. As a scene of love and jealousy expanded to include the language of Sin and Repentance, it seems logical that Blake might decide to locate the source of controversy in Jerusalem, a victimized biblical figure of increasing importance in his later writings. Moreover, both elements share a common relative lateness in the manuscript.[47] Basically, the emotional conflict between Tharmas and Enion remains the same in this love triangle, except that Tharmas has "Hidden <Jerusalem [instead of Enitharmon] in Silent Contrition>" (4:10), and he now asks Enion, "<Why hast thou taken sweet Jerusalem from my inmost Soul>" (4:12). Blake did not, however, carry out these revisions in Tharmas's plea "It is not Love I bear to Enitharmon It is Pity" (4:14) or in the story told by the messengers from Beulah on page 22, and this fact leads me to assume either that the change was only very tentative or that Blake "accidentally neglected making the same change here as in lines 9 and 11, and 5:7" (E.819). Moreover, Blake's incomplete revision of the Enion-Tharmas-Jerusalem triangle may have signalled his temporary abandonment of the text of pages 5–7.

In the process of developing and later deleting the text of pages 4–6, Blake put his characters through a series of interesting changes. Blake's tampering with this text is revealing in terms of his development of the relationship between Tharmas and Enion and their characterization. In lines 9–15 on page 6 Tharmas is described in "self admiring raptures" (6:13),

> wishing that the heavens had eyes to See
> And courting that the Earth would ope her Eyelids & behold
> Such wondrous beauty repining in the midst of all his glory
> That nought but Enion could be found to praise adore & love.   (6:9–12)

In a subsequent passage (6:26–35) Tharmas finds that Enion does not admire him half as much as he does himself, rebukes her for her accusations of sin (26–8), asserts his own moral purity against her supposed sins (29–31), and proclaims himself god over her tortured soul (32–5). Finally, he accuses her of being a false temptress (7:12–17) who first wants him to "hide thee with my power and delight thee with my beauty" (13) but then "darknest in my presence" (14) when he does appear. Thus he decides "In my jealous wings / I evermore will hold thee when thou goest out or comest in" (15–16). Throughout these lines we see Blake developing the most negative aspects of the Spectre he later calls the "Selfhood." The net effect of these passages is to polarize the innocent and evil sides of Tharmas into two distinct characters. On the one hand we have the innocent Tharmas, a victim of the Fall caused by the war between Luvah and Urizen; on the other we find the malevolent Spectre of Tharmas, the perversion of the victimized Tharmas, bent on dominating and destroying Enion. It is not surprising to find that as Tharmas grows more evil, Enion becomes a more sympathetic (or simply pathetic) victim.

In her first speech in this section (5:46–55, 57) Enion repents of weaving Tharmas into a Spectre, an act in which "Love is changd to deadly Hate" (48), and laments the feeling that her "Soul has lost its splendor & a brooding Fear / Shadows me oer & drives me outward to a world of woe" (53–4). Following the description of Tharmas's "self admiring raptures," Enion laments her solitude and calls out for Tharmas, whom she does not recognize in his Spectre form (6:16–25). Finally, she repents for slaying Tharmas's Emanations and defies the Spectre's perceived temptation that she "murder my own soul & wipe my tears & smile" (6:36–7:11). In Blake's rather patchy narrative here it appears that the victimized Tharmas sinks beneath the waves of Enion's "filmy Woof" (5:14) after turning "round the circle of Destiny" (5:11). This "innocent" Tharmas receives only a passing reference at 11:27 and then does not reappear until pages 43–4, where he arises from the ruin of Urizen's world. Enion, through her weaving, draws out the Spectre of Tharmas from the nerves and veins of the innocent Tharmas. The narrative then follows the Spectre's rape of Enion, after which he seems to disappear from the narrative. Blake leaves some clues suggesting that, in mingling with Enion, the Spectre becomes one with her in a perverse attempt to dominate and at the same time unite with her. His influence continues in the birth of Los and Enitharmon and the "Spectrous Life" (9:4) they draw from Enion. Ultimately, this spectrous quality would seem to emerge in the Spectre of Urthona. In a sense this chronicle reinforces the connection between Tharmas and Urthona as brothers in Eternity and allies in the war against Urizen while trapped in the fallen world. Again, the revisions of these opening pages make Tharmas a more central figure. In his Spectre form, he stands as the starting-point for the spectrous qualities that enter the fallen world.

Blake seems uncertain, however, about the degree of malevolence to attribute to the Spectre of Tharmas. Like the Spectre of Urthona – perhaps the first use of the idea of a Spectre – the Spectre of Tharmas arises as the product of sexual dissension and division, a perverted *Doppelgänger* for an eternal identity,[48] and represents a spirit of despair and self-destruction. In particular, the Spectre of Tharmas seems an inversion of Tharmas's unanswered desire for pity into a tyrannical attempt to instil terror and dominate or destroy the appearance of weakness in others, especially Enion. This entirely negative presentation of the Spectre seems more in keeping with the bat-winged, devouring figure in *Jerusalem* and lacks the potentially redemptive memory of eternity that we see in the Spectre of Urthona in Night vii[a].[49] Thus at some point Blake sought to moderate this confrontation of extremes and deleted all the above passages with grey wash, diagonal ink strokes, or both. The result was to neutralize the characterization of Tharmas somewhat and to confine his violent nature to the union with Enion (7:21–6). But another problem arises as a result of such extensive dele-tions. Enion has now lost much of the sympathetic quality that her laments gave her, and the keynote of her repentance is entirely lost. She is now merely a character acting out of sorrow and terror, weaving her lover into a terrible Spectre. Therefore, Blake may have decided to circle certain passages to be readmitted to the final version of Night 1.

At one time the ink circles around certain passages on pages 5, 6, and 7 were seen as part of Blake's process of deletion, but Andrew Lincoln has demonstrated that these circles were actually used by Blake to set off material that was to be saved from the mass of deletions on the page and that the poet added to these passages after they were struck out and circled.[50] Blake leaves the passage concerning Tharmas's "self admiring raptures" deleted, possibly because the line preceding it − "Glorying in his own eyes Exalted in terrific Pride" (6:8) − carries the essential significance of the 7 deleted lines (6:9–15). Blake also leaves out the previously deleted passage in which Tharmas condemns Enion as a temptress (7:12–17). This passage is useful in offering a clear explanation for Tharmas's violent attack, but perhaps Blake felt that the venom in the one passage he returned to the text was strong enough to get his point across. Thus, Tharmas's rebuke of Enion and his proclamation of himself as a god of moral purity over her tortured soul (6:26–35) is circled in order to be retained for a later version of the poem. The modified version of these lines (6:26–7, 29–35)[51] expands Tharmas's accusation that Enion is a "sinful Woman" (the deleted line 7:12), and perhaps this is another partial explanation for leaving 7:12–17 deleted. Further, Blake probably retained these lines because they present an essential expression of the Spectrous aspect of Tharmas's character and also because they establish an aspiration to godhood and moral purity that is characteristic of Tharmas and the rest of the Zoas and increasingly becomes a central concern for Blake. In these respects, this passage seems to supersede the characterization developed in the passages that Blake did not circle to retain for later use.[52]

Of the three Enion passages, Blake circled two and left the other deleted. He retains most of Enion's first lament, "What have I done ... accursed wretch! What deed ..." (5:46–57), but drops the last two lines. This passage is of importance in returning the sympathetic and lamenting quality to Enion. It establishes her realization of error that drives her "outward to a world of woe" (5:54), where she wanders throughout the course of the poem. Also, a modified form of the passage at the top of page 7 is retained in part as a continuation of the circled passage at the bottom of page 6 (Tharmas's assertion of godhood over Enion). "The final text at the top of page 7," argues Lincoln, "... should probably include lines 3, 4, 5, 6, 7, 8, & 11."[53] This passage expands on Enion's understanding of the murder of Tharmas's Emanations and adds a heightened pathos to her character with her statement, "now I find that all those Emanations were my Childrens Souls / And I have murderd them with cruelty above atonement" (7:5–6). The depth of pathos here puts her characterization quite in line with that of her other laments at 17:2–18:7 and 35:1–36:13, and her sense of murder without atonement explains further why she never answers to Tharmas's call as she wanders in the "dark deep" (34:98).

This passage also strengthens Enion's connection with her mythological antecedent, Demeter, who wanders the earth in search of her child Persephone.[54] Enion's laments show her wandering through a spiritual wasteland, lamenting for her surviving children, who flee from her "cruelty into the desarts / Among wild beasts to roam" (7:7–8). Yet Blake goes beyond his Greek sources to depict a mother who drives all love from her life and thereby exiles her creative potential, as represented by her offspring. Indeed, her self-absorption creates children who draw away her own life and vitality. Blake, however, remains unwilling to condemn Enion whole-heartedly. The one passage Blake did not circle to be reclaimed (6:16–25) does not evoke the same degree of pathos as the two circled passages, nor does it contain any statement of self-realization or repentance. Enion seems to show less awareness in this than in the previous speech. This deleted passage is merely a lament in solitude and a call for Tharmas that does not really fill out the narrative. Some confusion seems to remain in the setting, since Enion first stands "on the Rocks" before "her woven shadow glowing bright" (5:57), then hides "in the darksom Cave" (6:15), then sits "among the Rocks" (6:22), and finally sleeps "in a Chasm of the Valley" (6:24). I may perhaps be seeking a greater degree of consistency here than Blake saw necessary; however, because of the deletion of the material around this passage, it does not seem easily refitted into the narrative at this point. Yet just as importantly, Blake could not logically undermine Enion's laments at the ends of Nights I and II; she makes a central statement about the actual effect of the Fall in these laments that is true not only for the world of the poem but also the failings in contemporary British life that Blake attacked throughout his career. The pathos in her laments represents the spirit of pathos shut out from the sublime at the Fall.[55]

Throughout this process of revision we can see a tendency in Blake's writing, first to fill out the symbolic and conceptual elements in his character, then to revise these elements to fit the character they apply to. Thus, he works out the Spectre-like aspect of Tharmas to its fullest and then attempts to revise it in this case to limit the singular evil that the Tharmas character seems to take on. With Enion, Blake shifts the degree and expression of her pathos in relation to the ferocity of Tharmas. Such a process of revision brings a balance between the two characters. Of course, the fact that Blake revised the opening of Night 1 long after he had already written most of the poem also means that he had to consider whether he should accommodate his revisions to make later appearances of Tharmas consistent. It is not clear whether he was wholly committed to abandoning the consistency necessary to the relatively linear narrative of *Vala* in favour of a more non-linear form such as that of *Jerusalem*.

Although Blake worked extensively with the Tharmas-Enion story in Night 1, I suspect that this painstaking work eventually contributed to his abandonment of the manuscript. It seems that Tharmas's significance began to outstrip his role as one of the Four Zoas. Even as Blake elaborates on the identity of Tharmas, he develops him beyond the immediate needs of the narrative. In the poem's narrative he stands at the nodal point of the Fall into the chaotic sea of time and space and acts as a source for the conditions of fallen existence. Enion's weaving of Tharmas into the Circle of Destiny and the form of the Spectre suggests that Tharmas's fall introduces fate and error. The weaving imagery also suggests Tharmas's incarnation into the limitations of the physical body, while the notion that he holds the Emanation Jerusalem within suggests the potential for redemption of the body when it contains the City of God. These associations suggest that Tharmas is analogous to the universal human form of the One Man, Jesus Christ.

Such associations give Tharmas a symbolic equivalence with Albion. Indeed, as he developed the Tharmas character more fully, at the same time working on *Jerusalem*, Blake may have begun to transfer some of Tharmas's characteristics to Albion. In the design on plate 25 of *Jerusalem* Albion's fibres, like Tharmas's, are drawn out by female figures to create the vegetated world. Also, Albion's Spectre, like Tharmas's, emerges at the opening of the poem and moves to the west – Tharmas's dark domain (4:6) – where he remains "a black Horror" (J.5:68; E.148). Moreover, the action of Tharmas's hiding Jerusalem "in the Soft recess of darkness & silence" (4:13) from Enion may be compared to Albion's hiding of Jerusalem "in jealous fears" (J.4:33; E.147) "From the vision and fruition of the Holy-one" (J.4:17; E.146). In addition, lines addressed by Enion to Tharmas in *Vala* (4:18–21) are transferred to *Jerusalem*, where they are spoken by Vala to Albion (J.22:1, 10–12; E.167).[56] Of these lines Paley remarks that, "although it cannot be proved that the traffic goes from *FZ* to *J* here, it seems as if Blake were quarrying material from his nearly abandoned Zoas myth for the later myth of Jerusalem and Albion."[57] That Tharmas became a model for Blake's development of Albion thus seems quite possible; such a revision would render Tharmas a redundant character in *Jerusalem* and explain his relative absence from that poem.

Yet the shifting portrayal of Tharmas in particular suggests that Blake conceived of his characters' significances as more fluid than many critics have yet suggested. He seems more than willing to experiment freely with a character in a particular episode. Indeed, in the case of Tharmas, Blake seems to become obsessed with the scene before him, giving it a greater immediacy by straining certain attributes to their limits. Under this obsession, Blake relaxes concerns with narrative consistency (whatever value that term may have to a poet who often undermines consistency) for the effect of immediacy. None the less, with *Vala* Blake seems again to modify the immediacy of a scene to fit with the consistency of the thematic whole. Blake perhaps felt uncertain about how to resolve the tension emerging in the revisions to *Vala* between a sequentially coherent and consistent narrative structure – what Donald Ault has called the "Newtonian" narrative – and a subversively disjunctive and disruptive narrative – "anti-Newtonian," in Ault's terms.[58] The Newtonian narrative is necessary in conveying a fixity of events that may be understood and interpreted by the reader. Interpretation of such narrative involves a rational assemblage and comparison of events along a temporally and spatially limited schema, but the anti-Newtonian narrative offers expanded possibilities in educating the reader. The anti-Newtonian narrative, with its lack of explicitness and interpretive closure,[59] exerts pressure on the reader, forcing the use of individual imaginative vision to unify rather than assemble potential meaning in the text.

Blake found his answer to this tension in *Jerusalem*. In reading *Jerusalem*, we find that Blake demonstrates that immediacy of scene is all; overall effect derives from the imaginative unification of disparate parts. Thus meaning emerges from an accretion of disjunctive parts rather than from a linear narrative imposed by the consistencies of time and space. In *Vala* Blake seems still to feel a certain stress between diachronic and synchronic, sequential and disjunctive narratives and does yet not fully abandon one for the other. Perhaps the stress between these two forces caused additional delays in Blake's work on the poem and created fractures in the framework of his epic that he found he could never completely or satisfactorily repair.

# 4 Completing the Four Zoas

Pages 43–84, which comprise the end of Night III through the first two-thirds of Night VII[a], form a discrete unit with its own special distinctions and problems. The narrative content of these pages is in large part derived from Blake's earlier works, particularly *The Book of Urizen*, although considerably expanded for inclusion in *Vala*. Thus large portions of this text contain a narrative that had been developed elsewhere and was, by the time Blake transcribed it in *Vala*, relatively consistent in plot, character, and theme. It is not surprising, therefore, that there is relatively little revision of the text of these pages, suggesting that they represent a fair copy Blake remained content with as a unit throughout his revision of *Vala*.[1] Moreover, besides the physical facts that these pages are all written on *Night Thoughts* proof sheets, have a consistent average of about thirty lines per page, and were at one time bound together by Blake, the tone of these pages also exhibits a unique consistency. Wilkie and Johnson observe that "In its mood, events, and settings … [the middle section of the poem contains] almost unrelieved gloom, the darkness of the mindscape brightened fitfully by ambiguous moments of hope."[2] Even Donald Ault, who argues persuasively for the cohesiveness of narrative structure, notes a change in Night III, a Night consisting of the final pages of the early copperplate text with little revision and the transition, at page 43, to the *Night Thoughts* proof sheets written in Blake's ordinary hand. Ault demonstrates clearly that the narrative complexity of the first two Nights disappears in Night III. There are "no multiple sub-embedded layers" or "narrative leap" to an eternal world as in Night I; Night III, continues Ault, lacks the "radical discontinuous jumps between perspectives" that characterize Night II. The only serious narrative shift is "a shift of emphasis from one perspective (or plot) to another about two-thirds of the way through the Night."[3] The location of this "shift of emphasis" roughly corresponds to the change in paper and handwriting styles. At the very least it appears to suggest that Blake did not revise the text of pages 43–84 as extensively as he did the first two Nights. The simpler narrative style following this change seems symptomatic of an earlier stage of composition.

In this chapter, I propose to examine this portion of Blake's text as an important midpoint in Blake's composition of *Vala* as he expanded and settled his ideas about the poem. In particular I will discuss Blake's development of two new characters for his poem – Tharmas and the Spectre of Urthona – two crucial characters who complete the mythic shape of the poem and in effect transform it from *Vala* to *The Four Zoas*. Blake's copperplate transcription of pages 1–42 – the portion of the poem first transcribed – contains only two passing references to Tharmas[4] and no mention of the Spectre of Urthona. In the second phase of transcription, however, when Blake changed to the *Night Thoughts* proofs and his usual hand for recopying, Tharmas appears more regularly and the Spectre of Urthona quite frequently. Their virtual absence from the copperplate text suggests that Blake may not have developed, or fully developed, these two crucial characters until after he began transcribing the poem. The origin of these characters seems specifically related to the text of pages 43–84, and their development seems highly interrelated.

## THARMAS AND THE SPECTRE OF URTHONA

In what they contribute to *Vala*, Tharmas and the Spectre of Urthona have much in common. They greet one another as long-separated companions, and their memory of a past glory adds an elegiac tone to the poem that has also been either absent or highly localized in the speeches of Enion and Ahania. After his first appearance the Spectre of Urthona greets Tharmas with a recognition of a common past: "Tharmas I know thee. how are we alterd our beauty decayd / But still I know thee tho in this horrible ruin whelmd" (49:27–8). Tharmas's response acknowledges this common past and signals a note of amicability so rare to *Vala*, especially as it is later revised. He replies to the Spectre, "Art thou

Urthona My friend my old companion, / With whom I livd in happiness before that deadly night / When Urizen gave the horses of Light into the hands of Luvah" (50:29–31). Ironically, this amicability arises from Tharmas's misconception that he sees Urthona rather than Urthona's Spectre. As is fitting in a fallen world, recognition emerges through misunderstanding and consequently will be the source of an uncertain future relationship of both hope and despair.

Tharmas and the Spectre's exchange, however, not only develops a common bond between the two characters but also adds to the *ubi sunt* tone prevalent in these Nights.[5] The greeting speeches of these two characters echo Beelzebub's first words to Satan after the Fall in *Paradise Lost*: "O how fallen! how changed / From him, who in the happy realms of light / Clothed with transcendent brightness didst outshine / Myriads though bright" (1.84–7). The sense of epic loss and the emotional torment of figures "Vaunting aloud, but racked with deep despair" (1.126) intensifies the tone of this scene and sets it firmly within a suggestive literary context. In Blake's poem Tharmas and the Spectre of Urthona reveal that they share a common fate as victims of the Fall caused by Luvah and Urizen. Although Blake invokes the comparison with the fallen devils of *Paradise Lost*, he does not wholly condemn them or their energies. Together, Tharmas and the Spectre of Urthona, however misguided or tormented, seek to repair the damage caused by this Fall, and their actions add a redemptive thread to the poem which has been absent hitherto. Moreover, in their speeches a new version of the Fall emerges that includes material not present in the existing copperplate text and intertwines the stories of Tharmas and the Spectre of Urthona with the existing mythology of the poem and with each other. Such additions not only add to the complexity of Blake's own poem but act to correct Milton's fault of consigning those tormented by desire (along with the powerful poetic speeches they render) to a life of suffering without hope of redemption.

Tharmas and the Spectre of Urthona's narratives of the Fall seem designed by Blake to elaborate the sketchy outlines of his Fall narrative in the earlier copperplate text and also to give these new characters a place in the story. The new Fall narratives develop the copperplate text's story of Luvah's theft of "the Horses of Light" (10:13) and offer details and possibilities not suggested by the earlier text. The rebellion in heaven is described in the later *Night Thoughts* proofs as a full-scale war against the Man (see 50:1–10, 51:24–5, 58:23–5, 83:23–7, 83:31–2). Although Luvah seems the principal aggressor in this war, Urizen's role becomes more

complicated than it was in the copperplate text. He does not simply fall
asleep or succumb to Luvah's persuasion "To give the immortal steeds
of light to his deceitful hands" (39:5), but exchanges the horses of light
for "the wine of the Almighty" after he is made drunk by Luvah (65:5–
8). Thus, the degree of Urizen's culpability for the Fall is heightened.
He laments that he refused to give "the Lord of day" his horses (64:14)
and guide the "Son who wanders on the ocean" (64:24); instead, he hides
himself "in black clouds of … wrath" (64:25) and appears to muster forces
of rebellion against the Man (64:26–8). Also, the story of his fate after
the Fall is radically different from anything hinted at in the copperplate
text.

In Night VII[a] Enitharmon tells of Urizen's birth from the union of
the Man and Vala and of how he grew up on the plains of Beulah (83:7–
22). Here, Tharmas and Urthona are given a place in the Fall as victims
of the chaos that Urizen and Luvah's rebellion unleashes. In particular,
the Spectre of Urthona twice relates his surprise at the Fall as he is
divided and swept away on tides of blood, only to emerge from Enion
(see 50:10–25, 84:16–32). In the Spectre's narrative Blake first introduces
the idea of an identity between Los and the Spectre of Urthona and
even the idea that Urthona creates Los as a counterpart for Enitharmon
(84:25–31). Tharmas curses Urizen and Luvah for causing the Fall (48:2)
and is also identified as the father of Los. He hopes Los will rebuild the
chaos of the fallen world. In the speeches of the Spectre and Tharmas
are reminiscences of their companionable existence together in eternity
(49:27–31, 50:29–31), which not only emphasize the extent of their fall
but also demonstrate Blake's attempt to integrate these new characters
into the context of the Fall as described in the copperplate text.

### THARMAS

It seems significant that Tharmas's first major appearance in the base
text of *Vala* occurs immediately after Blake's change from the copper-
plate text to his fair copy in the usual hand on *Night Thoughts* proof
sheets. Although there are a number of possible reasons for the change
in paper and fair-copy style,[6] it is possible that Blake's development of
Tharmas may have contributed to the change. Blake may well have had
great difficulty in developing Tharmas in his working drafts as he first
conceived the character and subsequently became more tentative in
producing an elaborate fair copy.[7] As he developed Tharmas into a sig-
nificant character at the end of Night III and the beginning of IV, Blake

may have come to realize that repeated revisions would be required for his copperplate text of pages 1–42, which did not include Tharmas as a significant character. Thus, the introduction of Tharmas, if it did originate at this stage in the poem's development, may have contributed to Blake's abandonment of his elaborate copperplate fair copy beyond page 42 in favour of a more simplified transcription. It is also possible that Blake had simply run out of blank sheets; however, taken together, the appearance of new characters, along with a new method of transcription, more likely suggests a fresh start on the poem.

The appearance of Tharmas in Night i, although sequentially earlier in the narrative, is chronologically later in the development of the poem. The surrounding symbolism, which includes the mention of Emanations and Beulah, is all of a period later than that of the basic transcription of pages 43–84. These ideas only appear in portions of the manuscript added after the whole was transcribed. Even the term Spectre is only applied specifically to Urthona and once to Los (at 139:5) in the rest of the poem. This term used in conjunction with Tharmas does not appear in any other part of the poem except in additions to Night i, and thus seems a very late addition. Many of the added passages in the Tharmas portion of Night i are also used in *Jerusalem*;[8] this fact suggests that they may have been developed in the latter stages of Blake's work on *Vala*, when he was turning his attention to *Jerusalem*. Moreover, revisions to the copperplate text reveal a split between two opposing concepts of Tharmas, as, first, an innocent victim, and, second, a cruel tyrant.[9] This split seems an implicit development of the Tharmas on pages 43–84, where he appears mainly as victim but, as a result of his victimization, seeks to destroy himself and that which he commands Los to destroy.

In the speeches attributed to Tharmas in Night iv we get a more complete picture of his early characterization than that presented in the brief allusion made in the copperplate text of Night ii. Separated from Enion, Tharmas appears as a figure of doubt or despair forever separated from hope. In his despair Tharmas would destroy himself and others, but presumably an immortal nature preserves him: "Ah Enion, Ah Enion," he laments at the opening of Night the Fourth,

    All my hope <is gone> for ever <fled>
    Like a famished Eagle Eyeless raging in the vast expanse
    Incessant tears are now my food. incessant rage & tears
    Deathless for ever now I wander seeking oblivion
    In torrents of despair in vain. for if I plunge beneath
    Stifling I live. If dashd in pieces from a rocky height

> I reunite in endless torment. would I had never risen
> From deaths cold sleep beneath the bottom of the raging Ocean
> And cannot those who once have lovd. ever forget their Love?
> Are love & rage the same passion? they are the same in me
> Are those who love. like those who died. risen again from death
> Immortal. in immortal torment. never to be deliverd
> Is it not possible that one risen again from Death
> Can die! When dark despair comes over can I not
> Flow down into the sea & slumber in oblivion.   (47:9–23)

These powerful lines show Tharmas as a counterpoint of unlimited rage and despair to Enion's laments about the limited state of fallen existence. Tharmas exhibits a disturbed emotionalism by confusing "love & rage [as] the same passion" (47:18) and by constantly driving off Enion, the one person he loves and seeks in order to complete himself. But Tharmas's problem, as revealed in the above speech, appears to arise in part from his self-entrapment, his obsession with his own pain and torment. He represents, quite vividly, the curse of immortal life when that life is full of self-perpetuating despair. The juxtaposition of "love," "arisen," and "immortal" with the words "dead," death," "torment," and "die," in lines such as "Are those who love. like those who died. risen again from death / Immortal. in immortal torment. never to be deliverd / Is it not possible that one risen again from Death / Can die!" demonstrates the burden of immortality in a fallen existence. Blake's equation of Tharmas with a convulsive sea makes his portrayal even more vivid. Tharmas as a "raging Ocean" devours life because he, like it, cannot die. The random, directionless motion of stormy waters reinforces the idea of confused emotionalism, and the destructive energy of water that seems bent on destroying itself and whatever it crashes into develops the notion of a figure who would destroy himself and others. Further, water is an element that, in itself, is basically formless. It always takes the form of that which contains it. Thus, in his fallen form Tharmas is described as "<Struggling to utter the voice> of Man struggling to take the features of Man. Struggling / To take the limbs of Man," but as the facial expressions in the sketches on pages 44 and 46 reveal, Tharmas experiences only pain or anger in his human form.[10]

The Tharmas of Night IV, despite his doubt and despair, sets himself up as a god over the watery chaos that succeeds the Fall of Urizen's Golden World. Tharmas, a god of water, chaos, and darkness, is juxtaposed to Urizen, a god of sky, order, and light. Blake emphasizes the symbolic juxtaposition of these two characters at the moment in Night IV where Urizen and his Golden World fall and Tharmas emerges (44:6–21). The latter, as Ault points out, "re-surfaces into the poem in the midst of a welter of participles that virtually identify Urizen and Tharmas as inversions of each other."[11] Yet this symbolic polarity only underlines the thematic parallel Blake seeks to develop among Tharmas, Urizen, and also Luvah. All three figures seek godhood at different times for different reasons. In the Fall narratives Urizen and Luvah are said to seek dominion in eternity, thereby leading to the Fall, but Tharmas seeks dominion only after becoming a victim of the Fall caused by Urizen and Luvah. Blake thus introduces Tharmas into the narrative as an equal partner in eternity along with Urizen, Luvah, and Urthona but emphasizes his status as an innocent victim attempting to overcome his despair about the Fall through rebuilding the fallen world. Yet his impulses appear in a confused sense of purpose that cannot separate love and hate or creation and destruction.

Blake offers a symbolic commentary on this confused state by making Los the son of Tharmas. Tharmas calls Los his "Son Glorious in brightness comforter of Tharmas" (48:3). This connection with Los serves several purposes. First, it gives Tharmas a position in the narrative compatible with Blake's relatively early mythological characters. Second, the relationship with Los reinforces Tharmas's association with Urthona, since Urthona and the Spectre of Urthona are presented as different aspects of Los. Thus, the reasons behind the co-operative efforts of these characters against Urizen's control over the fallen world become more obvious. Finally, and perhaps most significantly, the interconnection between Tharmas and Los allows Blake a significant commentary on the relationship between destruction and creation. Tharmas, as chaos, is father to Los, the human creative principle. Blake seems to suggest that the human impulse to create is born of the chaos of matter, the *prima materia* for creation. The human impulse to survive dictates a need to create a human world from the threatening seas of time, space, and matter. Moreover, the interdependence of chaos and creation, decay and development, cannot be far from Blake's mind when he composes Tharmas's command for Los to

> Go forth Rebuild this Universe beneath my indignant power
> A Universe of Death & Decay. Let Enitharmons hands
> Weave soft delusive forms of Man above my watry world
> Renew these ruind souls of Men thro Earth Sea Air & Fire
> To waste in endless corruption. renew thou I will destroy.   (48:4–8)

Creation and decay are linked in a dialectical struggle for omnipotent control over a fallen world. Ironically, Tharmas's desire for a creation that he can destroy is linked to his desire to regain a lost portion of his eternal self, to regain his partner in eternity, Enion. While Los renews and he destroys, Tharmas holds out the tortured hope that "Enion may resume some little semblance / To ease my pangs of heart & to restore some peace to Tharmas" (48:9–10). It is possible, then, that this linking of creation and destruction, love and hate, allowed Blake to emphasize Tharmas's character first as the innocent victim and later the malicious tyrant in Night I.

Tharmas plays perhaps his most significant role in pages 43–84 in bringing about Los's separation from Enitharmon and the Spectre of Urthona, thus continuing the general disintegration of the Fall. This action, of course, allows Blake to bring the Spectre of Urthona into the narrative in preparation for his confrontation with the Shadow of Enitharmon in Night VII[a]. Tharmas then disappears from the narrative until "Night the Sixth," where he proposes a suicide pact with Urizen but is completely ignored (69:6–22). This pact has no real effect on the plot and may only have been added by Blake to keep Tharmas visible, in preparation for the transfer of power into Los later in the poem. Indeed, Tharmas has only very local and very limited effect on the plot of *Vala*, especially after ordering Los to rebuild Urizen's ruined world in Night IV. This factor would further support the notion that the major developments in his character came after the copperplate text was transcribed and possibly even after much of the following text of the poem was composed. In Night IV, for example, Tharmas's confrontation with Urizen (68:28–69:23) has no effect on Urizen or the plot, and may simply have been part of an attempt to introduce his character consistently throughout the work after he was developed for the particular turn of events in Night IV.

Yet Tharmas's role remains crucial in terms of the thematic structure of the work. He appears in the work more often to articulate a symbolic moment in the life of humanity than to change the course of the plot. His appearances in Nights I and III, for instance, provide dramatic enactments of the Fall of the Man and Urizen respectively. His cries of anguish at these turning points punctuate stages in the movement from eternity. After initiating the pact of creation and destruction with Los in Night IV, Tharmas next appears before Urizen with the proposed suicide pact in Night VI. These pacts seem to articulate the desires and fears within the fallen Man and his faculties as represented by the other characters in the work. Tharmas, lacking the intellectual and emotional coherence to enact even the perverse desire to commit suicide, turns to the more active figures of Los and Urizen, attempting to engage their co-operation. The pact with Los works, although with horrific results initially; that with Urizen fails but manages to express their mutual despair as Urizen begins his journey to find the apparent source of life in his ruined universe – Orc. Ault points out that Tharmas emerges in Night VI representing "the monstrous chaos in response to which Urizen created his closed geometrical world of fixed measurements in Night II";[12] as such, Tharmas represents a symbolic elaboration of narrative form rather than an integral element of sequential narrative development.[13] His addition to Blake's work seems part of a consistent attempt to move away from the restriction of narrative sequence and causality, a force that strongly underlies the structure of Creation, Fall, Last Judgement, and Apocalypse in *Vala*. As Frye has pointed out, *Milton* and especially *Jerusalem* achieve the narrative discontinuity to which *Vala* aspires.[14] The introduction of a character such as Tharmas, symbolizing an irrational chaos, marks an important step in Blake's mythology and in his use of a non-continuous narrative.

### THE SPECTRE OF URTHONA

Along with Tharmas, the Spectre of Urthona first appears on the *Night Thoughts* proofs pages 43–84. He appears suddenly in the narrative, so suddenly that Stevenson has remarked that "this passage [49:11ff.] reads as if the spectre was invented by B[lake] for this particular occasion."[15] It seems more likely, of course, that the Spectre gradually evolved through the course of Blake's composition and transcription of *Vala* and the later poems.[16] For the most part the Spectre appears in the base text of pages 43–84 as a willing and helpful accomplice to Los's recreation of Tharmas's ruined world. In the later works, *Milton* and *Jerusalem*, Blake's conception of the Spectre changes, and it takes on more distinctly sinister qualities. The Spectre in the base text of pages 43–84 is not the malevolent bat-winged figure in *Jerusalem*.[17] Only in additions to the manuscript do we read "that the Spectre is in Every Man insane brutish / Deformd ... a ravening devouring lust continually / Craving & devouring" (84:36–40; cf. 5:40–5), and thus it seems that the Spectre began as a more favourable, though still ambiguous, character or concept. Indeed, the Los of *Vala* carries more of the later, evil qualities of the *Jerusalem*

Spectre than the Spectre portrayed in the base text of *Vala*. Lincoln notes that "Throughout much of *The Four Zoas* Los appears as a spectral figure,"[18] and it is possible that Blake first developed the Spectre of Urthona as a fallen but redemptive counterpart to the violence-prone Los. Possibly, as time went on, Blake began to see Los in a more favourable light and transferred Los's evil tendencies into the Spectre of Urthona and then developed the more general idea of the Spectre as "An Abstract objecting power, that Negatives every thing [,] / ... the Holy Reasoning Power" (J.10:14–15; E.153), "separated / From Imagination" and that attempts "To destroy Imagination" (J.74:10–13; E.229). Whatever Blake's precise reasons for introducing the Spectre of Urthona into *Vala*, his appearance in the poem introduces new events and ideas not prepared for in the copperplate text.

Although Blake works the Spectre smoothly into the narrative scheme of Night IV, his first speech brings curious inconsistencies into the poem. Donald Ault expresses the central inconsistencies of the Spectre's appearance most succinctly: "the 'Spectre of Urthona' enters the narrative proper at the moment Tharmas separates Los from Enitharmon, but the Spectre retells this event as if it had not just occurred but had happened in the distant past, at the original 'Fall,' associated with an utterly different causal background. Significantly, he has no memory of, or makes no reference to, his immediate separation in the narrative proper."[19] In addition, the Spectre makes no reference to any of the events in the copperplate text, such as the Creation and Fall of Urizen's Golden World. The Spectre's speech may mark a fresh start on the poem, in which Blake attempted to integrate new characters. The Spectre's version of the Fall also introduces events that are not clearly part of the copperplate text. He claims that he issues "into the air" "from the breathing Nostrils / Of Enion" (50:23–4), an event never added to the copperplate text. Moreover, in Night VII[a] the Spectre of Urthona tells the Shadow of Enitharmon that at the Fall

> I sunk along
> The goary tide even to the place of seed & there dividing
> I was divided in darkness & oblivion thou an infant woe
> And I an infant terror in the womb of Enion
> My masculine spirit scorning the frail body issud forth
> <From Enions brain> In this deformed form leaving thee there
> Till times passed over thee but still my spirit return<ing> hoverd

And formd a Male to be a counterpart to thee O Love
Darkend & Lost In due time issuing forth from Enions womb
Thou & that demon Los wer<t> born.   (84:20–9)

Los and Enitharmon's birth from Enion is clearly a part of the revision to the copperplate text, but it is not clearly a part of the base text of Night I. It is possible, then, that Blake's invention of the Spectre of Urthona's Fall narrative came after the copperplate text, and it was an attempt to forge relationships among Tharmas, Enion, the Spectre of Urthona, Los, and Enitharmon. Therefore, Blake may have returned to the copperplate text and made the early revisions that make Enion and Tharmas the parents of the two infants, Los and Enitharmon, around the time he was working on the text of pages 43–84. Yet this assumption is open to question, since Blake did not make the story of Los and Enitharmon's birth in Night I entirely consistent with the Spectre of Urthona's Fall narrative in Night IV. The most glaring inconsistency created by the Spectre's story, however, is his total absence from pages 5–7 of Night I. The action of the Spectre in creating Los as a male "counterpart" to Enitharmon, for example, is never even hinted at in the copperplate text or in any additions to it.

The ambiguity of the Spectre's character is emphasized throughout his appearances in *Vala* and makes him a difficult figure to interpret with any degree of certainty. The Spectre is presented as both a product of the Fall, since he emerges from the separation of Los and Enitharmon, and an agent of restoration when Tharmas commands him to "Make … a resting place for Los & Enitharmon" (49:20). His ambiguous nature is particularly revealed in his praise of the tree of Mystery in Night VII[a]. While it may be true that the tree of Mystery is, as he tells the Shadow of Enitharmon, "given us for a Shelter from the tempests of Void & Solid / Till once again the morn of ages shall renew upon us / To reunite in those mild fields of happy Eternity" (84:2–4), it is also true that the tree symbolically stands in the narrative as the birthplace of deception. After all, the result of the Spectre of Urthona and Shadow of Enitharmon's conferring "among the intoxicating fumes of Mystery" (85:5) is the birth of the Shadowy Female, the very incarnation of Blake's notion of feminine deceptiveness. By stressing either side of the Spectre's character through changes in his physical description or activities, Blake could emphasize either his sincerity or duplicity.

In terms of the simple narrative of Night IV, the introduction of the Spectre of Urthona there seems necessary to resolve the standoff between

Los and Tharmas, and begins the work of recreation depicted in the following pages. Tharmas commands Los to "Rebuild this Universe beneath my indignant power" (48:4), but Los proves obstinately defiant and threatens to "drink up" the power of Tharmas as he and Enitharmon did that of the Eternal Man (48:13–14). Only after the Spectre emerges does the process of rebuilding begin (51:7–10), but he proves to be a complex agent of regeneration. He emerges as a product of Tharmas's separation of Los and Enitharmon and therefore is a victim (and symbol) of the continuing fragmentation after the Fall; yet his memory of and longing for eternity give him (and Los) a vision to strive towards.

The Spectre acts as a mediator, since his past affinity with Tharmas allows for the co-operative venture of creation and destruction to go forward between Tharmas and Los. Moreover, with the advent of the Spectre of Urthona, Blake develops a rationale for Los's creative failure as evidenced in the Lambeth books and the middle Nights of *Vala*. Blake's initial interest in the Spectre is highly specialized. As Ault notes, "the Spectre appears in Nights IV and V only in the context of jealousy: once the binding of Urizen officially began in Night IV (53:20), the Spectre dropped out and did not return until the narrative circled around and returned to a second binding, that of Orc."[20] This relatively narrow field of interest for the Spectre indicates the nascent stage of his development in Blake's mind. While the exigencies of the narrative at hand may enforce some limitations on a character, it seems clear that the Spectre's (and Los's) role expands radically in the late additions to *Vala* (most notably those at the end of Night VII[a]) and in *Jerusalem*.

Within *Vala* itself the identification between the fallen Spectre of Urthona and Los seems part of an attempt to give the Spectre a logical relationship to other characters in the narrative of events after the Fall. It also creates an alter ego for Los, giving him a connection in eternity with Tharmas, Urizen, and Luvah. The development of the Spectre of Urthona as part of Los's fallen identity, however, not only emphasizes the divine source of Los's creative activities but also, ironically, explains his limitations. Together, Los and the Spectre of Urthona represent man's creative potential, but they are parts of a fragmented personality and trapped in the fallen world. The Spectre of Urthona seems to carry the memory of eternity and all its splendour which Los lacks (or lost at the Fall, hence his name); without this memory of past glory, or a present revelation of what was lost, Los is unable to build a completely renewed world from the materials of fallen existence. Moreover, Los's recalcitrance in his rebellion against Tharmas (48:11–26) and his apparent failure in the recreation of Urizen (Night v) are given a clearer rationale with the introduction of the Spectre of Urthona as another aspect of himself; after his separation from his own Spectre, each of these acts becomes a function of his fragmented nature. In addition, the Spectre of Urthona points out that Los is only a temporary, vegetated counterpart who has no eternal existence. Thus, Los becomes a mere product of the Fall who will disappear at the end of time.[21] It is not surprising, then, that the Spectre and Los's joint effort to rebuild Tharmas's world proves limited; their creative activities at best attempt to give body to visions of eternity, but at the same time their creations are only recreations or imitations. The result of such creative activity can appear more horrifying than uplifting when they see how far short of perfection created forms are: Los's reaction to his creation of Urizen in Night v (55:10–17) reveals the horror of this kind of realization.

Yet, in the narrative of Nights iv and vii[a], Urthona is also a limited agent of redemption, and this is perhaps why Blake invented the intermediate agent, the "Spectre" of Urthona. The Spectre is but a ghost or "Shadow" (51:2) of an eternal identity acting in the fallen world.[22] His memory of eternity offers a positive vision from which to rebuild the fallen world, but it also instils in him a sense of despair when he sees how far all has fallen. He remembers the "mild fields of happy Eternity" where he and Enitharmon "in undivided Essence walkd about / Imbodied … / Mutual there … [they] dwelt in one anothers joy revolving" (84:4–7); presently, he finds himself "poor divided dark Urthona now a Spectre wandering / The deeps of Los the Slave of that Creation I created" (84:30–1). It seems, then, that this early form of the Spectre is characterized by despair rather than malevolence. The Spectre of Urthona's animosity and "jealous fear" (49:25) extend only to Enitharmon, whom he lost at the fall. His jealous response to Enitharmon is not unlike that of Tharmas towards Enion.

Like Tharmas, the Spectre of Urthona links creation and destruction in his efforts to regain eternity. Both, in their creative actions, seek to regain the feminine counterparts with whom they enjoyed an idyllic life in eternity. Their limited success and the increasing distance they fall from this ideal only seem to increase their destruction of and despair over what they create. In these two characters Blake seems to present a mechanism of history depicted through single characters. The presentation of history in terms of a dialectic between two characters like Urizen and Orc who turn into two alternatives of the same destructive dialectic is now supplanted by the individual faculty's struggle with creation and

destruction, hope and despair. Each duo–Urizen and Orc/Luvah, Thar-
mas and Urthona – seems to represent a different kind of attempt to
gain control of fallen existence and, presumably, an attempt to return to
eternity. As he transcribed pages 43–84 of *Vala*, though, Blake began to
emphasize the struggle of Tharmas and the Spectre of Urthona over that
of Urizen and Orc/Luvah.

Blake seems to have realized, even during the composition of *Vala*,
that those who caused the Fall, Orc and Urizen, could not repair the
damage; alternate figures were necessary to rebuild eternity from the
fallen world. The Fall was caused by a power conflict between two figures
attempting to assert one will over another, and mere physical force could
not break the mental chains of the participants locked in such a battle.
Therefore, Blake turned to the victims of the Fall and their struggle
against their despair over the loss of Eternity. This changing focus,
narrowing on to the victims of the Fall, however, did more than expand
Blake's narrative and his cast of characters. The introduction of figures
as important as Tharmas and Urthona (through his Spectre) brought a
change in the mythic structure of the poem. It represents a move away
from the duality of the Urizen-Orc, Urizen-Luvah struggle towards a
fourfold struggle between reason and passion and also imagination and
raging despair. We cannot say exactly when Blake saw the potential in
this fourfold myth, but its effects on the manuscript seem wide-ranging.
The move from a duality to a quaternity seems to have brought Blake
back to the start of his poem and caused him to rework the opening
pages of Night 1. Moreover, such a change in the approach to his own
myth eventually brought Blake to rename his poem *The Four Zoas*.

## THEMATICS OF THE FOURFOLD

In terms of Blake's overall mythology, then, the introduction of Tharmas
and the Spectre of Urthona was crucial to the completion of the fourfold
mythological structure that came to dominate his later work. This four-
fold division of the universe suggested by "the Four Zoas" reflects a
subtle symbolic shift in his thought. The early story of *Vala*, that before
the Christian additions and the love-and-jealousy motif in the first
Nights, centres around a conflict between Urizen (reason) and Luvah
(passion) that upsets the psychological equilibrium of the Eternal Man
and brings about the Fall. The conflict here seems essentially a devel-
opment of the doctrine of contraries first outlined in *The Marriage of
Heaven and Hell* and then dramatically portrayed in the strife between

Urizen and Orc in *America* and *Europe*. The twofold structure of Blake's myth creates a tension between polar opposites in which constant action and reaction of conflicting forces balance one another. In the early form of *Vala* Blake demonstrates the result when one force, reason, wins over the others. As the basis of the early *Vala*, after Luvah's revolt, Urizen establishes a tyranny that seeks to stop the free flow of contraries. This fixed form of existence then results in our fallen world.

The twofold centre of *Vala* leaves Tharmas and Urthona-Los as merely victims of a Fall resulting from the disputes between Luvah and Urizen. Blake seems to have developed the importance of Tharmas as the "Parent power" (4:7) in the opening of Night I and Urthona-Los as a central figure in the invocation to Night I and the end of Night VII[a] to supersede the twofold basis of his myth. The growing complexity of his myth and the increasing cast of characters contributed to a distinct shift in the mythological and poetic structure of the work. Thus it seems that as the poem grew and particularly as he revised the copperplate text of the poem, Blake came to recognize the aptness of a fourfold structure in his mythic universe.[23] Since the poem has generally been referred to simply as *The Four Zoas*, we often forget that this title is actually a relatively late addition to the manuscript.[24] Indeed, Blake's only direct use of the Zoas appears over a series of erasures at the beginning of the poem. His invocation addresses "Four Mighty Ones [who] are in every Man" (3:8), "the Living Creatures the Heavenly Father only / Knoweth <no> Individual [*Man*] Knoweth [*not*] nor Can Knoweth in all Eternity" (3:11–12). This singular appearance of the fourfold in the text of the poem suggests that Blake may not have used the idea consciously until after the whole poem and many of its revisions were transcribed.

From the perspective of the Eternal Man's psychology, a fourfold mental process symbolized by four Zoas allowed Blake to present a more detailed account of the intricacies of the falling and fallen human mind, and, through each Zoa's relationship with his Emanation, the various faculties' relationships with the fallen world. The added subtitle, "The torments of Love & Jealousy," seems to be related to the title change from *Vala* to *The Four Zoas*, since it characterizes the relationships among the four Zoas and their Emanations as they appear mainly in the revisions to the copperplate text. Thus it is likely that these title and subtitle changes were made after the revisions to the opening Nights.

Blake's change to a fourfold cosmology also arises from such biblical influences as the temples described in Ezekiel and Revelation. Blake demonstrates a conscious awareness of establishing an ordered symbolic orientation in his mythology in the first chapter of *Jerusalem*, for example, where he aligns each Zoa with a compass point and connects each with various elements, metals, and so on (see J.12:45–13:29; E.156–7). The composite picture, developed from the Bible and other Christian sources,[25] is that of the New Jerusalem, and Blake seeks to present the temple of the New Jerusalem as a containing human form for all of existence. Thus Blake connects the Four Zoas with every aspect of a fourfold map of the cosmos. Such symbolic structures founded on the idea of the quaternity, as Maria-Louise von Franz points out, "emphasize the establishment of an order"[26] rather than the flux of divine creative energy. Thus such an elaborate four-part symbolism presents a static icon of eternal existence. In the sequence of Blake's poetic development, however, this fourfold cosmos arises out of a mythology of contraries, and the fourfold model of established divine order is combined with the twofold model of active divine energy. Thus Blake is able to present a static picture of the form of eternity within which eternal process continues. Stillness and motion, product and process, repose and activity, reason and energy, therefore, gain equal significance in Blake's portrait of eternity.

Throughout this account of his development of pages 43–84 we can see the fluidity of Blake's myth. The earlier Lambeth material seems in no way limiting; it is merely the raw material available for further embellishment and ornamentation. Newer material created explicitly for dramatic purposes in *Vala* gradually becomes subsumed into the poet's evolving concept of the psyche of the Eternal Man. The place of the Spectre of Urthona and Tharmas in the myth is embellished as Blake sees greater potential use for them. Although the Spectre of Urthona and Tharmas may not have been an integral part of Blake's plan for *Vala* when he began the poem – indeed, he may not have conceived of them until after he began transcribing the poem – their late entrance into the manuscript in terms of the chronology of composition did not limit their later ascendance to the role of principal powers in later revisions.

In the extensive (and relatively late) revisions to Night 1 Blake made Tharmas into a "Parent power" (4:7), giving him what appears to be a symbolic ascendancy over the other Zoas. "Since he is the parent power of the other faculties," argues Bloom, "the fall of Tharmas – who is the body's instinctual energy, which can comprehend and hold together the rival energies of intellect, imagination, and emotion – must necessarily bring all the rest down with him."[27] Thus in the process of revision, Blake increasingly moves Tharmas into the centre of the mythology that underlies the whole poem: now, if Tharmas falls, all fall. His cry, "Lost! Lost! Lost! are my Emanations" (4:8) begins the action of the poem and expresses the universal anxiety felt by all the characters in the work.

In this centrality, however, Tharmas threatens to usurp the role of the Eternal Man, the encompassing form for all the characters in *The Four Zoas*, including Tharmas. With the addition of references to characters and symbols in *Jerusalem* to the opening of *The Four Zoas*, Tharmas begins to assume a role similar to that of Albion in the later poem. Indeed, lines addressed by Enion to Tharmas in *The Four Zoas* (4:18–21) are transferred to *Jerusalem*, where they are spoken by Vala to Albion (J.22:1, 10–12; E.167).[28] Moreover, although the analogy may not be perfect, the action of Tharmas's hiding Jerusalem "in the Soft recess of darkness & silence" (4:13) from Enion may be compared to Albion's hiding of Jerusalem "in jealous fears" (J.4:33; E.147) "From the vision and fruition of the Holy-one" (J.4:17; E.146).

As the mythology develops, Tharmas outgrows his status as one of the Four Zoas and seems more significant than the Eternal Man, who acts virtually not at all. Perhaps for these reasons, Blake underplayed the character of Tharmas in *Milton* and *Jerusalem* in favour of adapting certain elements of his character for Albion. Therefore, while Tharmas marked a significant addition to his fourfold mythological construct, Blake sought to develop the human anguish of the Fall through the universal man, Albion, and his emanations, Jerusalem. The Spectre of Urthona, by contrast, grew in importance, particularly in *Jerusalem*, only because of his crucial role in Blake's dramatic depiction of the artist's struggle with the materials of fallen existence. As Blake repeatedly revised the end of Night VII[a], the potential significance of Los, the Spectre, and Enitharmon grew to become a model for the individual's struggle with sin and Eternal Death. In *Jerusalem* Blake sought to exploit the artistic response of the fallen man to his dismal environment and did so largely through elaborating the struggle at the end of Night VII[a]. In this sense, the later use of Tharmas and the Spectre of Urthona reflects Blake's continuing re-evaluation of his mythic universe's potential for expansion. Ultimately, then, the revisions of *Vala* demonstrate the flexibility, the growing inclusiveness, and the shifting structures of Blake's myth.

# 5 The Revelations of Rahab

Since Blake revised his poetics in the course of transcribing his poem, it is not surprising that he would encounter points where inconsistencies between old and new methods would clash. The creation of Rahab is just such a creative crux. It is not that her character is constructed inconsistently (indeed, inconsistency and inconstancy are central to her existence), but she does seem to have been created and modified largely after the poem was transcribed, and her character seems to be revised in keeping with a complex synchronic poetics, whereby her interconnections with Blake's own characters and with biblical archetypes of the harlot who shelters Joshua's spies (Joshua 2:1–21) and of the Dragon conquered by Yahweh in primordial combat[1] become extensive enough to defy easy analysis.[2] She is at once Rahab, Tirzah, Vala, the Females of Amalek, Babylon, Mystery, and others. This synchronic association of characters might not be so trying if they were not inscribed into the most deterministic moment in the narrative: the crisis of apocalyptic transformation. In essence, Rahab may be taken as an instance of synchronic characterization placed within the framework of diachronic narrative. The consequent tensions created by conflicting poetic modes lead Blake through a large number of additions and deletions that render Night VIII, in particular, sometimes bewildering but always instructive.

In Erdman's edition of Blake's works, Bloom's commentary on Night VIII offers a succinct summary of its aims: "Blake's principal purpose in Night VIII is to integrate his contemporary political, social, and religious context, which he chooses to call Deism or Natural Religion, into the mythic structure of his poem."[3] While offering a useful overview of the Night as it is produced in most standard editions of Blake's work, this comment does not take into account the late entry of Rahab into the manuscript. Described only once in the base text of the poem and then only in Night VIII, the last transcribed Night, Rahab has a relatively minor role as an alternate form of Tirzah and the "Daughters of <Amalek> Canaan & Moab" (105:28), mocking the Lamb of God at the crucifixion:

> Sometimes as twelve daughters lovely & sometimes as five
> They stood in beaming beauty & sometimes as one even Rahab
> Who is Mystery Babylon the Great the Mother of Harlots.   (106:4–6)

From this rather limited beginning, Rahab's role and character are elaborately embellished to become "the Female Will incarnate, the mystery of State Religion hid in war, and so the final product of Urizen's delusions."[4] Because of the radical evolution of Rahab in the latter stages of the manuscript's composition and revision, her character offers a unique opportunity to trace Blake's attempts to integrate a new figure into an already constructed narrative. Not only is she interesting as a late addition to the manuscript, but her role in the poem proves a crucial impediment to the reconstruction of the climax, sometime after the Christian dialectic between the Lamb and Satan enters it. Thus, she does seem to be part of Blake's last attempt to reconstruct the transition to the Apocalypse.

The late addition of Rahab to the work is facilitated by a general poetics of interinvolved character and narrative that emerges in the synchronic dimensions of later revision. In moving to more synchronic modes, Blake probably found the introduction of new characters initially quite easy; the only requirement would be to equate the new character (or narrative) with an already existing one. In general, this process of interinvolvement may seem to constitute what Ault describes as "an asymptomatic approach to total confusion: at the same time that more and more characters with seemingly distinct identities crowd into an ever-condensing web of events, all of these characters and events more explicitly than before become aspects of one another, with key features interfusing and crossing over from each character and event to all the others." In particular, this poetics of interinvolvement begins fairly simply for the introduction of Rahab; as Ault again points out, "her role significantly overlaps that of the 'Shadowy Female' ... These two female forms intersect by virtue of their relationship to the name 'Vala.'"[5] Just as the Lamb of God and Satan complement (or supersede?) the narrative of Los and Urizen, the construction of Rahab is designed to complement the place of the Shadowy Female in the earlier form of the poem. The attempt to consolidate contemporary social, political, and religious concerns into a series of archetypal constructs for human delusion, constructs at least as old as the Bible, leads to configuration of character notable for its allusiveness, compactness, and inclusiveness. This poetics of character, emerging as it does with the narrative crisis of the poem, defines the range of difficulties Blake encounters as he attempts to develop Rahab beyond her initial overlap with the Shadowy Female.

As the earliest transcribed passage containing direct reference to Rahab shows, Blake initially introduces her in antithesis to the Lamb, as a singular form for the composite figures of Tirzah and the "Daughters of <Amalek> Canaan & Moab" and as analogous to the Whore of Babylon from Revelation. Each of these aspects serves a particular function. Her antithesis to the Lamb gives her a structural function as feminine error placed in opposition to masculine vision; metaphoric identity with Tirzah creates an intersecting point of relational identity with already existing characters in the narrative, as well as a symbolic context for her actions; and finally, the allusion to the Bible creates an intertextual matrix that completes Blake's narrative of the Lamb and Satan and interconnects it with the larger mythological structures produced in and by the Bible. The actual meaning of Rahab at this point, the manifestation of her identity at the crucial moment of Crucifixion, ruptures the narrative in a determined way, however, forcing Blake into a number of embellishments of her character. His extensive reworking of Rahab's actions around the Crucifixion attests to the difficulties inherent in elaborating character in alignment with its plot function. All revisions point to her place in the narrative as an agent of consolidation, defining human error in antithesis to divine vision so that vision may triumph and error be cast out at the Last Judgement. One of the few surviving drafts stands as witness to this struggle between character revision and narrative continuities.

Behind this initial modification of Rahab lies one of the few surviving drafts for the poem. Page 145, originally a draft for the Crucifixion scene on page 105, survives as part of an early attempt to describe how Rahab's "harlot form appeard / In all its turpitude beneath the divine light" (145:21–2). Included in this draft are some ten lines describing how

"Rahab stripd off Luvahs robes from off the lamb of God" (145:20). As a result of this action, the Lamb's "glory" and Rahab's "turpitude" are revealed, the dead in Beulah descend, and Urizen is tormented by the "female" influence. To some extent these cataclysms – particularly the descent of the dead from Beulah – repeat and perhaps intensify those at the end of vii[a] (85:18) and vii[b] (95:11), but the accumulation of these multiple events at this point in Night viii tends to overpower any need for the continuation of the narrative following pages 106. In particular, the mutual revelations of the Lamb's glory and Rahab's turpitude act as unveilings designed to inaugurate directly the Apocalypse. The final line of page 145 – "he felt the female &c." – indicates, however, that this scene was to be grafted back on to the narrative at 106:35, to be followed by at least four pages of text before arriving at the actual unveiling of the Apocalypse.[6] The apocalyptic elements of divine revelation, exposure of error, and descent of the dead seem out of keeping with the material following, outlining delays occasioned by Urizen's stony stupor, the return to the battle of Los, Tharmas, and Urthona against Urizen, and the laments of Ahania and Enion. More problematically, Rahab's action of stripping Luvah's robes becomes a determining factor in the processes of revelation that follow; the redemptive power of the Lamb seems largely incidental. While Blake adapted much of the material from page 145 to page 105, he did not retain the lines devoted to Rahab's actions in relation to the Lamb of God.

Passages added to the margins of page 105 develop Rahab's role in a twofold way. On the one hand, her character is developed in synchronic alignment with other characters and concepts inside and outside Blake's poem. On the other, pressures of plot direct certain aspects of her character towards the demands of a diachronic narrative, demands particularly forceful since she becomes the crucial agent in the final turn towards the Apocalypse at the end of Night viii. Blake's revisions to the scenes immediately preceding the Crucifixion develop her synchronic dimensions through her interidentification with Satan, Tirzah, and the "Daughters of <Amalek> Canaan and Moab." The additions associate her with the Synagogue of Satan (105:14), reinforce biblical allusions in identifying her directly with the figure of "Mystery" in Revelation (105:15), and place her within the perceptual universe of *Jerusalem*:

> When viewd remote She is One when viewd near she divides
> To multitude as it is in Eden so permitted because
> It was the best possible in the State calld Satan to Save
> From Death Eternal & to put off Satan Eternally.   (105:16–19)

In *Jerusalem*, this shifting perspective is attributed to the Divine Family in a speech to Albion:

> Mutual in one anothers love and wrath all renewing
> We live as One Man; for contracting our infinite senses
> We behold multitude; or expanding: we behold as one,
> As One Man all the Universal Family; and that One Man
> We call Jesus the Christ: and he in us, and we in him,
> Live in perfect harmony in Eden the land of life.   (34[38]:16–21 e.180)

Set in juxtaposition, these passages generate a synchronic irony in terms of their respective objects of perception and yet offer a consistent analogy as a text of instruction. Rahab and Christ would seem the total antithesis of human experience in Blake's structural universe, but the mode of recognizing them as singular or multiple forms is the same. Recognition of the authority of perception in determining the content of states of human experience becomes a crucial element of characterization. It seems to supersede interest in character development, making the recognition of character types in whatever form, singular or multiple, the ascendent interest for the reader.

The structural antithesis to the Lamb of God continues in the second half of the addition with a description of Rahab's origin: "The Synagogue Created her from Fruit of Urizens tree" (105:20). Any myth of origination would seem to be inspired by concerns for the emergence of crucial figures in the diachronic development within time and space. Within this origin, however, Blake is careful to interconnect older elements of the poem – Urizen and his tree – with newer ones – the actions of the Synagogue of Satan. The interconnections contextualize Rahab's existence and create an increasingly inclusive set of equations; Urizen's tree, the Synagogue of Satan, and Rahab are all complicit and synchronically aligned in the work. Her mockery of the Lamb, the Synagogue's crucifixion, and Urizen's military assault on Orc, Los, Tharmas, and Urthona (among others) all are given roughly the same symbolic value through such developing interconnections. The vague temporalities and spatial contexts of this myth of origins undermine the horizontal teleology of the passage, making it an event in an eternal present rather than a distant past. Such vague atemporalities serve as reminders that teleology does not entirely define error, despite human desires to locate it in terms of determinate beginnings, development, recognition, and correction.

Through a series of later additions Rahab rapidly becomes indispensable as a link among a series of established characters and as a crucial object requiring the enactment of an idealized mode of perception. The final lines of the addition to page 105 offer a physical and symbolic location for Rahab in relation to Satan but counterbalance the apparent concreteness of spatial location by cancelling out any stability of time and by making space a symbolic antithesis rather than a palpable form: after her creation, Rahab

>           there was hidden within
> The bosom of Satan The false Female as in an ark & veil
> Which christ must rend & her reveal.   (105:24–6)

This depiction reveals Rahab to be the feminine version of error and also shows her as a demonic parody or inversion of Jerusalem, within whose veil the Lamb of God appears:

> And Enitharmon namd the Female Jerusa[*le*]m the holy
> Wondring she saw the Lamb of God within Jerusalems Veil
> The divine Vision seen within the inmost deep recess
> Of fair Jerusalems bosom in a gently beaming fire.   (104:1–4)

Moreover, the internalization of Rahab within Satan reinforces her motivational essentialism in the consolidation and action of error and offers a symbolic enactment of the way she is inscribed into the core of the narrative. The attempt to describe origins, to define the perceived essence of Rahab as a multiple or singular element of an eternal State, and to locate her within the bosom of Satan reinforce an atemporal dimension to her character at this point. At the same time, it should be noted that this addition ultimately confines Rahab's apparent autonomy within the actions of the Lamb. No longer the active agent of the Lamb's unveiling as depicted on the draft on page 145, she now becomes the veiled object "Which christ must rend & her reveal" (105:26). Forces of redemption are now given a commanding agency in the Apocalypse. While this passage offers a combination of atemporal character traits in combination with a teleology of vaguely defined origins and ends, perhaps the most difficult aspect of her development comes in the steps towards the conclusion of Night VIII and her fully revealed state.

The diachronic demands of narrative development return as Blake attempts to complete the story of Rahab's revelation with a series of additions to the end of Night VIII, additions made after the Night was transcribed complete with the finis, "The End of the Eighth Night." In

his first attempt Blake has Rahab place the Lamb in a Sepulchre she
has created and weep "over the Sepulcher weaving / Her web of Religion
around the Sepulcher" (110:32–3). As she buries the Lamb and begins to
weave the Lamb's garment into part of her own religion of "Death" (see
106:7–13), however,

> the bottom of the Sepulcher
> Rent & a door was opend thro the bottom of the Sepulcher
> Into Eternity And as she wove she heard a Voice behind her calling her
> She turnd & saw the Divine Vision & her [...]   (110:34–7)

Blake's addition drops off here, and although he may have not been sure
how to complete this scene, the thematic outlines are clear. Like the
draft on page 145, the addition describes the revelation of the "Divine
Vision" to Rahab. The new ending to Night VIII, however, relocates the
Revelation several pages after rather than at the Crucifixion, and creates
a symbolic as well as chronological separation between Crucifixion and
Revelation (both of the Divine Vision and of Rahab's error). The loca-
tion of the Revelation at the end of the Night, however, presents an
effective climax, with the revelation of truth and repudiation of error as
the turning-point of the Last Judgement at the opening of Night IX.[7]
Thus the new conclusion of Night VIII temporarily presents the epiph-
any of the Lamb at the time of his burial. At this moment, in the burial
of Christ, begins the false religion that worships his Crucifixion and
death but fails to look beyond the moment of burial to the Resurrection.
Yet Blake shows that in this burial "the bottom of the Sepulcher / Rent
& a door was opend ... / Into Eternity" (110:34–6). At this time there
is a polarization between a religion of life and one of death, leading to
a revelation about the source of life in this religion of death.

Blake appears to have struck out this passage before completing it,
but then placed a similar passage again near the Crucifixion scene when
he added the latter half of page 113 plus the text on pages 115–16 to his
manuscript. He created a narrative connection between the two texts by
the addition of lines 7–16 to page 106 and 40–6 to page 113. This
connection between his existing narrative and the material on the extra
pages contains essentially the same matter he had tried unsuccessfully to
develop on pages 145 and 110. Blake's addition of this new text (pages
113–16), however, reflects the growing importance of Los in *Vala* rather
than an essential concern with Rahab's character development. The
addition attributes the creation of the Lamb's sepulchre to Los and

introduces Los's extended diatribe on "the Sons of Los & Enitharmon" (115:1). The placing of 113–16 at this point in the manuscript also returns the revelation of Rahab's state closer to the Crucifixion. In this arrangement the Crucifixion is followed immediately by the preparation of the Lamb's tomb, and Rahab's true state is revealed at the tomb when she cuts "off the Mantle of Luvah from / The Lamb of God" (113:40–1). In this moment "Rahab in all her turpitude" (113:43) is revealed as "the Temple & the Synagogue of Satan & Mystery" (113:42). Blake had stopped and cancelled this passage in his previous attempts to portray Rahab's fate; with the addition of page 113, however, he directed attention away from Rahab at this crucial point in her story to Los, before whom she stands "among the Furnaces / Dividing & uniting in Delusive feminine pomp questioning him" (113:44–5).

The change in dramatic focus reflects Blake's renewed interest in Los as a redemptive force in *Vala*, but it also elides the ultimate fate of Rahab. An addition to Night IX on page 120 suggests that Rahab will somehow be redeemed, but the text between pages 113 and 120 does not specify how this redemption will take place. The Eternal Man argues in Night IX that Urizen's Dragon form will be burned

> With Mystery the Harlot & with Satan for Ever & Ever
> Error can never be redeemd in all Eternity
> But Sin Even Rahab is redeemd in blood & fury & jealousy
> <That line of blood that stretchd across the windows of the morning>
> Redeemd from Errors power.　(120:47–51)

It is impossible to determine exactly when Blake added these lines, but they involve his doctrine of the forgiveness of Sins developed in *Jerusalem* and thus would seem to be later rather than earlier. Further, they presuppose an attempt to develop a redemptive potential in the Rahab story that, although perhaps suggested in the earlier abortive attempts to fill out her narrative, is not resolved until the addition of page 111 to the manuscript. Lines 47, 48, 49, and 51, the original addition to page 120, were quite probably added before page 111, probably at the same time Blake was working on the texts of 145:20–3, 110:30–7, 106:7–16, and 113:40–5, since these texts all contain a reasonable degree of symbolic consistency. Moreover, line 50, a later addition to this passage, with its explicit reference to the biblical story of Rahab of Jericho, appears to date from the transcription of page 111 and seems designed to make the rest of the passage more consistent with the later characterization of Rahab on page 111.

On page 111, Blake presents a masterful compression of his entire mythology from the earliest to the latest elements in *Vala*. He synthesizes aspects of his earlier narrative, including the fates of Orc, "Urizens Dragon form," and Ahania's and Enion's laments with Rahab, the Synagogue of Satan, and a commentary on the origin of Deism and Natural Religion. This passage completes the story of Rahab as the ultimate form of female error (in opposition to the male error of Satan), placing her epiphany in a climactic moment just prior to the Last Judgement. Page 111 also depicts her with a degree of ambiguity that allows for her redemption as described on page 120 of Night IX.

Behind the characterization of Rahab on page 111 lie two particular biblical allusions that serve to heighten the presentation of her deceptive nature, allow for her potential redemption as described on page 120, and demonstrate the seriousness of the evil she represents. First, when Blake writes that in her repentant mood Rahab "commund with Orc in secret She hid him with the flax" (111:11), he refers to the Old Testament story of Rahab of Jericho, who hid Joshua's spies under "stalks of flax, which she had laid in order upon the roof" (Josh. 2:6). As a result of her actions she is spared from the burning of the city and accepted as a member of the Hebrew tribe. Rahab thus stands as a symbol of both the redeemed heathen and the repentant harlot saved before God's wrath is unleashed on the unrepentant. Blake's use of the Old Testament story reinforces the depiction of his Rahab as a potentially repentant character. However, he carefully chooses to ally his figure with the secretive and deceptive activities of the Old Testament Rahab, maintaining some consistency in his vision of Rahab as a figure of feminine delusiveness.

Blake adds to the ambiguity of the portrait by associating his Rahab with the Queen of Sheba as depicted in 1 Kings. Certainly both figures are associated with a wealth of gold, jewels, and great beauty, but Blake's comparison is far more specific than this. Rahab's vacillation between Orc and Satan begins "when she saw the form of Ahania weeping on the Void / And heard Enions voice sound from the caverns of the Grave." The text then states that as a result of this vision, "No more spirit remained in her" (111:8–10), thus drawing on the biblical story of the Queen of Sheba. In the Old Testament tale we are told that when Sheba "had seen all Solomon's wisdom, and the house that he had built … there was no more spirit in her" (1 Kings 10:4–5), and she too seems in a potentially repentant state. In both cases a figure of pomp associated with gold and jewels is rendered powerless before a figure of spiritual wisdom. There seems no reason to suspect any duplicity on Rahab's part in her reaction to the sight of Ahania and the voice of Enion. She certainly does not gain from her sympathy with them; in fact, the encounter causes an internal division within Rahab that ultimately brings about her own destruction. Yet there is an underlying note of uncertainty in the comparison with the Queen of Sheba, since she is the first of a long line of "many strange women" (1 Kings 11:2) from foreign countries who "turned … [Solomon's] heart after other gods" (1 Kings 11:4).[8] His lust for Sheba and others like her leads him into idolatry, and Blake seems to imply by comparison or allusion that those who follow the religion of Rahab and "The Daughters of <Amalek> Canaan & Moab" (105:28) also fall into an equally repugnant form of idolatry.

Through these biblical allusions, then, Blake presents a complex but striking image of delusive beauty. Rahab's vacillation on page 111 makes her actions difficult to interpret, since an essential attribute of her character is its deceptive nature.[9] Therefore, it is not entirely clear whether she is dissembling in her trysts with Orc, or how ambivalent she actually feels about her place in the Synagogue of Satan. It does seem that her repentance before Orc is genuine, since her sympathy with him only serves to unite the Synagogue of Satan against her. Moreover, their temporary reunion directs attention to their former unfallen life as Luvah and Vala,[10] and perhaps suggests a genuinely redemptive movement in their communion. The allusions to the Queen of Sheba and Rahab of Jericho, however, allow us to see both sincere and ironic motives behind Rahab's actions, and the secrecy surrounding their meetings suggests that Rahab is still concerned more with the appearance than the rightness of her actions. Furthermore, Rahab's apparent repentance is set against her less repentant moods, when she returns "to the Synagogue of Satan in Pride" (111:16), "kissing her Robes & Jewels & weeping over them" (111:15). Her pride and its connection with the "Robes & Jewels" she wears symbolically reinforce her identity with the Whore of Babylon, who is "arrayed in purple and scarlet colour, and decked with gold and precious stones and pearls" (Rev. 17:4).[11] And it seems that Rahab is equally sincere in this role. Of course, in this case Rahab fits more easily into our expectations of her, arising from other passages in *Vala* and particularly in *Jerusalem*. Yet she becomes all the more treacherous for this apparently ambiguous appearance.

While it is true that this ambiguity may be part of her "Delusive feminine pomp" (113:45), I think Blake offers more subtle possibilities in this latest development of Rahab's character. Although the reader may not be able to gauge accurately the degree of Rahab's sincerity, it is also possible that neither can she. Rahab is now doubly duplicitous and doubly dangerous. She deludes others but also deludes herself, since she appears at ease with her own contradictory behaviour. Such an interpretation reflects on earlier passages in the text, such as Tirzah's song of torture. Tirzah, another form of Rahab, believes that she tortures the "poor human form" (105:31) for its own good. She tells her sisters not to weep, because "our life depends on this [torture] / Or mercy & truth are fled" (105:52–3). On page 111 Blake brings this double-edged delusion to its most concise form in connection with Rahab and manages to condemn her activity while still allowing for repentance and redemption from this state of self-delusion. Rahab's irresolute state is cut short when the Synagogue of Satan "resolvd in open Sanhedrim / To burn Mystery with fire & form another from her ashes" (111:19–20). From the divine perspective this action is part of a providential scheme leading to the Last Judgement. From the Satanic perspective the Synagogue's action may be an attempt to reproduce Rahab's error, apart from any tendency towards repentance. From a literary perspective the burning of Rahab acts as a parody, a kind of anti-revelation, preceding the fiery consummation of the Last Judgement.

Blake's revisions ultimately place Rahab at the pivotal point of the Apocalypse, supplanting the male error of Urizen and Satan. According to Blake's additions to Night VIII, she is the motivating force in the torture and Crucifixion of the Lamb. Yet she is also God's agent in demonstrating the transcendence of the Lamb. Ironically, her religion of mystery and death places her at the centre of the revelation of man's eternal existence. Blake goes to great lengths, however, to allow for her redemption; otherwise, he would find himself with a Judas-scapegoat figure who has no place in a system of belief that holds that "every thing that lives is Holy" (*MHH*, Song of Liberty; E.45). True error, if there is such a thing, is attributed to Satan, who is not a being but a state of mind consumed in the mental flames of the Apocalypse. There is a distinct change in emphasis from the earlier story, of fallen existence progressing to a stony stupor shattered by the awakening of the Eternal Man, to the later narrative of a progression of forces of truth and error to a nodal point at which error brings about its own collapse and the

Last Judgement emerges from the "Universal Confusion" this Fall creates. This nodal point in history is a revelation of evil following its apparent triumph over good. Blake identifies this evil as the triumph of the natural over the spiritual, leading to a recurrent cycle of natural existence. In *Vala* such a moment occurs after Rahab or Mystery is burned and

> The Ashes of Mystery began to animate they calld it Deism
> And Natural Religion as of old so now anew began
> Babylon again in Infancy Calld Natural Religion.   (111:22–4)

By identifying Babylon or Mystery with Natural Religion or Deism, Blake appeals to a symbol of error made universal in Revelation and particularizes it in terms of a contemporary but far-reaching form of religious error. This kind of addition grounds the poem in specific historical process while universalizing this particular error in history as a synchronous representation of all error. As a mental state the nature of error never changes, even though it appears in a variety of forms.

Although Blake constantly refined his definition of Rahab, the introduction of so many new characters and narrative elements into Night VIII created inconsistencies in the transition to Night IX. Rahab does not appear in the basic text of Night IX or in the pages added to the opening of the Night; Blake explains the fate of Rahab only in additions to this Night. She, along with Tirzah, appears in a single line added to the general consummation, where they "wail aloud in the wild flames they give up themselves to Consummation" (118:7). Rahab's only other appearance is in the Eternal Man's address to Urizen, where he threatens to burn all forms of error until they are either consumed or purified and redeemed. These lines purport to show that the destruction and bloodshed of the Last Judgement are part of a process that redeems Rahab, yet Rahab is virtually absent from the Apocalypse. With this addition Blake attempts to redress the imbalance of importance given to Rahab in the additions to Night VIII, but her absence from Night IX undermines the effectiveness of this revision. Further, Blake does not actually show how Rahab is redeemed, except perhaps through the implicit identification of Rahab with Vala: in terms of this identification the earlier story of Vala and Luvah's redemption in Night IX would also account for Rahab's redemption. However, the symbolic significance of Rahab perhaps became too complicated to be explained in these terms, and so her character merely adds further stress to the diachronic structure of *Vala*. Developed as a synchronic principle of error, and drawing in a multitude of allusions, she plays a pivotal role in contextualizing the nature of error coherently through history. Yet the synchronic poetics that Blake uses to enrich her character create a centrality unprepared for and undeveloped in the diachronically based narrative. She is left a central character with only a minimum of narrative space to describe the importance of her actions.

# Conclusion: Revisionary Poetics

In my Preface I invoked De Quincey's comparison of the mind to a palimpsest as a fitting description of the tension between the layers of text that comprise the *Vala* manuscript. Later layers, added in succession, threaten to bury preceding "layers of ideas, images, [and] feelings," while the unextinguished presence of the underlying layers glows with an uneasy and sometimes unassimilated light. The tension between the "heaven-created palimpsest, the deep memorial palimpsest of the brain," which demands order, coherence, and intelligibility, and the "grotesque collision of those successive themes," which seem to have "no natural connexion, which by pure accident have consecutively occupied the roll," emanates from the physical manuscript of *Vala* and shapes, distorts, and frustrates interpretive approaches to the poem.

The pursuit of palimpsests involves the critic in a series of activities, each of which complicates the last. If we imagine the manuscript as an archeological site, the complexity of the process of interpretation emerges. In the presence of overwritten portions of text, the critic is inevitably engaged in a vertical process of uncovering successive textual strata. Yet this vertical physical layering is further complicated by what might be figured as adjacent lateral or horizontal material, marginal additions whose temporal relationship to the base text is often difficult to ascertain. Exposing layers of text involves the vertical separation of earlier and later strata and an attempt (however conjectural at times) to reconstruct the physical and conceptual relationship between them. This process is complicated by the horizontal layers of adjacent materials, often of different stages of composition. Interpolation is inevitably brought in with at least some concern to develop or even to disrupt surrounding narrative, character, and context, and so our understanding of vertical layerings must exist in conjunction with the continuities or discontinuities of contiguous units of text. A radical suspension of finalities, the very definition of manuscript form itself, qualifies all critical statements about it.

With the above in mind, therefore, I have tended to avoid much of the debate on issues of completion or the lack thereof in the poem. Such debates are, at least in part, the result of acts of containment that strive towards making an intelligible whole out of what Frye has called a "cultural disaster."[1] The problem, however, is that such debates direct attention away from the vital processes evidenced by the manuscript itself. A manuscript as long and complex as *Vala* is naturally forbidding, but it becomes more tractable when placed in context alongside the current critical reception of Blake's other works. Joseph Viscomi's arguments about the illuminated poems are a case in point. He posits that in the production of the illuminated works, no preliminary or transfer drawings were used.[2] As a result, the copperplate becomes a medium with the flexibility of the sketchpad rather than the fixity of a resistant metal. Throughout his study Viscomi shows how Blake constantly revised his works, how the poems and designs subtly changed through all stages in the process of production. Fluidity and change become the norm within the partially fixed designs of the plate, and Blake, for commercial reasons, sought to give a sense of uniqueness to each copy of each work, even when, as Viscomi points out, an edition of several copies was produced in one printing session. Viscomi's notion of editions balances the sense of a containing form or design against the accidents in the materials and methods of production that give a sense of the unique and the different emerging from this identity. In commenting on the theoretical implications of similarity and difference between copies of the illuminated works, Viscomi argues:

With variations technically inevitable and aesthetically acceptable and concepts of uniformity and final form permitting diversity, variations not only occur but can be thought of as deliberately allowed to occur. Such variations among copies of the same edition, then, do not represent a rethinking of the poem or page but a sensitivity to the generative powers of execution, to the logic of the tools, materials, and processes – and to the original contributions of an assistant.[3]

It has been my contention throughout this study that the manuscript of *Vala* operates in a similar manner. Just as the exploitation of variation through manipulation of the fixed medium of the copper plate by masking borders, varying ink colours, adding watercolours (or leaving the copy monochrome), and so on changes the conventions of reproduction in a mechanical medium from those associated with identical repetition to the appearance at least of radical variation within distinct borders, so too the revisions to *Vala* are radical variations on a central design. Indeed, the vitality of the manuscript is present in that it retains the containments of nine Nights, for instance, but allows the ruptures and excesses of revision to remain in conflict with the sense of design most critics search for in their readings of the poem. Such a process of revision gives a flexibility to this design that stretches all normative measures of consistency and coherence. This flexibility also tests fallen perception and all acts of mental containment, whether they be the exertions of editors, theorists, specialized Blake critics, casual readers, or any combination of these. In particular, the conventions of freedom within the genre of the manuscript are subtly challenged here. While the author presumably has the total freedom to delete large passages, to throw out pages or to go so far as to destroy the whole bundle of pages, this is not obviously the case in *Vala*, which is more a record of accretion than of erasure. Bentley's argument that "Blake's general method of revision was to add and expand, rather than to delete and compress" (B.164) seems an accurate assessment of the remains of the *Vala* manuscript. While there are possibilities of rejected and now lost drafts, transcriptions, and pages, the remaining manuscript tells a tale of steady addition and enlargement. Indeed, only the opening pages of the copperplate text show evidence of extensive erasures and extensive rewriting. Nowhere else do we see so much evidence of lost text, and at the same time such visible sign of growth and expansion. The result is a literary form that accumulates and records its own growth, united with a minimal censuring of its past development (or developments). The evolution of design or identity can be seen simultaneously as progress towards unity and the emergence of recessive tendencies in conflict with the sense of overall design. Thus, coherence and conflict mark the manuscript physically and thematically. Unlike the illuminated works, however, *Vala* shows this coherence and conflict within one flexible design, one physical manifestation, rather than across the production of several versions or editions of the same work. The sense of identity within difference and difference within identity marks the manuscript more distinctly than it does the illuminated work, but the principle remains constant.

The manuscript, like Blake's illuminated works, seems to play out the conflict inherent in Barthes's distinction between "work" and "text."[4] As a "work" the poem attempts to close itself on a signified, to strive towards some system with centre and end to it.[5] The Ninth Night, for instance, leads to a point of narrative and thematic culmination satisfying enough to lead critics like Northrop Frye to say, "There is nothing like the colossal explosion of creative power in the Ninth Night of *The Four Zoas* anywhere else in English poetry."[6] Yet, as we have seen, the kinds of additions made to the end of Night VII[a] render Night IX an anticlimax. David Aers' dissatisfaction with the "collective passivization" in Night IX, one that makes "agency ... extrinsic to the peoples supposedly involved in revolutionary transition," finds some appeasement (not surprisingly) in the ending of Night VII[a].[7] Aers' comments speak to the desire to approach *Vala* as text, as a "network" of signifiers capable of being "broken" and that practise "an infinite deferment of the signified."[8]

This approach to the work as text, as a network of signifiers, delivers the work into the order of language and writing in at least two ways. First, "like language, it [the text] is structured but off-centred, without closure."[9] Second, *Vala* exhibits what Derrida calls the fissured value of writing integral to all language. Derrida argues that writing attempts to reappropriate presence at the same time that "it consecrates the dispossession that had already dislocated the spoken word."[10] A passage in Night VIII on page 99 about the "Council of God," for instance, illustrates this bluntly (99:1–19). Added in the later states of revision, mainly after all but the Eighth Night was transcribed, the description of the Council appears to offer a stable centre of being for the conflicted world experienced by the Zoas and Emanations. However, lines about Christ as a Good Shepherd guiding the fallen Man are erased and written over,[11] only to be transferred to page 8 (10–11), where they are again struck out and then transferred to page 21 (1–7), a page with no clear location in the sequence of connected pages. Despite the antitheses of translucence they set against the "Limit of Contraction" established for Albion, the heavy weight of revision makes these passages into leaden angels, their design as presence obscured by the blurs and blots of revision.

It should be clear by now that the manuscript also materializes the poststructuralist problematic of the author. According to Barthes, "A classic narrative always gives this impression: the author first conceives the signified (or the generality) and then finds for it, according to the chance of his imagination, 'good' signifiers, probative examples; the classic author is like an artisan bent over the workbench of meaning and selecting the best *expressions* for the concept he has already formed." In such classic narratives "the *author* is always supposed to go from signified to signifier, from content to form, from idea to text, from passion to expression; and, in contrast, the *critic* goes in the other direction, works back from signifiers to signified." The poststructuralist text instead supplants the author with the performative aspects of writing itself and with the reader "who holds together in a single field all the traces by which the written text is constituted."[12]

Working with the *Vala* manuscript, relentlessly faced with the physical manifestation of Blake's revisionary shaping of his poem, leaves me in no doubt that any study of the manuscript will be heavily driven by such conceptualizations of author as intentional consciousness. Systematic revisions such as the change of "Man" to "Albion" in the first 56 pages (see B.172) suggest an attempt to achieve coherence and consistency. That this revision does not go beyond page 56, however, calls into question the use of a unified conception of an author embodying conscious and singular intentionality. Did Blake forget, give up, or get careless? How much is accident and how much intention? Robert Essick's argument that "the sharing of creative responsibility between artist and medium blurs conventional distinctions between what is intended by the artist and what is an unintended 'accident' or 'error'"[13] takes on crucial importance. That we are able to see and describe such a change emphasizes the sense of an author, but such an author figure can only be reconstructed as embodying multiple conceptions of the poem simultaneously rather than as presenting a unified or consistent consciousness. We have a manuscript in which we must see "plurality" rather than unity, a "weave of signifiers" leaving the reader "at a loose end"[14] rather than a fully intelligible structure closing on an elusive signified. Thus the "cacophony of voices" that Otto sees in the poem itself need not achieve resolution in authorial origins. As he points out in commenting on the significance of the poem, "In *The Four Zoas* ... truth is inevitably mediated by interpretation and position. It is only in an embrace of the multitude of voices and memories which are found in the fallen world that truth, albeit in an equivocal and still conditioned fashion, is presented."[15] Such statements point to a self-reflexivity that inscribes the reader fully within the signifying process of the text and leaves the posited identity of the author a diversified and problematic one.

In the textuality of *Vala* the sense of design, of teleology, and of order is modified by flexibility, inconclusiveness, and disruption. The flexible design of the manuscript asks its readers to hold the two poles of textuality in constant tension and suspension. As other Blake texts are read as an analogous form of manuscript poetics – always a poetics of revision – the flexible design radically refigures the identity of the poem, author, and reader as multiplicity, diversity, and difference. While it would be impossible in this conclusion to explore fully the impact of extending the analogy of the flexible design to Blake's works as a whole, two brief examples may act as indices to the kinds of readings that might follow.

At its simplest level the kind of poetics of revision I have investigated here might be taken beyond *Vala* or *The Four Zoas* into the kinds of practical and theoretical cruxes we find in the typographic example of the "Mad Song" in the *Poetical Sketches*. According to Michael Phillips, seven copies of the *Poetical Sketches* record the emendation of "the rustling *beds* of dawn" (7; E.415) to "the rustling *birds* of dawn" (emphasis mine).[16] In traditional approaches, an either/or choice might be forced between "beds" and "birds."[17] Such a choice reinforces the stability of authorship and intentionality and delimits to a certain extent the play of language in the poem. Yet a poetics of revision might be able to entertain the juxtaposition of these two possibilities instead of suppressing one. The tension between "beds" and "birds" literally plays out the differential functions of language described by Saussure and elaborated on repeatedly within poststructuralism. "Birds" plays up the literal logic of morning and flights from the earth; "beds" embellishes the figurative association of the place of awakening with human actions in that place. The incorporation of such conflicting variants opens out the play of signifiers in the text and leads to a degree of suspension of critical judgement that opens out multiple vectors of meaning.

My second example comes from *America* and involves two instances of variants attached to the poem. The first arises from one of three "variant" plates printed for but not included in any completed copy of *America*.[18] The first – known as plate a – is a variant of plate 3, offering slight alterations in text and design. The second – plate b – contains designs similar to those in *America*, plate 4, but with an entirely different text. Finally, the third – plate c – has no direct correlation to any other plate in the poem and seems more a discarded supplement than a variant.[19] In this instance the relation between variant and final form carries out the same tensions of the poetics of revision at a more complex level and in two very different kinds of variation. Existing as each does in a single monochrome copy and poorly printed, these plates are normally accorded the status of experimental alternatives or rejected passages. Yet their presence calls into question the closure and autonomy of the so-called finished copies of *America*. They become less finished, more like a manuscript, as the possibilities suggested by these "cancelled variant[s]" are considered.

While the different degrees of variation found in each of these plates disrupt *America* in a variety of ways, the variant known as plate b invokes the most complex dimensions of the poetics of revision. "Plate b," as Erdman points out, "is a variant of Plate 4 in the illustrations, but quite different in text" (E.802). In both versions the plate depicts two flying forms, a human male holding a sceptre and a dragon, across the top of the plate and at least one crouched human figure grasping his head at the bottom of the plate. Plate 4 of *America* adds an additional crouched figure embracing a small child to the bottom tableau and transforms the clouds at the bottom left to a form Erdman describes as "a beached sea monster."[20]

These visual variants are relatively minor and serve mainly as markers drawing the very different text on the two plates into curious alignment. The text, however, varies not just in its wording and content but in its representational strategy. The strategies of occlusion, for instance, engaged in by refiguring the forces of oppression as Albion's Angel or Urizen lapse for a crucial moment in the cancelled plate, and "George the third" (b:9) is directly named as the central embodiment of British oppression for the only time in Blake's prophetic books.[21] The only other "George" present (or absent) in the prophetic books appears in a cancelled line of *Jerusalem*. The line, "Edward Henry Elizabeth James Charles William George" (73:37; E.228), is deleted and covered by vines in all copies (except for posthumous ones) of the poem.

Morton Paley, in commenting on the specific reference to "George," remarks, "The inclusion of George – whichever one may have been meant – may have caused second thoughts in a man who had once been tried for sedition and so have led to the deletion of the line."[22] The shift in strategy from dark figures to explicit statements, from the kind of sublime allegory "addressed to the Intellectual powers while it is altogether hidden from the Corporeal Understanding" (letter to Thomas Butts, E.730) to a more directly historical referentiality, challenges the critical convention of prophetic design. Indeed, Paley's comment on *Jerusalem* suggests the important asset Blake found in the symbolic indirectness of prophetic style. Verbal occlusions protect the prophetic writer and empower the satiric force of the text. The page containing a direct reference to "George the third" acts as an odd supplement that is part of and yet not part of the totality of *America*. On cancelled plate b the source of error is momentarily focalized in the historical personage of "George the third" and brings Blake's method more solidly under the rubric of *roman à clef* or naïve allegory, but the tenuous relationship of such a supplementary identification to the completed work creates a sense of textuality that both invites and resists such an act of incorporation. Including the plate in an interpretation of the poem creates a text and a Blake who invites direct allegory; rejection of it creates a text and a Blake who rejects such allegorization, presumably in favour of more complex, more indirect representations. The radical suspension of alternatives, however, removes text, author, and reader from a state of singular unified identity into one marked by multiple potentialities.

A second type of variant appears (and disappears) on plate 2 at the end of the Preludium to *America*. The final four lines on the plate in copies A, G, and N-Q dramatize a "Bard's" reaction to the story of Orc's rape of the Shadowy Female:

> The stern Bard ceas'd, asham'd of his own song; enrag'd he swung
> His harp aloft sounding, then dash'd its shining frame against
> A ruin'd pillar in glittring fragments; silent he turn'd away,
> And wander'd down the vales of Kent in sick & drear lamentings.
>
> (2:18–21; E.52)

The identification of a narratorial response to events in the Preludium gives these lines potential importance in shaping critical response: whether reliable or not, an explanation of the extremity of reaction by a poet figure to such an utterance seems necessary for a thorough explanation of *America*. However, these lines were masked on the copper plate during printing and do not appear in copies B-F, H-M, R, and the Morgan Pull.[23] This crux, therefore, invites a reading, but its tenuous relationship to the rest of a poem where it sometimes appears and sometimes does not confounds the interpretive act.

Located at a representational crux where sexual violence is brought into conjunction with political liberation, the Bard's reaction could be viewed as a moment of guidance for interpretation, a surrogate response for the reader, or an author's authoritative sanction stabilizing the act of reading. These lines might be read as supporting definable responses to this event: on the one hand, the Bard's rejection of his song might be a rejection of the act within the song; on the other, it might encompass a pessimism about the possibility of apocalyptic fulfilment and speak of the song only as a purely symbolic representation of revolutionary consciousness (male) acting on a passive object of transformation (female). While the political contexts of *America* largely celebrate the force of revolution, the rape of the Shadowy Female has a shocking violence that qualifies wholehearted endorsement of actions that lead to such violations. Making the illuminated book an analogy of the manuscript might additionally lead to a consideration of this passage, not in light of its influence on the interpretation of the role of the events of the Preludium within *America* as a whole, but instead of the effect of its absence and presence in the act of interpretation itself.

In the crux of presence and absence, the Bard becomes a part of the shifting possibilities of interpretation the moment he becomes reader of his own text. The reflexivity of the passage in turn makes the reader part of the layered potentiality of interpretation. Analogy of Bard and reader draws attention to the potential variousness of interpretation and the presence, absence, and uncertainties of motives for response. While the Bard might be equated with the author, it seems more fruitful to consider instead the author's role in choosing to include or exclude this passage. The writer and engraver of *America* sees fit to indicate the Bard's response; the printer chooses to mask or erase this response. We do not speak of the death of authorial intent here so much as a radical dispersion of different intentional identities across different moments of textual production. Such an authorial event disperses the identity of the poem; it becomes a different poem in different copies of *America*. In this instance *America*, like *Vala*, becomes a flexible design that radically refigures the identity of reader, author, and poem as a layered event that compounds and confounds the processes of interpretation.

Let me return then to the title of the poem, as it emerges finally on Blake's manuscript (see Plate 1). The "Ancient Man" is "Eternal" only in palimpsest; "A DREAM of Nine Nights" offers form to the poem only under fairly sharp and definite ink strokes; "The Four Zoas" and their "Torments of Love & Jealousy" appear only pencilled in above the bold calligraphy of "VALA"; "VALA" itself remains with only a slight pencil mark through it, a mark distinct enough to be registered but not definitive enough to cancel out its potential status as title. It seems to me that the pull towards the title of *The Four Zoas* in Blake criticism generally registers a desire for a return to the work after the cacophony of textual revision. The elaborate fourfold structuring of the Zoas offers the critic some reassuring symmetries of the type found in Frye's famous chart of overlapping fourfold categories in *Fearful Symmetry*,[24] but this totalized structure leaves behind the enigma of the title *Vala*. She is hardly present in the poem, yet continues to exist under an erasure that leaves her literally more visible than "The Four Zoas," added to "complete" the structure of human consciousness in the Eternal Man, the Fallen Man, or Albion (is he a trinity of three in one? or just one figure?). The added subtitle – "The torments of Love & Jealousy in" – postulates a continued state of being in antithesis to the evolving developments of "Death and Judgement," but it is perhaps unfair to say one takes precedence over the other because one was added later. Their simultaneous presence records the ongoing conflict of work and text in the poem's flexible design.

# APPENDIX A
# The Copperplate Text of *Vala*

The following text represents an attempt to isolate the earliest remaining copperplate-hand version of *Vala*. I have begun this transcription from the middle of page 7 because some of the heavy erasures on the pages before have rendered the copperplate lines virtually irrecoverable. I have indicated erased text in angle brackets <>, but left out even Blake's earliest additions to the copperplate text in an attempt to present the earliest possible text. B refers to Bentley's edition of *Vala*, E to Erdman's *The Complete Poetry and Prose*, and M to Margouliouth's *Blake's Vala*.

VALA

*Night the First*

PAGE 7
Twisting in fearful forms & howling <                    >
<          > harsh shrieking, mingling their bodies join in burning anguish
Mingling his horrible brightness with her tender limbs; then high she soar'd
Above the ocean; a bright wonder that Nature[1] shudderd at
Half Woman & half Serpent,[2] all his lovely changing colours mix
With her fair crystal clearness; in her lips & cheeks his poisons rose
In blushes like the morning, and his scaly armour softening
A monster lovely in the heavens or wandering on the earth,

With Serpent[3] voice incessant wailing, in incessant thirst
Beauty all blushing with desire mocking her fell despair

Wandering desolate, a wonder abhorr'd by Gods & Men

PAGE 8
Till with fierce pain she brought forth on the rocks her sorrow & woe
Behold two little Infants wept upon the desolate wind.

*[5 erased copperplate lines]*[4]

Enion brooded, oer the rocks, the rough rocks <                    >
The barked Oak, the long limbd Beech;[5] the Ches'nut tree; the Pine.
The Pear tree mild, the frowning Walnut, the sharp Crab, & Apple sweet,
The rough bark opens; twittering peep forth little beaks & wings
The Nightingale, the Goldfinch, Robin, Lark, Linnet & Thrush
The Goat leap'd from the craggy Rock[6] the Sheep awoke from the mould
Upon its green stalk rose the Corn, waving innumerable
Infolding the bright Infants from the desolating winds
*[2 erased copperplate lines]*

PAGE 9
*[3 erased copperplate lines]*[7]
*[erased ?copperplate lines?]*[8]
*[1 erased ?copperplate line]*[9]

Nine Times they livd among the forests, feeding on sweet fruits
And nine bright Spaces wandered <                         >
Snaring the wild Goats for their milk they eat the flesh of Lambs
A male & female naked & ruddy as the pride of summer

Alternate Love & Hate his breast; hers Scorn & Jealousy[10]
In embryon passions. they kiss'd not nor embrac'd for shame & fear

His head beamd light & in his vigorous voice was prophecy
He could controll the times & seasons, & the days & years
She could controll the spaces, regions, desart, flood & forest
They wanderd long, till they sat down upon the margind sea.

Thy name is Enitharmon; said the bright prophetic boy

PAGE 10

But Enitharmon answerd with a dropping tear & smiling
Bright as a dewy morning when the crimson light appears

To make us happy how they weary their immortal powers
While we draw in their sweet delights <                    >
<                              > for if we grateful prove
They will withhold sweet love, whose food is thorns & bitter roots
Hear! <                  > Death! it is a <      > of Vala![11]

The Eternal Man takes his repose: Urizen sleeps in the porch Luvah and Vala
    wake & fly up from the Human Heart
Into the Brain; from thence upon the pillow[12] Vala slumber'd.
And Luvah siez'd the Horses of Light, & rose into the Chariot of Day
<      > in the visions of Vala <                         >
<                    > among the branches, & among sweet flowers.
Why is the light of Vala darken'd in her dewy morn[13]
Why is the silence of Vala lightning & her smile a whirlwind
Uttering this darkness in my halls? in the pillars of my Holy-ones

Why dost tho weep O Vala? & wet thy veil with dewy tears.
In slumbers of my night-repose, infusing a false morning?

PAGE 11

I heard the sounding sea: I heard the voice weaker and weaker;
The voice came & went like a dream, I awoke in my sweet bliss.

Los answer'd, darkning with foul indignation hid in smiles
*[2 erased copperplate lines]*[14]
Seeking to comfort Vala, ?but[15] she will not be comforted
She rises from his throne and seeks the shadows of her garden
Weeping for Luvah <                              >
Sickning lies the Eternal Man his head sick his heart faint
I see, invisible descend into the Gardens of Vala
Luvah walking on the winds, <                    >
*[1 erased copperplate line]*
<      > in the Brain of Man we live, & in his circling Nerves.
<      > this bright world of all our joy is in the Human Brain.
<      > Urizen & all his Hosts hang their immortal lamps
<                  > cold expanse where watry Tharmas mourns

*[2 erased copperplate lines]*

PAGE 12
The <            >[16] Man bow'd his <      > head and Urizen descended
Indignant muttering low thunders; <                    >
*[2 erased copperplate lines]*
Ten thousand thousand were his hosts of spirits on the wind:
Ten thousand thousand glittering Chariots shining in the sky:
They pour upon the golden shore beside the silent ocean.

The Earth spread forth her table wide. the Night a silver cup
Fill'd with the wine of <         > waited at the golden feast
But the bright Sun was not as yet; he filling all the expanse
Slept as a bird in the blue shell that soon shall burst away
They eat the <       > bread, they drank the <        > wine

PAGE 13
They listend to the elemental Harps & Sphery Song
They view'd the dancing Hours, quick sporting thro' the sky
With winged radiance scattering joys thro the <      > changing light

The purple night the crimson morning & the golden day descended[17]
<      >[18] the clear changing atmosphere display'd green fields among
The varying clouds, like paradises stretch'd in the expanse
With towns & villages and temples, tents sheep-folds and pastures
Where dwell the children of the elemental worlds in harmony.
Not long in harmony they dwell, their life is drawn away
And wintry woes succeed: successive driven into the Void
Where Enion craves: successive drawn into the golden feast

And Los & Enitharmon sat in discontent & scorn
The Nuptial Song arose from all the thousand thousand spirits
Over the joyful Earth & Sea, and ascended into the Heavens
For Elemental Gods their thunderous Organs blew; creating
Delicious Viands. Demons of Waves their watry Eccho's woke! Bright
Souls of vegetative life, budding and blossoming

PAGE 14
Stretch their immortal hands to smite the gold & silver Wires
And with immortal Voice soft warbling fill all Earth & Heaven.

With doubling Voices &[19] <        > Horns wound round sounding
Cavernous dwellers fill'd the enormous Revelry, Responsing!
And Spirits of Flaming fire on high, govern'd the mighty Song.


*[Song at the Feast of Los and Enitharmon]*[20]


PAGE 17
And Enion Blind & age-bent wept upon the desolate wind


Why does the Raven cry aloud and no eye pities her?
Why fall the Sparrow & the Robin in the foodlesss winter?
*[1 erased copperplate line]*[21]


Wearied with seeking food across the snowy waste; the little
Heart, cold; and the little tongue consum'd, that once in thoughtless joy
Gave songs of gratitude to the waving corn fields round their nest.


Why howl the Lion & the Wolf? why do they roam abroad?
Deluded by the summers heat they sport in enormous love
And cast their young out to the <              > sandy desarts


PAGE 18
Why is the Sheep given to the knife? the Lamb plays in the Sun
He starts! he hears the foot of Man! he says, take[22] thou my wool


But spare my life, he knows not that the winter cometh fast


The Spider sits in his labourd Web, eager watching for the Fly
Presently comes a famishd Bird & takes away the Spider
His Web is left all desolate, that his little anxious heart
So careful wove: & spread it out with sighs and weariness.
This was the Lamentation of Enion round the golden Feast


*End of the First Night*


PAGE 23


*Night the* <          >[23]


The[24] Man calld Urizen & said. Behold these sickning Spheres

Take thou possession! take this Scepter! go forth in my might
For I am weary. & must sleep in the dark sleep of Death
Urizen rose from the bright Feast like a star thro' the evening sky
Exulting at the voice that calld him from the Feast of envy
First he beheld the body of Man pale, cold, <                    >
<              ` > shot thro' him as he stood in the Human Brain
And all its golden porches grew pale with his sickening light
Pale he beheld futurity; pale he beheld the Abyss
Where Enion blind & age bent wept in direful hunger craving
All rav'ning like the hungry worm, & like the silent grave


PAGE 24
Mighty was the draught of Voidness to draw Existence in


Terrific Urizen strode above, in fear & pale dismay
He saw the indefinite space beneath & his soul shrunk with horror
His feet upon the verge of Non Existence; his voice went forth


Luvah & Vala trembling & shrinking. beheld the lord of ?day[25]
And heard his work! Divide ye bands influence by influence
The Bands of Heaven flew thro the air singing & shouting to the lord[26]
Some fix'd the anvil, some the loom erected, some the plow
And harrow formd & framd the harness of silver & ivory
The golden compasses, the quadrant & the rule & balance
They erected the furnaces, they formd the anvils of gold beaten in mills
Where winter beats incessant, fixing them firm on their base
The bellows began to blow & the Lions of Urizen stood round the anvil


PAGE 25
And the leopards coverd with skins of beasts tended the roaring fires
The tygers of wrath called the horses of instruction from their mangers
They unloos'd them & put on the harness of gold & silver & ivory
In human forms distinct they stood round Urizen prince of Light
Rattling the adamantine chains & hooks heave up the ore
In mountainous masses, plung'd in furnaces, & they shut & seald
The furnaces a time & times; all the while blew the North
His cloudy bellows & the South & East & dismal West
And all the while the plow of iron cut the dreadful furrows


Luvah was cast into the Furnaces of affliction & sealed
And Vala fed in cruel delight, the furnaces with fire

Stern Urizen beheld urg'd by necessity to keep
The evil day afar, & if perchance with iron power
He might avert his own despair; in woe & fear he saw


PAGE 26
Vala incircle round the furnaces where Luvah was clos'd
In joy she heard his howlings, & forgot he was her Luvah
With whom she walk'd in bliss, in times of innocence & youth
Hear ye the voice of Luvah from the furnaces of Urizen


If I indeed am Luvah's Lord[27] & ye O sons of Men
The workmanship of Luvahs hands; in times of Everlasting
When I calld forth the Earth-worm from the cold & dark obscure
I nurturd her I fed her with my rains & dews, she grew
A scaled Serpent, yet I fed her tho' she hated me
Day after day she fed upon the mountains in Luvahs sight
I brought her thro' the Wilderness, a dry & thirsty land
And I commanded springs to rise for her in the black desert
Till she became a de <      >[28] winged bright & poisonous
I opend all the floodgates of the heavens to quench her thirst


PAGE 27
And I commanded the Great deep to hide her in his hand
Till she became a little weeping Infant a span long
I carried her in my bosom as a man carries a lamb
I loved her I gave her all my soul & my delight
I hid her in soft gardens & in secret bowers of Summer
Weaving mazes of delight along the sunny Paradise
Inextricable labyrinths, She bore me sons & daughters
And they have taken her away & hid her from my sight
They have surrounded me with walls of iron & brass,
*[3 erased lines]*[29]
Because I love for I am love & hatred <      > in me
The hand of Urizen is upon me because I blotted out
That Human terror to deliver all the sons of God
From bondage of the Human form, O first born Son of Light
O Urizen my enemy I weep for thy stern ambition
But weep in vain O when will you return Vala the wanderer[30]


PAGE 28
These were the words of Luvah patient in afflictions

And when Luvah age after age was quite melted with woe
The fires of Vala faded like a shadow cold & pale
An evanescent shadow. last she fell a heap of Ashes
Beneath the furnaces a woful heap in living death

Then were the furnaces unseald with spades & pickaxes
Roaring let out the fluid, the molten metal ran in channels
Cut by the plow of ages held in Urizens strong hand
In many a valley, for the Bulls of Luvah dragd the Plow

Then siezd the Lions of Urizen their work, & heated in the forge
Roar the bright masses, thund'ring beat the hammers, many a globe[31]
Is form'd & thrown down thund'ring into the deeps of Non Entity
Heated red hot they hizzing rend their way down many a league
Till resting. each his center finds; suspended there they stand
Casting their sparkles dire abroad into the dismal deep
For measurd out in orderd spaces the Sons of Urizen
With compasses divide the deep; they the strong scales erect

PAGE 29
That Luvah rent from the faint Heart of the Eternal Man
And weigh the massy Globes, then fix them in their awful stations
And all the time in Caverns[32] shut, the golden Looms erected
First spun, then wove the Atmospheres, there the Spider & Worm
Plied the wingd shuttle piping shrill thro' all the list'ning threads
Beneath the Caverns roll the weights of lead & spindles of iron
The enormous warp & woof rage direful in the affrighted deep
While far into the vast unknown, the strong wing'd Eagles bend
Their venturous flight, in Human forms distinct; thro darkness deep
They bear the woven draperies; on golden hooks they hang abroad
The universal curtains & spread out from Sun to Sun
The vehicles of light, they separate the furious particles
Into mild currents as the water mingles with the wine.

While thus the Spirits of strongest wing enlighten the dark deep
The threads are spun & the cords twisted & drawn out; then the weak
Begin their work; & many a net is netted; many a net

PAGE 30
Spread & many a Spirit caught, innumerable the nets

Innumerable the gins & traps; & many a soothing flute
Is form'd & many a corded lyre, outspread over the immense
In cruel delight they trap the listeners, & in cruel delight
Bind them, together[33] the strong energies into little compass
Some became seed of every plant that shall be planted; some
The bulbous roots, thrown up together into barns & garners

Then rose the Builders; First the Architect divine his plan
Unfolds, The wondrous scaffold reard all round the infinite
Multitudes without number work incessant: the hewn stone
Is placd in beds of mortar mingled with the ashes of Vala
Severe the labour, female slaves the mortar trod oppressed

Los joyd & Enitharmon laughd, saying Let us go down
And see this labour & sorrow; They went down to see the woes
Of Vala & the woes of Luvah, to draw in their delights
And Vala like a shadow oft appeard to Urizen

PAGE 31
The King of Light beheld her mourning among the Brick kilns compelld
To labour night & day among the fires, her lamenting voice
Is heard when silent night returns & the labourers take their rest

O Lord wilt thou not look upon our sore afflictions
Among these flames incessant labouring, our hard masters laugh
At all our sorrow. We are made to turn the wheel for water
To carry the heavy basket on our scorched shoulders, to sift
The sand & ashes, & to mix the clay with tears & repentance
The times are now returnd upon us, we have given ourselves
To scorn and now are scorned by the slaves of our enemies
Our beauty is coverd over with clay & ashes, & our backs
Furrowd with whips, & our flesh bruised with the heavy basket
Forgive us O thou piteous one whom we have offended, forgive
The weak remaining shadow of Vala that returns in sorrow to thee.
Thus she lamented day & night, compelld to labour & sorrow
Luvah in vain her lamentations heard; in vain his love
Brought him in various forms before her still she knew him not

PAGE 32
Still she despisd him, calling on his name & knowing him not

Still hating still professing love, still labouring in the smoke

And Los & Enitharmon joyd, they drank in tenfold joy
From all the sorrow of Luvah & the labour of Urizen

For infinitely beautiful the wondrous work arose
In songs & joy a Golden World whose porches round the heavens
And pillard halls & rooms recievd the eternal wandering stars
A wondrous golden Building; many a window many a door
And many a division let in & out into the vast unknown
Circled in infinite orb immoveable, within its arches all
The heavens were closd <                                    >
[1 erased line]34

Then went the Planters forth to plant, the Sowers forth to sow
They dug the channels for the rivers & they pourd abroad

PAGE 33
The seas & lakes, they reard the mountains & the rocks & hills
On broad pavilions, on pillard roofs & porches & high towers
In beauteous order, thence arose soft clouds & exhalations
Wandering even to the sunny orbs of light & heat
For many a window ornamented with sweet ornaments
Lookd out into the world of Tharmas, where in ceaseless torrents
His billows roll where monsters wander in the foamy paths
On clouds the Sons of Urizen beheld <                   >
They weighd & orderd all & Urizen <                >35
The wondrous work flow forth like visible out of the invisible
[4 or 5 erased lines]36

Thus were the stars of heaven created like a golden chain
To bind the body37 of Man to heaven from falling into the abyss38
Each took his station, & his course began with songs & joy

PAGE 34
And Los & Enitharmon were drawn down by their desires
Descending sweet upon the wind among soft harps & voices

Urizen saw & envied & his imagination was filled
Then he contemplated the past in his bright sphere

Terrified with his heart & spirit at the visions of futurity
That his dread fancy formd before him in the unformd void

Now Los & Enitharmon walkd forth on the dewy Earth
Contracting or expanding their all flexible senses
At will to murmur in the flowers small as the honey bee
At will to stretch across the heavens & step from star to star
Or standing on the Earth erect, or on the stormy waves
Driving the storms before them or delighting in sunny beams
While round their heads the elemental Gods kept harmony

Thus <      > Los driving Enion far into the <        > infinite
Ah happy blindness she sees not the terrors of the uncertain
And oft thus she wails from the dark deep, the golden heavens tremble

PAGE 35
I am made to sow the thistle for wheat: the nettle for a nourishing dainty
I have planted a false oath in the earth, it has brought forth a poison tree
I have chosen the serpent for a councellor & the dog
For a schoolmaster to my children
I have blotted out from light & living the dove & nightingale
And I have caused the earth worm to beg from door to door
I have taught the thief a secret path into the house of the just
I have taught pale artifice to spread his nets upon the morning
My heavens are brass my earth is iron my moon a clod of clay
My sun a pestilence burning at noon & a vapour of death in night

What is the price of Experience do men buy it for a song
Or wisdom for a dance in the street? No it is bought with the price
Of all that a man hath his house his wife his children
Wisdom is sold in the desolate market where the none come to buy
And in the witherd field where the farmer plows for bread in vain
It is an easy thing to triumph in the summers sun
And in the vintage & to sing on the waggon loaded with corn
It is an easy thing to talk of patience to the afflicted
To speak the laws of prudence to the houseless wanderer

PAGE 36
To listen to the hungry ravens cry in wintry season
When the red blood is filld with wine & with the marrow of lambs

It is an easy thing to laugh at wrathful elements
To hear the dog howl at the wintry door, the ox in the slaughter house moan
To see a god on every wind & a blessing on every blast
To hear sounds of love in the thunder storm that destroys our enemies house
To rejoice in the blight that covers his field, & the sickness that cuts off his
    children
While our olive & vine sing & laugh round our door & our children bring fruits
    & flowers

Then the groan & the dolor are quite forgotten & the slave grinding at the mill
And the captive in chains & the poor in the prison, & the soldier in the field
When the shatterd bone hath laid him groaning among the happier dead

It is an easy thing to rejoice in the tents of prosperity
Thus could I sing & thus rejoice, but it is not so with me![39]

*End of the Second Night*

PAGE 37

*Night the <            >*[40]

Now sat the King of Light on high upon his starry throne
And bright Ahania bow'd herself before his splendid feet

O Urizen look on thy Wife, that like a mournful stream
Embrace round thy knees & wet her bright hair with her tears:
Why sighs my Lord! are not the morning stars thy obedient Sons
Do they not bow their bright heads at thy voice? at thy command
Do they not fly into their stations & return their light to thee
The immortal Atmospheres are thine, there thou art seen in glory
Surrounded by the ever changing Daughters of the Light
Thou sitst in harmony for God hath set thee over all

She ceas'd the Prince his light obscurd & the splendors of his crown

PAGE 38

Infolded in thick clouds, from whence his mighty voice burst forth
O bright Ahania a Boy is born of the dark Ocean
Whom Urizen doth serve, with Light replenishing his darkness

I am set here a King of trouble commanded here to serve
And do my ministry to those who eat of my wide table
All this is mine yet I must serve & that Prophetic boy
Must grow up to command his Prince & all my Kingly power
That Vala [?]may become a Worm in Enitharmons Womb
Laying her seed upon the fibres soon to issue forth
And Luvah in the loins of Los a dark & furious death
Alas for me! what will become of me at that dread time?

Ahania bow'd her head & wept seven days before the King
And on the eighth day when his clouds unfolded from his throne
She rais'd her bright head sweet perfumd & thus with heavenly voice

O Prince the Eternal One hath set thee leader of his hosts

PAGE 39
Raise then thy radiant eyes to him raise thy obedient hands
And comforts shall descend from heaven into thy darkning clouds
Why didst thou listen to the voice of Luvah that dread morn
To give the immortal steeds of light to his deceitful hands
No longer now obedient to thy will <                              >
To <           > the curbs of iron & brass to build the iron mangers
To feed them with intoxication from the wines presses of Luvah
They call thy lions to the fields of blood, they rouze thy tygers
Out of the halls of justice, till these dens thy wisdom framd
Golden & beautiful but O how unlike those sweet fields of bliss
Where liberty was justice & eternal science was mercy
Then O my dear lord listen to Ahania, listen to the vision
The vision of Ahania in the slumbers of Urizen
When Urizen slept in the porch & the Eternal Man was smitten
The Eternal Man walkd on the steps of fire before his halls
And Vala walkd with him in dreams of soft deluding slumber
He looked up & saw the< > Prince of Light with splendor faded
But saw not Los nor Enitharmon for Luvah hid them in shadow

PAGE 40
Of a soft cloud outstretch'd across, & Luvah dwelt in the cloud
Then Man ascended mourning into the splendors of his palace
Above him rose a shadow from his wearied intellect
Of living gold, pure, perfect, holy; in white linen pure he hover'd

A sweet entrancing self delusion, a watry vision of Man
Soft exulting in existence all the Man absorbing

Man fell upon his face prostrate before the watry shadow
Saying O Lord whence is this change thou knowest I am nothing
And Vala trembled & coverd her face, & her locks. were spread on the pavement
I heard astonishd at the Vision & my <          > trembled within me
I heard the voice of the Eternal Man & thus he spoke
O I am nothing when I enter into judgment with thee
If thou withdraw thy breath I die & vanish into Hades
If thou dost lay thine hand upon me behold I am silent
If thou withhold thine hand I perish like a fallen leaf
O I am nothing & to nothing must return again
If thou withdraw thy breath, behold I am oblivion

He ceasd: the shadowy voice was silent; but the cloud hoverd over their heads

PAGE 41
In golden wreathes, the sorrow of Man & the balmy drops fell down
And Lo that Son of Man, that shadowy Spirit of the Eternal One
Luvah, descended from the cloud; the Eternal Man arose

Indignant rose the Eternal Man & turnd his back on Vala
I heard the Voice of the Eternal starting from his sleep

Why roll thy clouds in sickning mists. I can no longer hide
The dismal vision of mine Eyes, O love & life & light!
Prophetic dreads urge me to speak. futurity is before me
Like a dark lamp. Eternal death haunts all my expectation

Whence is this voice crying Enion that soundeth in my ears
O cruel pity! O dark deceit! can Love seek for dominion

And Luvah strove to gain dominion over the Eternal Man
They strove together above the Body where Vala was inclos'd
And the dark Body of Man left prostrate upon the crystal pavement
Coverd with boils from head to foot. the terrible smitings of Luvah

Then frownd the Eternal Man & put forth Luvah from his presence

PAGE 42[41]

Saying, Go & die the Death of Man for Vala the sweet wanderer
I will turn the volutions of your Ears outward; & bend your
Nostrils Downward; & your fluxile Eyes englob'd, roll round in fear
Your withring Lips & Tongue shrink up into a narrow circle
Till into narrow forms you creep. Go take your fiery way
And learn what 'tis to absorb the Man you Spirits of Pity & Love

They heard the Voice & fled swift as the winters setting sun
And now the Human Blood foamd high the Spirits[42] Luvah & Vala
Went down the Human Heart where Paradise & its joys abounded
In jealous fears in fury & rage, & flames roll'd round their fervid feet
And the vast form of Nature like a Serpent play'd before them
And as they went in folding fires & thunders of the deep
Vala shrunk in like the dark sea that leaves its slimy banks
And from her bosom Luvah fell far as the east & west
And the vast form of Nature like a Serpent roll'd between.

She ended. for his wrathful throne burst forth the black hail storm[43]

[*Night Thoughts* proof pages follow.]

# Stages in the Development of Nights VII through IX of *Vala* or *The Four Zoas*

### PHASE 1

Phase 1, largely a conjectural reconstruction, consists of events and characters developed from Blake's Lambeth prophecies. This phase contains no mention of Christian imagery and characters, and the roles of Los and the Spectre of Urthona are fairly limited.

Night VII     The present transcription of Night VII[a] (pages 75–85:22)

?Night VIII     This may have been a rough draft, including a version of the present Night VII[b] (in order 91:1–98:31) plus some form of the present Night VIII 101:1–103:31 and 106:18–110:28.

?Night IX     Probably a rough draft similar to the present transcription, beginning at 117:14 and following through to the end of the Night.

### PHASE 2

Phase 2 is based more directly on existing text. It results in attempts to include Christian additions. Most of these additions are to Night VIII; the expansion causes it to grow beyond the size of any other Night, and so Blake recopies the ?Night VIII from phase 1 in the form of two Nights, Night VII[b] and the base text (the text before additions) of the present Night VIII.

Night VII[a]     The present transcription of Night VII[a] with the addition of 85:18–21, 23–31.

Night VII[b]   The present transcription of Night VII[b] (in order 91:1–98:31). Blake may consider changing the order of VII[b] at this point.

Night VIII   The present base-text transcription of Night VIII, including pages 99–110:28. Note that the text of 110:29–41, page III, and pages 113–14 and 115–16 are not part of this version.

Night IX   Probably the present transcription beginning at 117:14 and following through to the end of the Night.


PHASE 3


Phase 3 includes the present text and the addition of Los and Enitharmon's redemptive labours in Night VIII (99:20–100:26, 101:35–37, and 103:32–104:4). This overall stage may have included additions to the end of Night VII[a].


Night VII[a]   The present transcription of Night VII[a], with the addition of 85:32–47, all of 86 and 87, and 90:1–58.

Night VII[b]   Most certainly in its reversed order (95:15–98:31, 91:1–95:14), since it no longer fits new ending of VII[a].

Night VIII   The present "base text" transcription of Night VIII, including pages 99–110:28. Note that the text of 110:29–41, page III, and pages 113–14 and 115–16 are not part of this version.

Night IX   All of the present transcription, including the new opening lines on page 117.


SUBSEQUENT ADDITIONS


Night VII[a]   90:59–68
Night VIII   leaves 113–14, 115–16

# Notes



1 See *Blake: An Illustrated Quarterly* 12.2 (1978).

2 Kilgore, Lincoln, "Revision," and Lefebvre engage in a debate about the placement of Night VII[b], a debate that was instrumental in causing Erdman to integrate VII[b] into the end of VII[a].

3 Lincoln, "*The Four Zoas*," and Erdman, "*The Four Zoas*," discuss the potential reconstruction of the text on pages 5, 6, and 7.

4 The Santa Cruz Blake Study Group's review of Erdman's *Complete Poetry* offers a trenchant commentary on the critical influence of typographic editions on the understanding of Blake. See 13–16 for specific commentary on *Vala*.

5 The debate begins with Mann, "The Final State," and Essick, "*The Four Zoas*," continues with Otto, "Final States," and culminates in the exchange between Mann, "Finishing Blake," and Otto, "Is There a Poem in This Manuscript?"

6 Grant, "Visions in *Vala*," 143.

7 Even readings of the poem that place less emphasis on the manuscript's development relegate discussion of the designs to a rather subsidiary role. Both Lincoln, *Spiritual History*, 291–2, and Rosso, *Blake's Prophetic Work-shop*, 164–79, confine their examinations of the designs to appendices. Magno and Erdman's facimile (25–102) is still the most extensive commentary on the illuminations. The drawings also receive general treatment in Bentley's facsimile (180–3).

8 Kermode, "Introduction to the New Testament," *The Literary Guide to the Bible*, ed. Alter and Kermode, 377. For a brief treatment of synoptics in relation to Blake's *Jerusalem*, see Jeanne Moskal, *Blake, Ethics and Forgiveness*, 173–7.

9 *Fearful Symmetry*, 205.

10 Bloom, *Blake's Apocalypse*, argues, "Therefore it is more than accident that Winter's appearance should anticipate that of Urizen, the fearful limiter of desire and oppressive sky-god of Blake's pantheon" (17).

11 *William Blake Printmaker*, xix.

12 Viscomi, *Blake and the Idea of the Book*.

13 "Blake's Revisions of *The Tyger*," 669.

14 *Words of Eternity*, 115.

15 Santa Cruz Blake Study Group, "What Type of Blake?" 326.

16 Ault, *Narrative Unbound*, xii.

17 Rosso, *Blake's Prophetic Workshop*, 15.

18 Lincoln, "Revision," 115–33.

19 De Quincey, "Suspiria de Profundis," 144.

20 Ibid.

21 See Aristotle, *Poetics*, 8–9, for a discussion of the "qualitative" aspects of literature and the definition of plot as the "soul" of tragedy.

22 James, "The Art of Fiction," 39.

23 Rimmon-Kenan, *Narrative Fiction*, 34–6.

24 Paley, *The Continuing City*, 294–313.

25 For an excellent survey of narrative theory see Martin, *Recent Theories of Narrative*.

26 Smith, "Narrative Versions, Narrative Theories," 227–8.

27 Barthes, "Introduction to the Structural Analysis of Narratives," 87.

28 For a fuller discussion of the development of these oppositions within structuralism see "The Linguistic Foundation" in Culler, *Structuralist Poetics*, 3–31, and Terence Hawkes, *Structuralism and Semiotics*.

29 Derrida, *Positions* 12, 24.

30 Rimmon-Kenan, *Narrative Fiction*, offers a vigorous defence of the structural independence of character but allots only two chapters (3 and 5) to the poetics of character. Jonathan Culler, *Structuralist Poetics*, offers only a subsection on character in his "Poetics of the Novel" (see 230–8).

31 Barthes, *S/Z*, 190–1.

32 Magno and Erdman, *The Four Zoas*, 50.

33 Ibid., and John E. Grant, "Visions in *Vala*," 163. Rosso, *Blake's Prophetic Workshop*, 170, sees "Urizen on page 44 with his left arm, Lazarus on page 45 with his right."

34  Grant, "Visions in *Vala*," 164.

35  This line (line 689 [Blake's lineation] in Night iv of *Night Thoughts*) is marked as connecting with the illustration. See *William Blake's Designs for Edward Young's Night Thoughts*.

INTRODUCTION

1  Although Blake states in a letter dated 30 January 1803, "I now have it in my power to commence publication with many very formidable works, which I have finishd & ready" (E.726), and in another dated 25 April 1803,

none can know the Spiritual Acts of my three years Slumber on the banks of the Ocean ... unless he should read My long Poem descriptive of those Acts for I have in these three years composed an immense number of verses on One Grand Theme Similar to Homers Iliad or Miltons Paradise Lost ... an immense Poem Exists which seems to be the Labour of a long Life   (E.728–9)

it is not at all clear whether the "immense poem" refers to *Vala, Milton, Jerusalem,* or any combination of these works. Further, Blake's letters do not specify whether or not this "immense Poem" was in manuscript form or engraved at the time he wrote these letters.

2  Erdman, "The Binding (et cetera) of *Vala*," 112.

3  For the purposes of this discussion I am setting aside Bentley's fourth group, which consists of "three small scraps of paper which are now bound in at the end of the manuscript as pages 141–6" (B.196). These pages contain drafts, used and unused, for revisions to *Vala*. I will consider these later along with the relevant sections of the poem.

4  For Bentley's overall discussion of these groupings see his "A Description of the Manuscript" in the *Vala* facsimile, 193–6.

5  There is another style of handwriting on these pages Bentley calls the "modified copperplate hand," which "looks rather as if Blake had been writing the copperplate hand in something of a hurry" (B.196).

6  See Appendix A for a transcription of the extant copperplate text of *Vala*.

7  Erdman, "The Binding (et cetera) of *Vala*," 125.

8  Mann, "The Final State of *The Four Zoas*," 205.

9  Essick, "*The Four Zoas*: Intention and Production," 216, 218, 219.

10  See also Bentley's "The Date of Blake's *Vala* or *The Four Zoas*," 96–100.

11  See B.162–3 and Erdman, *Blake, Prophet against Empire*, 295–6, for a more extensive discussion of the dating of these pages.

12  In particular, the long list of the Sons and Daughters of Los and Enitharmon includes characters who do not appear elsewhere in *Vala*, and the

allusions to Rintrah, Palamabron, and the conflict with Satan are drawn from the Bard's Song in *Milton* although the events alluded to are not used anywhere in *Vala*.

13 Although leaf 111–12 does have stitch marks, several other factors suggest that its text, like that on 19–22, 86–90, and 113–16, is a later addition. It does not have line numbering; it contains more than 30 to 38 lines of text; and it has text that contains symbolism later than the base text of *Vala*.

14 Andrew Lincoln, "Revision," 121, points out:

> In IX* the Christian references have no ... controlling effect, but are subordinate in a narrative which is otherwise conceptually compatible with the basic text of pages 43–85. The limited importance of these references suggests that they were not introduced as part of a carefully planned revision; they seem to have been introduced as an immediate response to the major model for the Last Judgment, the Book of Revelation, and Blake may even have decided to introduce them while he was actually transcribing the Night.

15 Ibid., 119.

16 It should also be noted that, besides *Paradise Lost*, Blake's other immediate models, the Bible and Young's *Night Thoughts*, have a generally loose structure and would not tend to inspire Blake to construct a more rigorously controlled narrative. In addition, Beer, *Blake's Visionary Universe*, 4, points out that Blake's episodic method of composition was inherent in the nature of the work he was undertaking. Beer writes, "The problems of construction – greater than Milton's, since nothing was 'given' – led Blake to adopt the looser form of Young's *Night Thoughts* and to try to organize his poem around an idea – the idea (represented by his figure Vala) that 'nature,' seen by eighteenth-century man as the ultimate revelation of creative purpose in the universe, was no more than a partial source of truth." For the influence of Young on Blake, see Rosso, *Blake's Prophetic Workshop*, 48–50, 56–8; and Lincoln, *Spiritual History*, 34–5. Although these are contributing factors to Blake's piece-by-piece method of composition and revision, I suspect that this method may have been a common practice for Blake throughout his career.

17 De Luca, "The Changing Order of Plates in *Jerusalem*, Chapter II," 192.

18 De Luca, "The Changing Order of Plates in *Jerusalem*," 192.

19 Cf Blake's comments in the *Descriptive Catalogue* that "the antiquities of every Nation under Heaven, is no less sacred than that of the Jews. They are the same thing as Jacob Bryant, and all antiquaries have proved" (E.543).

20 Paley, *The Continuing City*, 303.

21 Benzel, "Vision and Revision in *The Four Zoas*: The Evidence of the Manuscript," 50.

22 Ault, *Narrative Unbound*, 115.

23 See "Introduction" to *Songs of Experience* (E.18).

24 Margoliouth, *William Blake's Vala*, xix.

25 In *Milton* Blake makes the identification of Urizen and Satan explicit in the line "Then Los & Enitharmon knew that Satan is Urizen" (10[11]:1; E.104).

26 See B.173 and E.839–40 for a discussion of Blake's use of this passage.

CHAPTER ONE

1 Bentley, *Blake Books*, 682–3.

2 Brisman, *Romantic Origins*, 228.

3 Frye, *Fearful Symmetry*, 108.

4 Anderson, *Creation versus Chaos*, 114, 136–7.

5 Frye, *Fearful Symmetry*, 386.

6 Gen. 1:1. All quotations will be taken from the King James Version unless noted otherwise.

7 In addition to the sources discussed here, see Eichrodt, "In the Beginning," 65–73, and Josipovici, *The Book of God*, 53–74.

8 This quotation and the alternative translation of Genesis is taken from Robinson, *Inspiration and Revelation in the Old Testament*, 18–19. See also the discussion of this passage in *The Interpreter's Bible*, 1:466–8.

9 Gilkey in *Maker of Heaven and Earth*, 43, defines *creatio ex nihilo* as God's bringing "the finite world into being out of nothing through a 'purposive' act of His free will."

10 Curry, *Milton's Ontology, Cosmogony and Physics*, 26.

11 Ibid.

12 Heninger, *The Cosmographical Glass*, 15, discusses the syncretic development of the Western creation myth from classical and Christian traditions.

13 Danielson, *Milton's Good God*, 26. See Schwartz, *Remembering and Repeating*, for an extended discussion of Milton's views of creation.

14 Danielson, *Milton's Good God*, 28.

15 In the opening invocation to *Paradise Lost* Milton addresses the Holy Spirit as

> Thou [who] from the first
> Wast present, and with mighty wings outspread
> Dove-like satst brooding on the vast Abyss
> And mad'st it pregnant   (1.19–22).

All citations of Milton's poetry from *Complete Poems and Major Prose*, ed. Hughes.

16 For a more detailed discussion of Blake and creation, see Esterhammer, *Creating States*, 145–73.

17 Stevenson, "Two Problems in *The Four Zoas*," 15–16.

18 Bentley, *William Blake's Writings*, 2:1088.

19 Margoliouth, *William Blake's Vala*, 99.

20 Brisman, *Romantic Origins*, 228–9.

21 Erdman contradicts this reading in his argument that "'Third' is written over one or two erasures, possibly in the sequence: [*Third*] <[*Fourth*]> <Third>" (E.830).

22 The phrase "succession of events" is offered as a basic definition of narrative by Rimmon-Kenan in *Narrative Fiction* , 2–3.

23 *The Return of Eden*, 17–21.

24 Said, *Beginnings*, 43.

CHAPTER TWO

1 Ault, *Narrative Unbound*, 327, 336.

2 For this section in the chapter all references to *Vala* or *The Four Zoas* will be from Erdman's edition.

3 Erdman, *Blake, Prophet Against Empire*, 377–8.

4 Ibid.

5 Ault, *Narrative Unbound*, 280.

6 Lincoln, "Revision," 120.

7 Editors and critics who argue that vii[a] was written first include Bentley, ed., *Vala or The Four Zoas*, 162–3; Margoliouth, ed., *William Blake's Vala*, xiii; Keynes, ed., *Blake: Complete Writings with Variant Readings*, 706; Paley, *Energy and the Imagination*, 263; Kilgore, "The Order of Nights vii a and vii b in Blake's *The Four Zoas*," 107–13; and Lincoln, "Revision," 115–33. Those who hold that vii[b] was written first include . Erdman, "The Binding (et cetera) of *Vala*," 112–29, and his *Blake, Prophet against Empire*, 295–6; Sloss and Wallis, eds., *The Prophetic Writings of William Blake*, 1:137–8; Stevenson, ed., *The Poems of William Blake*, 371; Wilkie and Johnson, *Blake's Four Zoas*, 140; and Bloom, *Blake's Apocalypse*, 244–6.

8 Keynes, Bentley, and Stevenson (in his first edition) all present Nights vii[a] and vii[b] consecutively in their editions. Erdman, in his edition of *The Poetry and Prose*, and Sloss and Wallis present Night vii[b] as appendix to the whole poem.

9 These three articles are all contained in *Blake: An Illustrated Quarterly* 12 (1978): Kilgore, "The Order of Nights VIIa and VIIb in Blake's *The Four Zoas*," 107–13; Lincoln, "The Revision of the Seventh and Eighth Night of *The Four Zoas*," 115–33; and Lefebvre, "A Note on the Structural Necessity of Night VIIb," 134.

10 Erdman, "Night the Seventh: The Editorial Problem," 136.

11 Ault, *Narrative Unbound*, 475.

12 *Fearful Symmetry*, 298.

13 It is possible that Blake's re-evaluation of Los was "suggested by the dramatic enlightenment that followed Blake's visit to the Truchsessian Gallery in the Autumn of 1804," as Lincoln argues, since Blake still writes disparagingly of Los at least as late as 1802 in a verse letter to Thomas Butts. In the letter a Thistle across Blake's path states:

> Los the terrible thus hath sworn
> Because thou backward dost return
> Poverty Envy old age & fear
> Shall bring thy Wife upon a bier
> And Butts shall give what Fuseli gave
> A dark black Rock & a gloomy Cave   (35–40: E.721).

Blake's confrontation with Los in this verse is much like Los's confrontation with his Spectre of Urthona in *Jerusalem*, with Blake in the role of Los and Los in the role of the Spectre. Yet it is not until October 1804, in the Truchsessian Gallery letter, that Blake writes of completely overcoming his spectrous side. His announcement that "I have entirely reduced that spectrous Fiend to his station, whose annoyance has been the ruin of my labours for the last passed twenty years of my life … he is become my servant who domineered over me, he is even as a brother who was my enemy" (E.7567) is couched in language reminiscent of his first added ending to VII[a] (85:23–31) and may have led to a radical recasting of Los's role in *Vala*.

Of course a specific date or cause for such a change is difficult to determine. In relative terms we can say that the new Los appears before Night VIII was transcribed but after Night VII[b] was composed, with its warlike version of Los. This relative date suggests that Blake's rethinking of Los's characterization came after the Christianization of the poem. Besides any personal reasons Blake may have had for changing Los's character, he may also have chosen Los as the most likely character within the narrative to undergo a conversion experience. To begin with, Los, as a prophetic figure, would ideally be expected to develop an insight into divine truth. But Los also appears in all stages of the manuscript's development, from the early copperplate text to the latest transcription of Night VIII. His struggles with Enitharmon, Orc, Tharmas, and Urizen at different bibliographical and narrative stages in the manuscript make him a figure with significant potential for psychological development.

14 Bentley argues for the lateness of these pages based on paper, handwriting, and stitch marks, and the absence of line numbers (B.195–6). Lincoln, "Revision," 126, elaborates on these bibliographical indicators about the lateness of these pages in arguing, "The fact that the leaves were made by destroying a large print [of *Edward and Eleanor*] would suggest that they were among the very last to be added to the poem, used when Blake was having difficulty finding paper of an appropriate size, and when the overall appearance of the manuscript was less important to him than the inclusion of all relevant material."

15 Ault, *Narrative Unbound*, 333, 475.

16 Blake extended Night VII[a] in at least three distinct phases. In his first revision he erased "End of the Seventh Night" after 85:22, added lines 23–31, and again wrote "The End of the Seventh Night." He then erased this finis and added lines 32–47 plus the text on pages 86, 87, and 90 (lines 1–58). Finally, he added the additional lines 59–68 to page 90.

17 Kilgore, Lincoln, Lefevbre, and Erdman have interpreted the absence of a finis line as evidence that Night VII[a] was to be inserted in Night VII[b], but the repeated expansion of VII[a], causing Blake to erase his finis line twice, may have left Blake hesitant about adding an "End of…" to something showing potential for repeated expansion and development.

18 McGann, "The Idea of an Indeterminate Text," 321, 323.

19 Presumably this only occurrence of the "Spectre" of Enitharmon is simply a variation on the "Shadow of Enitharmon" in the added ending to Night VII[a].

20 Lincoln, "Revision," 119.

21 Paley, *Energy and the Imagination*, 165.

22 This first reading supplied by Erdman (839).

23 Wilkie and Johnson, *Blake's Four Zoas*, 161.

24 Note that this confrontation is little more than a manifestation of the two opposing camps and does not contain the same degree of dramatic intensity as Blake developed in the reconciliation of Los, Enitharmon, and Spectre of Urthona.

25 Lincoln, "Revision," 119, 125.

26 Frye, *Fearful Symmetry*, 298.

27 Probably these lines were among the very last added to the manuscript, since they undermine to such a great extent the lines that follow. Indeed,

it is presumably the effect of these lines that causes Lincoln, "Revision," 126, to postulate that the added ending for vii[a] was composed "before but transcribed sometime after, viii* was transcribed." It seems more likely that Blake wrote out vii[a] up to line 58 around the same time he transcribed viii, since vii[a] prepares for the redemptive labours of Los and Enitharmon in viii; however, lines 59–68 on page 90, clearly a later addition to that page, were probably written later than viii.

28 The connections between Urizen and Satan and the Spectre as a central figure become more obvious in Blake's later writings. In *Milton*, for example, Blake explicitly identifies Urizen with Satan (10[11]:1; e.104), and the Spectral figure is generally identified as Satanic in both *Milton* (14[15]:30–2; e.108) and *Jerusalem* (29[33]:17–24; e.175). However, the equation of the Spectre of Urthona with Satan is more subtle in the earliest form of vii[a]. In his temptation of the Shadow of Enitharmon with the fruit of the Tree of Mystery, he recalls the Satan of Genesis or, more particularly, of *Paradise Lost*. The Spectre is not as obviously malevolent here as he is in Blake's later works, but his seduction of the shadow of Enitharmon creates "a wonder horrible" (85:7) who causes "the dead [to] burst forth from the bottoms of their tombs" (85:18) and begin the Satanic war of Nights vii[b] and viii. On the positive side, though, the Spectre in the additions to the end of vii[a] offers Los fairly reasonable advice on the Eternal rewards to arise from their reunion, and even his advice to Enitharmon that the tree of Mystery "Is given us for a Shelter from the Tempests of Void & Solid / Till once again the morn of ages shall renew upon us" (84:2–3) appears to have some merit.

CHAPTER THREE

1 "Beech" (8:14) and "Rock" as first reading for "cliff" (8:18) taken from e.824.

2 Cf *BU* 3:37–9; e.71.

3 Bentley, *William Blake's Writings*, 2:1085.

4 Ault, *Narrative Unbound*, 132–3, notes that the above three passages chronicle a change in Los and Enitharmon's role in Night ii. They begin "drawing in" delights from Urizen and Luvah, then "drink in" joy from sorrow, and finally lose control when they are "drawn down" to cause division between Urizen and Ahania.

5 Bloom, *Blake's Apocalypse*, 202.

6 See, for example, Meyers, "The Dialogue as Interpretive Focus in Blake's *The Four Zoas*," 230–1; Stevenson, *The Poems of William Blake*, 306 (first

ed.) or 307 (second ed.); Wilkie and Johnson, *Blake's Four Zoas*, 32–3; and Webster, *Blake's Prophetic Psychology*, 207.

7 I will return to this problem later in my discussion of Luvah and Vala.

8 Bentley, *William Blake's Writings*, 2:1093.

9 It is also possible that these lines make Los more sympathetic only in order to make Enitharmon appear more cold and tormenting.

10 See 60:6–63:16.

11 Despite the fact that the poem is named for her, Vala plays a limited role in determining the narrative direction of the poem. She virtually disappears after Night 11 and seems to be replaced by the Shadowy Female in Night vii[b] and Rahab in Night viii. Luvah fares no better. He drops out of the narrative after Night 11, being replaced by Orc in Night v. He returns in Night ix only to make a token appearance with Vala and the other central characters in the apocalyptic celebration. On Vala's limited role in the poem, see, for example, Frye, *Fearful Symmetry*, 269–70; Margoliouth, *William Blake's Vala*, xviii–xxi; Erdman, *Blake, Prophet against Empire*, 293; Fisher, *The Valley of Vision*, 225–6; Harper, "Apocalyptic Vision and Pastoral Dream in Blake's *Four Zoas*," 121; and Stevenson, *Divine Analogy*, 123.

12 DiSalvo, *War of Titans*, 195. DiSalvo also notes that Blake used the war in heaven "as a reflection of power struggles on earth" (191), and the metaphor itself "provided a more explicitly political analysis of the human condition than the story of Adam's sin" (186).

13 It appears that Blake may have viewed the Phaeton myth as an archetypal example of the conflict of desire and reason in which reason wins and suppresses energy. Plate 5 of *The Marriage of Heaven and Hell* describes the suppression of desire, and the illustration, according to Erdman in *The Illuminated Blake*, 102, depicts a "Phaeton-like" figure "and a horse with saddle cloth and broken chariot wheel … [falling] into flames."

14 Ahania's account mentions a struggle between Luvah and the Man "above the Body where Vala was inclos'd" (41:14), but there is no mention of a knife, and the Man is clearly the victor in this encounter. Luvah does not wound the Man, although he does seem responsible for smiting the Man with boils.

15 As we shall see in the next section, the modifications to Urizen's narrative emphasize the negative connotations of his actions.

16 Dawson, "Blake and Providence," 140.

17 Paley, *Energy and the Imagination*, 155.

18 Guthrie, *Orpheus and Greek Religion*, 100, describes syncretism as "the religious phenomenon whereby the personalities of divinities once held to be distinct become blended and indistinguishable from each other." The character of Blake's Luvah develops by accretion just as the figures in Greek mythology do. He is both rebel and victim, a god of love and hate, and a figure whose past consists of a number of apparently contradictory myths about the same figure.

19 Ault, *Narrative Unbound*, 121.

20 In *Milton* Blake makes the identification of Urizen and Satan explicit in the line "Then Los & Enitharmon knew that Satan is Urizen" (10[11]:1).

21 Note that when Blake writes of Urizen's repentance in Night IX, he changes his mind about locating the causes of Urizen's error in the past or future. On page 121 he changes each reference to the "past" or "remembrance" to "futurity." Initially, he seems to have intended that Urizen repent of his creation of the physical world, the imprisonment of Luvah, his tormenting of Orc, and the war he initiates against Los and Tharmas as past acts. Repentance for acts in the past, however, is not necessarily productive and is certainly not preventative. Perhaps for this reason Blake redirects Urizen's repentance to his concern for futurity. After all, fear of the future is one of the emotions that initiates Urizen's creative action in Night II (23:15). Blake strengthened the idea of futurity as the source of Urizen's error by adding such warnings as "Why wilt thou look upon futurity darkning present joy" (37:11) and "Leave all futurity to him [the Eternal Man] resume thy fields of Light" (39:3) to Ahania's speech to Urizen at the beginning of Night II. For more on the role of past and future in *Vala* see Glausser, "The Gates of Memory in Night VIIa of *The Four Zoas*," 196–203.

22 Michael Benzel, "Vision and Revision in *The Four Zoas*," 50.

23 Note that Los is involved with another type of Vala but Urizen is not.

24 At 16:17–18 the manuscript states that Urizen sits at the feast of Los and Enitharmon, "forgetful of the flowing wine / And of Ahania his pure Bride but She was distant far"; however, I am assuming that this leaf was not added until after the love and jealousy theme was fully developed.

25 Paley, "Blake's *Night Thoughts*: An Exploration of the Fallen World," 152.

26 Heninger, *The Cosmographical Glass*, 34.

27 Quoted from Harper, *The Neoplatonism of William Blake*, 124.

28 Ibid.

29 Bidney, "Urizen and the Comedy of Automatism in Blake's *The Four Zoas*," 207–11, discusses the comedic nature of "Urizen's project of

constructing an artificial universe, complete with simulated sky, shutting out the real heavens."

30 The use of pyramids and cubes with negative associations appears liberally in Blake's pictorial art preceding the composition of *Vala*. One illustration for *Tiriel* uses pyramids in the background to connect Tiriel's despotic rule with the kind of rule imposed on the Israelites in Egypt. (See drawing 1, plate i, in Bentley's edition of *Tiriel*). Plate 21 of some copies of *The Marriage of Heaven and Hell* contains background images of pyramids (Erdman, *The Illuminated Blake*, 118), and, of course, the colour print of Newton is centred around the triangular shape of his compasses. Also, paintings such as *A Breach in a City, the Morning after the Battle*, from a drawing later adapted for the frontispiece to *America*, uses heavy block bricks in the construction of a wall breached by war and filled in with the bodies of those slain in the war. Moreover, Blake's depiction of *Pestilence* contains the conspicuous presence of massy forms as a background for the great plague.

 David Bindman, *Blake as an Artist*, 32, commenting on *A Breach in a City, Pestilence*, and a sketch for *War Unchain'd*, writes, "In all three designs Divine wrath is visited upon an apparently prosperous city, and the classical buildings in *Pestilence* and the probable study for 'War Unchained' carry implications of material pride, idol-worship and abstract reason." I would add that Blake took this association of divine wrath, judgement, and war against a backdrop of massy forms composed of cubes and angles used in his pictorial art before and during the composition of *Vala* and adapted it to his poetic revision of Urizen's character. As we have already seen, Blake's description of Urizen's descent in Night 1 already contained latent elements of a god of judgement and war, which were later made more explicit. Blake's revision of circular symbolism to angular in the descriptions of Urizen's created world are probably also a part of this general trend in revising Urizen's character.

31 Bidney, "Urizen and the Comedy of Automatism in Blake's *The Four Zoas*," 208.

32 Quoted from Harper, *The Neoplatonism of William Blake*, 124.

33 Cf Plato's description of the angular construction in the *Timaeus*, 53c–55c. All citations from Plato taken from *The Collected Dialogues of Plato including the Letters*, ed. Edith Hamilton and Cairns.

34 As well as in a pictorial presentation on 33[36]. See E.133.

35 Paley, "Blake's *Night Thoughts*," 133, comments on the image of humanity breaking from a shell as it appears in Young's *Night Thoughts* and as adapted by Blake in *The Gates of Paradise*. Frye, *Fearful Symmetry*, 168,

quoting the same passage in Young, suggests this "may have been the source of the 'Mundane Shell.'" The passage from Young, *William Blake's Designs for Edward Young's Night Thoughts*, reads,

> Embryos we must be, till we burst the Shell,
>
> Yon ambient, azure shell, and spring to Life,
>
> The life of Gods: O Transport! and of Man.   (I. 131–3)

Curry, *Milton's Ontology, Cosmogony and Physics*, 100–2, offers a survey of authors from Democritus and Lucretius to Milton who use the idea of a protective shell surrounding the World and protecting it from Chaos. It is possible that Blake may also have used Milton as a source for this image.

36 Percival, *William Blake's Circle of Destiny*, 62.

37 Interestingly, Blake does not use Tharmas and Enion later in his writings. The *Concordance to the Writings of William Blake* reveals that Tharmas's and Enion's names do not appear in Blake's work before *Vala*, and they appear only infrequently in *Milton* and *Jerusalem*. Tharmas's name appears 6 times in *Milton* and 11 in *Jerusalem*; Enion's, once in *Milton* and 6 times in *Jerusalem*. This absence may reflect Blake's later change of focus to the struggle of specific universal characters such as Milton and Albion.

38 Margoliouth, *William Blake's* VALA, xx.

39 This opposition is played out more fully in Night IV, where Tharmas enlists the help of Los to rebuild his watery world after the collapse of Urizen's golden one. It should be remembered that Tharmas first appears in Night III as a product of the confusion and chaos created by the separation of Urizen and Ahania, and therefore he appears as a figure in symbolic opposition to them. Although the lines in Night IV are physically later in the narrative of the manuscript, it seems likely that they were transcribed before the revisions to the early part of Night I describing Tharmas, since Night IV presents a more simplified picture of him and does not define him as a "Spectre."

40 Lincoln, "*The Four Zoas*," 91.

41 Raine, *Blake and Tradition*, 1:279–82, discusses the two-sided nature of Tharmas in terms of possible alchemical sources.

42 I hold some reservations about 6:5–8 in this grouping. They appear to be written higher on the page than the erased portion of text on page 6 and may have been added slightly later than the other lines I have included here. This idea is supported by the narrative connection between 5:57 – "But standing on the Rocks her woven shadow glowing bright" – and 6:9 – "Searching for glory wishing that the heavens had eyes to See." Perhaps,

then, the text on page 6 during this phase of rewriting began at line 6:9; however, lines 6:5–8 have little that would characterize them as distinctly later than the rest of this phase of rewriting. Presumably, they were added much earlier than the other obvious additions to pages 3–6.

43 Paley, "The Figure of the Garment in *The Four Zoas, Milton,* and *Jerusalem,*" 119–39, discusses the late occurrence of weaving imagery in Blake's poetry.

44 *Milton* 18[20]:30; E.111, and 22[24]:38; E.117. *Jerusalem* 21:11–12; E.166. 64:1–5; E.215. 80:62–5; E.237. 87:18–19; E.246. 88:19–20, 27–8; E.247.

45 Note that Enion's lines at 7:3–8 appear to be part of this revision.

46 Bentley, *Blake Books,* 342, notes that the earliest this poem could have been written in its present form is 1802 since it is written on blank leaves from Hayley's *Ballads* of that year. However, Bentley qualifies this late date by noting that "the dates of original composition may well be 1800–4 for the Ballads Manuscript poems." A date of soon after 1800 would correspond roughly with the time Blake was working on the Tharmas-Enion material.

47 If the addition of Enitharmon to the Tharmas-Enion conflict is concurrent with the addition of pages 20–2 to the manuscript, as I suggested earlier, then the addition of Jerusalem to the conflict (and also the language of Sin and Repentance) would be very late indeed, perhaps the latest addition to the entire poem.

48 Hilton, *Literal Imagination,* 151.

49 This factor suggests that Blake did not develop the story of the Spectre of Tharmas until after much of *Vala* was transcribed and he was well into work on *Jerusalem.*

50 Lincoln, "*The Four Zoas,*" 94. The passages discussed here are as follows (the undeleted form of these lines is based on Lincoln's arguments):

| *Stage 1: Passages marked for deletion* | | *Stage 2: Passages circled for return to final draft* | |
| --- | --- | --- | --- |
| Tharmas | Enion | Tharmas | Enion |
| 6:9–15 | 5:46–57 | 6:26–7, 29–35 | 5:46–55 |
| 6: 26–35 | 6:16–25 | | 6:36, 38–7:3–8, 11 |
| 7:12–17 | 6:36–7:11 | | |

51 Lincoln, "*The Four Zoas,*" 94–5, notes that in Blake's revision, "The end of the first line [6:26] and all of the second line ('Art thou not my slave & shall thou dare / To smite me with thy tongue beware lest I sting thee

also') were deleted and replaced by an addition of one-and-a-half lines
(the full line subsequently deleted):

    Who art thou Diminutive husk & shell

  [*Broke from my bonds I scorn my prison I scorn & yet I love*]."

Erdman, following Lincoln's reconstruction, prints this modified version
at 6:8–16 in his new edition.

52  Wilkie and Johnson, *Blake's Four Zoas*, 74, point out that in Night III,
"Urizen's insistence that Ahania is 'diminutive' repeats the pattern of
Tharmas's rejection of Enion in Night I; in both instances a domineering
character projects his own smallness or sense of it onto his more passive
partner." In a note to this discussion, Wilkie and Johnson (268) suggest
that 6:27 (and the remaining portion of this deleted passage) in particular
may have been reinstated to strengthen the parallels between the Thar-
mas-Enion and Urizen-Ahania stories.

53  Lincoln, "*The Four Zoas*," 95.

54  Frye, *Fearful Symmetry*, 279, notes this correspondence between Demeter
and Enion. See also Lee, "Ways of Their Own: The Emanations of
Blake's *Vala*, or *The Four Zoas*," 134, for a more detailed discussion of this
correspondence. Note that Blake strengthened these associations in addi-
tions to the poem that show that Enion's lament, at least in part, may be
traced to her children, Los and Enitharmon, who draw life and vitality
from their parent: "And then they wanderd far away she sought for them
in vain / In weeping blindness stumbling she followd them oer rocks &
mountains" (9:1–2).

55  In a unique version of the frontispiece to *Jerusalem* (see Keynes, "New
Lines from *Jerusalem*," 115–17) Blake wrote of the sublime and the pathos
at the fall:

    His [Albion's] Sublime & Pathos become Two Rocks fixd in the Earth

    His Reason his Spectrous Power, covers them above

    Jerusalem his Emanation is a Stone laying beneath

    O [*Albion behold Pitying*] behold the Vision of Albion.   (*J* 1:4–7; E.144)

Possibly, Blake began to see Tharmas and Enion's relationship as an icon
of the situation represented by these lines and continued to revise it
accordingly in late stages of revising pages 4–7. Tharmas and Enion, as
the Sublime and the Pathos, are fixed and separated by virtue of the
Spectrous power emerging from mutual distrust and jealousy over Thar-
mas's relationship with Jerusalem.

56  Paley, *The Continuing City*, 79–80, compares the use of these lines in *Vala*
and *Jerusalem*. See also 35–6.

57 Paley, *The Continuing City*, 80.

58 Ault, "Revisioning *The Four Zoas*," 105–9.

59 Ault, ibid., 108, sees a "narrative field in which the past is not closed and complete but open – unfinished and revisable" as one of the prime elements of the anti-Newtonian narrative.

CHAPTER FOUR

1 The essential narrative of Nights IV through VI is that of *The Book of Urizen*. Los's rebuilding of Urizen, taken directly from *Urizen*, the embrace of Los and Enitharmon, the birth and binding of Orc, and Urizen's exploration of his dens are common elements in *The Book of Urizen* and *Vala*, although all are more substantially developed in *Vala*. It seems likely that Blake developed Tharmas and the Spectre while expanding the earlier material for *Vala*, since these characters do not appear any earlier in his writings. By the time he transcribed all this material into its present form Blake seems to have brought old and new material together in this section with a stability that remained largely unshaken while he continued to revise *Vala*. Repeated revisions in the opening Night and the end of Night VIIa, however, indicate that he was less certain about the impact of Tharmas and the Spectre respectively on the rest of the narrative.

2 Wilkie and Johnson, *Blake's Four Zoas*, 81.

3 Ault, *Narrative Unbound*, 140.

4 The name "Tharmas" appears in the copperplate text at 11:27 and 33:6, where he is little more than a name. At 11:27 Los tells Enitharmon that she "<neer shalt leave this> cold expanse where watry Tharmas mourns," and at 33:6 Urizen and his sons "Lookd out into the world of Tharmas, where in ceaseless torrents / His billows roll where monsters wander in the foamy paths." In both cases Tharmas is associated with water and chaos, but his character and situation are developed no further. The lengthy dialogue between Tharmas and Enion on pages 4–7 is all added over several layers of erased text and shows signs of being a relatively late addition to the entire poem.

5 Blake attempted to make the tone of Nights IV-VI consistent by giving even Urizen a speech in Night V, in which he regrets the loss of eternity (63:24–65:12).

6 For a discussion of possible reasons for the change see Mann, "The Final State of *The Four Zoas*," 204–9, and Essick, "*The Four Zoas*," 216–20.

7 The extensive revisions to the text containing the violent interchange of Tharmas and Enion on pages 3–7 demonstrate that Blake's conception of

these characters was still undergoing development long after the manuscript was transcribed. Many of the revisions to these pages appear related to ideas that emerged during his work on *Jerusalem*. The repeated revisions to the first and most extensive appearance of Tharmas and Enion may have caused Blake uncertainty about the relative state of completion of what appears to be a fair copy of the manuscript.

8 Of the dialogue between Tharmas and Enion, lines 18–21, 27–8, and 30–4 on page 4 also appear in *Jerusalem* at lines 1, 10–12, 14–15, and 20–4 of plate 22. In *Jerusalem* these lines become part of a dialogue between Albion and Vala, reflecting the emergence of sin and jealousy in male-female relationships. Paley, *The Continuing City*, 79–80, discusses the use of these lines in the two poems.

9 Andrew Lincoln, "*The Four Zoas*," 91.

10 Although the sketch on page 44 is incomplete, it appears that the lower half of Tharmas's body may have been left indistinctly drawn on purpose. The sketch seems to illustrate Tharmas's emergence after the fall of Ahania, "struggling / To take the limbs of Man struggling to take the features of Man" (44:17–18) and thus may have been intended to show Tharmas's difficulty in emerging from the indistinct form of water to a more distinct, human form. The context of this picture is differently construed by John E. Grant, "Visions in *Vala*," 162–3.

11 Ault, *Narrative Unbound*, 158.

12 Ibid., 214.

13 Many of the later additions to *Vala* or *The Four Zoas* reflect a symbolic elaboration of the poem's narrative structure. Doctrinally shaped passages on the nature of Eternity and Beulah (5:31–9), passages on the significance of the Spectre (5:40–5; 84:36–42), the creation of time and space (9:9–19), and the Council of God (55:26–31; 99:1–15) show evidence of being late additions. While these passages do not add to the narrative progression of the poem, they are an essential part of Blake's elaboration of the symbolic universe within which characters act and plot develops.

14 Frye, "The Road of Excess," 162–3.

15 Stevenson, *Poems* (1989), 342–3.

16 The first datable use of the term "Spectre" occurs in a letter of 11 September 1801 to Thomas Butts: "my Abstract folly hurries me … over Mountains & Valleys which are not Real in a Land of Abstraction where Spectres of the Dead wander" (E.716).

17 See especially the text on plates 6–7 and the accompanying design on plate 6 of *Jerusalem*. The Spectre is described as "panting like a frighted wolf, and howling / He stood over the Immortal [Los], in the solitude

and darkness" (*J.* 7:1–2; E.149), while the design on plate 6 depicts the Spectre as a bat-winged creature hovering above Los's head. The devouring vampire-like aspect of the Spectre is also used by Blake in *Jerusalem* 11:6–7; E.154 and *Milton* 39[44]:16–21; E.140. See Stevenson, *Poems* (1989), 639–40, and Hilton, *Literal Imagination*, 147–72, for a fuller account of the different aspects of the Spectre.

18 Lincoln, "Revision," 125.

19 Ault, "Re-Visioning *The Four Zoas*," 117. In *Narrative Unbound*, 172–5, Ault offers a fuller discussion of the thematic significance of the discrepancies between Urthona's and the Spectre's versions of their division from that depicted in the narrative.

20 Ault, *Narrative Unbound*, 197.

21 This idea is borne out at the end of the poem, where the "Spectre Los" (139:5) disappears as "Urthona rises from the ruinous walls / In all his ancient strength to form the golden armour of science / For intellectual War" (139:7–9).

22 Stevenson, *Poems* (1989), 342–3.

23 Blake's first datable use of "fourfold" appears in a famous letter to Butts dated 22 November 1802, where he includes a poem "Composed <above> a twelvemonth ago" (E.720):

> Now I fourfold vision see
> And a fourfold vision is given to me
> Tis fourfold in my supreme delight
> And three fold in soft Beulahs night
> And twofold Always. May God us keep
> From Single vision & Newtons sleep   (83–8; E.722)

24 That Blake continued to write the title "Vala" at the top of the beginning page of each Night (even Night VIII, probably the last to be transcribed) suggests that he did not seriously consider using the title "The Four Zoas" until sometime after he had finished transcribing the whole poem.

25 For an excellent discussion of Blake's models and his use of them in creating the Golgonooza of *Jerusalem* see Paley, *The Continuing City*, 136–66.

26 von Franz, *Patterns of Creativity Mirrored in Creation Myths*, 169.

27 Bloom, *Blake's Apocalypse*, 195.

28 Paley, *The Continuing City*, 79–80, compares the use of these lines in *Vala* and *Jerusalem*. See also 35–6.


CHAPTER FIVE

1 See the *Interpreter's Dictionary of the Bible*.

2 Some central discussions of Rahab's biblical associations include Frye, *Fearful Symmetry*, 139–40, and Lincoln, *Spiritual History*, 268–9.

3 See Erdman's text, 962.

4 Ibid.

5 Ault, *Narrative Unbound*, 241, 320.

6 It should be remembered at this point that Night VIII originally ended on page 110.

7 The appropriateness of placing Rahab's epiphany at the end of Night VIII may have caused Blake to return to this point in his final addition to her narrative when he added page 111.

8 A sexual liaison between Sheba and Solomon is only implied in the biblical text: however, later Judaic traditions supply a range of intriguing details about Sheba and her relation to Solomon. Among these are stories implying Solomon and Sheba produced Nebuchadnezzar and that Sheba herself was associated with the demon Lilith. See Pritchard, *Solomon and Sheba*, 65–84.

9 In a confrontation with Los she is described as "Dividing & uniting in Delusive feminine pomp" (113:45).

10 See Wilkie and Johnson, *Blake's Four Zoas*, 205.

11 For more on the association of Rahab with the Whore of Babylon see Frye, *Fearful Symmetry*, 139–40.

CHAPTER SIX

1 Frye, *Fearful Symmetry*, 269.

2 Viscomi makes this argument most fully in chapter 2 of *Blake and the Idea of the Book*, 16–25.

3 Ibid., 175.

4 Mann, "Apocalypse and Recuperation," 3–6, has also observed the tension between "text" and "work" in Blake's method of production.

5 Barthes, "From Work to Text," 158–9.

6 Frye, *Fearful Symmetry*, 305.

7 Aers, "Representations of Revolution," 264–5, 269–70.

8 Barthes, "From Work to Text," 158.

9 Ibid., 159.

10 Derrida, *Of Grammatology*, 166.

11 See Erdman's reconstruction of these lines on pages 839–40 of his *Complete Poems*.

12 Barthes, *S/Z*, 173, 174; "The Death of the Author," 148.

13 Essick, *William Blake and the Language of Adam*, 190.

14 Barthes, "From Work to Text," 159.

15 Otto, "The Multiple Births of Los in *The Four Zoas*," 633, 641.

16 Phillips, "Blake's Corrections in *Poetical Sketches*," 44.

17 For an interesting outline of the choices editors and critics have made between "beds" and "birds," see Lowery, *Windows of the Morning*, 35–7.

18 See *Blake Books*, 99.

19 Erdman, *Illuminated Blake*, 394, argues that plate c "may have followed Plate b, some of its motifs being absorbed into the illuminations of Plate 5, some logically possible after plate 8."

20 Erdman, *The Illuminated Blake*, 393.

21 Mee, *Dangerous Enthusiasm*, 26, comments on the significance of this change in relation to *America*'s integration with *Europe*.

22 Paley, ed., *Jerusalem: The Emanation of the Giant Albion*, 253.

23 See Bentley, *Blake Books*, 87, for a description of these variations, and also his article, "The Printing of Blake's *America*," 46–57.

24 See Frye, *Fearful Symmetry*, 277–8.

APPENDIX A

1 B. reads "Beulah" as the original reading deleted when "Nature" was later added. E.822, however, reads "Nature" under "Beulah." Both agree that "Beulah" was later changed to "Nature."

2 B. reads "Spectre."

3 B. reads "Spectre."

4 The following stanza, written over five erased copperplate lines, appears to be an early addition to this Night. Although not part of the original transcription, these lines do help us to understand the narrative continuity of the Night.

> The first state weeping they began & helpless as a wave
> Beaten along its sightless way growing enormous in its motion to
> Its utmost goal, till strength from Enion like summer shining
> Raised the bright boy & girl with glories from their heads out beaming
> Drawing forth drooping mothers pity drooping mothers sorrow.

5 B. reads "Beach."

6 E.'s reading of erasure under "cliff."

7 E.824 notes "The first of three erased copperplate lines ... may read, at the end, '... embracd for' (compare line [9:]25); the second ends '... love.'" While these words may be detected on the manuscript, I am not entirely certain that they are necessarily part of the copperplate substrata.

8 Bentley marks the following lines as part of the copperplate text:

Ingrate they wanderd scorning her <drawing> her life; ingrate
Repelling her away [from them] by a dread repulsive power
Into Non Entity revolving round in dark despair.

While these lines at first appear to be part of the copperplate text, they are surrounded by a series of erased lines and additions and may be part of an early addition to the copperplate text. In particular the line "Into Non Entity revolving round in dark despair" does not appear to be spaced as evenly as other examples of the copperplate text and in fact appears to curve upwards slightly at the end of the line. Moreover, the malevolent tone indicated by these lines seems out of keeping with the tone of the rest of the base text of Night i and seems more characteristic of the later additions to the copperplate.

9  B.10 notes that in this erased line, "'Till they,' 'quite,' and the final 'Enion' are legible." E.824 reads this "erased ink line [as] 'Till they had?drawn the Spectre quite away from Enion' – which reappears slightly varied in 109:25–26 in Night viii, suggesting that the 'Spectrous Life' revisions of p 7 were made during the writing of viii."

10  While these lines appear to be a part of the copperplate text, they seem inconsistent with the overall tone of the base transcription. Could they have been added in the stanza break?

11  Several different readings have been offered for the words under the two "Song"s in this line. M.165 notes that a "D" is visible under each "Song" and conjectures that the word "Dream" is written under "Song." B.12 states, "The word under the second added 'Song' could be 'Dirge.'" E.825 concurs with B. but reads "Dirge" under the first "Song" as well.

12  B. reads "Pillow."

13  These four lines follow E.'s reading under the erasures (825). In the first line Blake changed "Vala" to "Enitharmon" and scratched out "her." In the second he changed "Vala lightning" to "Enitharmon a Cloud" and then changed "Cloud" to "terror." In the fourth line he changed "O Vala" to "as Vala."

14  The later version reads, "I die not Enitharmon tho thou singst thy Song of Death / Nor shalt thou me torment For I behold the Eternal Man." The last half of the second line, with its use of "Eternal Man," is probably close to the original transcription.

15  Conjectured by E.825.

16  De Luca suggests "Eternal" as the first reading here.

17  E.'s reading under "descending" (826).

18  E.826 tentatively suggests "Thro" was originally "While" but cautions that it also may have been "Where."

19 B. reads "and."

20 B.16 notes that the chronologically later text at the bottom of 14 is "written over an erasure of two stanzas of about nine lines." Blake included the continuation of this later version of the Marriage Song on the added sheet 15–16.

21 B.18 and E.827 agree that this line is written over an erased line that probably began with "Why." E. also determines that there was an "&" underneath this line.

22 E. reads "Take."

23 Both B.24 and E.828 agree that two erased "First"s can be seen. E. adds that an erased "Third" underlies one of the "First"s; however, I could not see a "Third" in the heading.

24 M. suggests "Then" as a possible first reading.

25 E.'s reading under "great Workmaster" (828). Cf. Urizen's identification of the Eternal Man as "Lord of day" at 64:14.

26 E.'s reading under "Urizen" (828).

27 Later replaced by "Valas King."

28 The "de" is apparently a slip for the word "Dragon" added to this line.

29 E.828 sees "I?die" under the first line. He also suggests that the next line perhaps began "Albion." The line that E. sees is probably an addition later than the original copperplate transcription.

30 It is difficult to say whether the "w" is upper or lower case. B. has lower case, while E. shows it as upper case.

31 Emended to "Globe."

32 B. reads "caverns."

33 "Condensing" added over "together" at some stage.

34 B.32 and E.829 agree that the erased line may end "within."

35 E.829 suggests the first reading may have been, like the draft above this line, "in comfort saw."

36 B.33 notes that the present lines about the Lamb of God are "written over an erasure of five lines, the third of which ends 'ing in triumph,' and the last 'Mundane Egg.'" E.829 argues that there are only "four revised and erased lines, traces of which are: 'And ?Luvah      lding fly / R      rejoicing & triumph / S      falling / A      walkd      of the Mundane Egg.'"

37 Emended to "Body."

38 Emended to "Abyss."

39 E.'s question mark seems more logical than B.'s double commas, but either reading is difficult to confirm from the manuscript. I would suggest an exclamation mark at this point.

40  B. reports originally written "Fourth"(?) and then deleted. E. argues "'Third' is written over one or two erasures, possibly in the sequence: [*Third*] <[*Fourth*]> <Third>." Although Erdman's argument that "Perhaps at one time Night 11 began on p 7, 11 was Third, 111 was Fourth" is ingenious, in my own examination of the manuscript I have been unable to confirm his readings.

41  E.831 claims that the first ten lines on this page are "over original copperplate erased."

42  E.831, so reads under "I saw that."

43  The status of this line as part of the original copperplate may be questioned because of the irregular spacing between it and the line above. Moreover, lines 21–3 were clearly added later in the copperplate hand, and it is possible that line 20 was added later, around the same time as 21–3, to create a sense of narrative continuity with pages 43 ff.

Barthes, Roland. *S/Z: An Essay.* Trans. Richard Miller. New York: Hill and Wang 1974.

– *Image–Music–Text.* Trans. Stephen Heath. New York: Noonday 1977. "Introduction to the Structural Analysis of Narratives," 79–124. "From Work to Text," 155–64.

Beer, John. *Blake's Humanism.* Manchester: Manchester University Press 1968.

– *Blake's Visionary Universe.* Manchester: Manchester University Press 1969.

Bentley, G.E., Jr. "The Date of Blake's *Vala* or *The Four Zoas.*" In *A Mirror for Modern Scholars: Essays in Methods of Research in Literature*, ed. Lester A. Beaurline. New York: Odyssey 1966. 96–100.

– "The Printing of Blake's *America.*" *Studies in Romanticism* 6 (1966): 46–57.

– "William Blake's Protean Text." In *Editing Eighteenth-Century Texts: Papers Given at the Editorial Conference, University of Toronto, October 1967*, ed. D.I.B. Smith. Toronto: University of Toronto Press 1968. 44–58.

– *Blake Records.* Oxford: Clarendon 1969.

– *Blake Books: Annotated Catalogues of William Blake's Writings in Illuminated Printing, in Conventional Typography, and in Manuscript and Reprints thereof, Reproductions of His Designs, Books with His Engravings, Catalogues, Books He Owned, and Scholarly and Critical Works about Him.* Oxford: Clarendon 1977.

Benzel, Michael Arnold. "Vision and Revision in *The Four Zoas*: The Evidence of the Manuscript." PhD, University of Toledo 1976.

Bidney, Martin. "Urizen and the Comedy of Automatism in Blake's *The Four Zoas.*" *Philological Quarterly* 56 (1977): 204–20.

Bindman, David. *Blake as an Artist.* Oxford: Phaidon 1977.

Bloom, Harold. *Blake's Apocalypse: A Study in Poetic Argument.* Ithaca: Cornell University Press 1963.

Bracher, Mark. *Being Form'd: Thinking through Blake's Milton.* Barrytown: Station Hill 1985.

Brisman, Leslie. *Romantic Origins.* Ithaca: Cornell University Press 1978.

Bronowski, Jacob. *William Blake and the Age of Revolution.* London: Routledge and Kegan Paul 1972.

Butlin, Martin. *The Paintings and Drawings of William Blake.* 2 vols. New Haven: Yale University Press 1981.

Cantor, Paul A. *Creature and Creator: Myth-Making and English Romanticism.* Cambridge: Cambridge University Press 1984.

Culler, Jonathan. *Structuralist Poetics: Structuralism, Linguistics and the Study of Literature.* London: Routledge & Kegan Paul 1975.

Curran, Stuart, and Joseph Anthony Wittreich, Jr, eds. *Blake's Sublime Allegory: Essays on The Four Zoas, Milton, Jerusalem.* Madison: University of Wisconsin Press 1973.

Curry, Walter Clyde. *Milton's Ontology, Cosmogony and Physics*. Lexington: University of Kentucky Press 1957.

Danielson, Dennis Richard. *Milton's Good God: A Study in Literary Theodicy*. Cambridge: Cambridge University Press 1982.

Damon, S. Foster. *William Blake: His Philosophy and Symbols*. Gloucester: Peter Smith 1958.

– *A Blake Dictionary: The Ideas and Symbols of William Blake*. Boulder: Shambala 1979.

Dawson, P.M.S. "Blake and Providence: The Theodicy of *The Four Zoas*." *Blake: An Illustrated Quarterly* 20 (1987): 134–43.

Deen, Leonard B. *Conversing in Paradise: Poetic Genius and Identity-as-Community in Blake's Los*. Columbia: University of Missouri Press 1983.

De Luca, V.A. "Ariston's Immortal Palace: Icon and Allegory in Blake's Prophecies." *Criticism* 12 (1970): 1–19.

– "The Changing Order of Plates in *Jerusalem*, Chapter 11." *Blake: An Illustrated Quarterly* 16 (1983): 192–205.

– "A Wall of Words: The Sublime as Text." In Hilton and Vogler, *Unnam'd Forms*, 218–41.

– *Words of Eternity: Blake and the Poetics of the Sublime*. Princeton: Princeton University Press 1991.

De Quincey, Thomas. "Suspiria de Profundis." *Confessions of an English Opium-Eater and Other Writings*. Ed. Grevel Lindop. New York: Oxford University Press 1985. 87–181.

Derrida, Jacques. *Of Grammatology*. Trans. Gayatri Chakravorty Spivak. Baltimore: Johns Hopkins University Press 1974.

– *Positions*. Trans. Alan Bass. Chicago: University of Chicago Press 1981.

DiSalvo, Jackie. *War of Titans: Blake's Critique of Milton and the Politics of Religion*. Pittsburgh: University of Pittsburgh Press 1983.

Eichrodt, Walther. "In the Beginning: A Contribution to the Interpretation of the First Word of the Bible." In *Creation in the Old Testament*, ed. Bernhard W. Anderson. Philadelphia: Fortress Press 1984. 65–73.

Erdman, David V. "The Binding (et cetera) of *Vala*." *The Library: A Quarterly Journal of Bibliography* 19 (1964): 112–29.

– and John E. Grant, eds. *Blake's Visionary Forms Dramatic*. Princeton: Princeton University Press 1970.

– *Blake, Prophet against Empire: A Poet's Interpretation of the History of His Own Times*. 3rd ed. Princeton: Princeton University Press 1977.

– "*The Four Zoas*: New Text for Pages 5, 6, & 7, Night the First." *Blake: An Illustrated Quarterly* 12 (1978): 96–9.

– "Night the Seventh: The Editorial Problem." *Blake: An Illustrated Quarterly* 12 (1978): 135–9.

Essick, Robert N. *William Blake: Printmaker.* Princeton: Princeton University Press 1980.

– "*The Four Zoas*: Intention and Production." *Blake: An Illustrated Quarterly* 18 (1985): 216–20.

– *William Blake and the Language of Adam.* Oxford: Clarendon 1989.

Esterhammer, Angela. *Creating States: Studies in the Performative Language of John Milton and William Blake.* Toronto: University of Toronto Press 1994.

Evans, James C. "The Apocalypse as Contrary Vision: Prolegomena to an Analogical Reading of *The Four Zoas.*" *Texas Studies in Literature and Language* 14 (1972): 313–28.

Fisher, Peter F. *The Valley of Vision: Blake as Prophet and Revolutionary.* Ed. Northrop Frye. Toronto: University of Toronto Press 1961.

Frye, Northrop. *Fearful Symmetry: A Study of William Blake.* Princeton: Princeton University Press 1947.

– *The Return of Eden: Five Essays on Milton's Epics.* Toronto: University of Toronto Press 1965.

– "The Road of Excess." *The Stubborn Structure: Essays on Criticism and Society.* London: Methuen 1970. 160–74.

– *The Great Code: The Bible and Literature.* Toronto: Academic Press 1982.

Gilkey, Langdon. *Maker of Heaven and Earth: A Study of the Christian Doctrine of Creation.* Garden City: Anchor 1959.

Glausser, Wayne. "The Gates of Memory in Night VIIa of *The Four Zoas.*" *Blake: An Illustrated Quarterly* 18 (1985): 196–203.

Grant, John E. "Visions in *Vala*: A Consideration of Some Pictures in the Manuscript." In Curran and Wittreich, *Blake's Sublime Allegory*, 141–202.

Guthrie, W.K.C. *Orpheus and Greek Religion: A Study of the Orphic Movement.* London: Methuen 1935.

Hagstrum, Jean. "Babylon Revisited, or the Story of Luvah and Vala." In Curran and Wittreich, *Blake's Sublime Allegory*, 101–18.

– "Christ's Body." In *William Blake: Essays in Honour of Sir Geoffrey Keynes*, ed. Morton D. Paley and Michael Phillips. Oxford: Clarendon 1973. 129–56.

Harper, George Mills. *The Neoplatonism of William Blake.* Chapel Hill: University of North Carolina Press 1961.

– "Apocalyptic Vision and Pastoral Dream in Blake's *Four Zoas.*" *South Atlantic Quarterly* 64 (1965): 110–24.

Hawkes, Terence. *Structuralism and Semiotics.* Berkeley: University of California Press 1977.

Heninger, S.K., Jr. *The Cosmographical Glass: Renaissance Diagrams of the Universe.* San Marino: Huntington Library 1977.

Hilton, Nelson. *Literal Imagination: Blake's Vision of Words.* Berkeley: University of California Press 1983.

– ed. *Essential Articles for the Study of William Blake, 1970– 1984*. Hamden: Archon 1986.

— and Thomas A. Vogler, eds. *Unnam'd Forms: Blake and Textuality*. Berkeley: University of California Press 1986.

*The Interpreter's Bible: The Holy Scriptures in the King James and Revised Standard Versions with General Articles and Introduction, Exegesis, Exposition for Each Book of the Bible*. 12 vols. Nashville: Abington 1952.

*The Interpreter's Dictionary of the Bible: An Illustrated Encyclopedia Identifying and Explaining All Proper Names and Significant Terms and Subjects in the Holy Scriptures, including the Apocrypha, with Attention to Archaelogical Discoveries and Researches into the Life and Faith of Ancient Times*. Ed. George Arthur Buttrick. 5 vols. Nashville: Abingdon 1962.

James, Henry. "The Art of Fiction." *The House of Fiction: Essays on the Novel by Henry James*. Ed. Leon Edel. London: Rupert Hart-Davis 1957.

Josipovici, Gabriel. *The Book of God: A Response to the Bible*. New Haven: Yale University Press 1988.

Kermode, Frank. "Introduction to New Testament." In Alter and Kermode, *Literary Guide*, 375–86.

Keynes, Geoffrey. "New Lines from *Jerusalem*." *Blake Studies: Essays on His Life and Work*. 2nd ed. Oxford: Clarendon 1971. 115–17.

Kilgore, John. "The Order of Nights viia and viib in Blake's *The Four Zoas*." *Blake: An Illustrated Quarterly* 12 (1978): 107–13.

Lee, Judith. "Ways of Their Own: The Emanations of Blake's *Vala*, or *The Four Zoas*." ELH 50 (1983): 131–53.

Lefebvre, Mark S. "Note on the Structural Necessity of Night viib." *Blake: An Illustrated Quarterly* 12 (1978): 134.

Lemieux, Gerard Alfred. "The Mantle of Mystery: Its Growth from *Vala* to *The Four Zoas*." PhD, Southern Illinois University at Carbondale 1977.

Lincoln, Andrew. "*The Four Zoas*: The Text of Pages 5, 6, & 7, Night the First." *Blake: An Illustrated Quarterly* 12 (1978): 91–5.

– "The Revision of the Seventh and Eighth Nights of *The Four Zoas*." *Blake: An Illustrated Quarterly* 12 (1978): 115–33.

– *Spiritual History: A Reading of William Blake's Vala or The Four Zoas*. Oxford: Clarendon 1995.

Lowery, Margaret Ruth. *Windows of the Morning: A Critical Study of William Blake's Poetical Sketches, 1783*. New Haven: Yale University Press 1940.

McFarland, Thomas. *Romanticism and the Forms of Ruin: Wordsworth, Coleridge and Modalities of Fragmentation*. Princeton: Princeton University Press 1981.

McGann, Jerome J. "The Idea of an Indeterminate Text: Blake's Bible of Hell and Dr. Alexander Geddes." *Studies in Romanticism* 25 (1986): 303–24.

McNeil, Helen T. "The Formal Art of *The Four Zoas*." In Erdman and Grant, *Blake's Visionary Forms*, 373–90.

Mann, Paul. "Editing *The Four Zoas*." *Pacific Coast Philology* 16 (1981): 49–56.

– "Apocalypse and Recuperation: Blake and the Maw of Commerce." *ELH* 52 (1985): 1–32.

– "The Final State of *The Four Zoas*." *Blake: An Illustrated Quarterly* 18 (1985): 204–9.

– "Finishing Blake." *Blake: An Illustrated Quarterly* 22 (1989): 139–42.

Margoliouth, H.M. *William Blake*. London: Oxford University Press 1951.

Martin, Wallace. *Recent Theories of Narrative*. Ithaca: Cornell University Press 1986.

Mee, Jon. *Dangerous Enthusiasm: William Blake and the Culture of Radicalism in the 1790s*. Oxford: Clarendon 1992.

Meyers, Victoria. "The Dialogue as Interpretive Focus in Blake's *The Four Zoas*." *Philological Quarterly* 56 (1977): 221–39.

Miller, Dan, Mark Bracher, and Donald Ault, eds. *Critical Paths: Blake and the Argument of Method*. Durham: Duke University Press 1987.

Milton, John. *Complete Poems and Major Prose*. Ed. Merritt Y. Hughes. Indianapolis: Bobbs-Merrill 1957.

Miner, Paul. "William Blake: Two Notes on Sources." *Bulletin of the New York Public Library* 62 (1958): 203–7.

– "William Blake's 'Divine Analogy.'" *Criticism* 3 (1961): 47–61.

Moskal, Jeanne. *Blake, Ethics, and Forgiveness*. Tuscaloosa: University of Alabama Press 1994.

Nurmi, Martin. "Blake's Revisions of *The Tyger*." *PMLA* 71 (1956): 669–85.

Ostriker, Alicia. *Vision and Verse in William Blake*. Madison: University of Wisconsin Press 1965.

Otto, Peter. "Final States, Finished Forms." *Blake: An Illustrated Quarterly* 20 (1987): 144–6.

– "Is There a Poem in This Manuscript?" *Blake: An Illustrated Quarterly* 22 (1989): 142–4.

– "Blake and Poststructuralism." Review of Ault, *Narrative Unbound*. *Southern Review* 23 no. 2 (1990): 158–71.

– "The Multiple Births of Los in *The Four Zoas*." *Studies in English Literature, 1500–1900* 21 (1991): 631–53.

Paley, Morton D. "Blake's *Night Thoughts*: An Exploration of the Fallen World." In *William Blake: Essays for S. Foster Damon*, ed. Alvin H. Rosenfeld. Providence: Brown University Press 1969. 131–57.

– *Energy and the Imagination: A Study of the Development of Blake's Thought*. Oxford: Clarendon 1970.

- "The Figure of the Garment in *The Four Zoas, Milton, Jerusalem*." In Curran and Wittreich, *Blake's Sublime Allegory*, 119–39.
- "The Truchsessian Gallery Revisited." *Studies in Romanticism* 16 (1977): 165–77.
- *The Continuing City: William Blake's Jerusalem*. Oxford: Clarendon 1983.

Percival, Milton O. *William Blake's Circle of Destiny*. New York: Octagon 1970.

Phillips, Michael. "Blake's Corrections in *Poetical Sketches*." *Blake Newsletter* 4 (1970): 40–7.

Plato. "Timaeus." Trans. Benjamin Jowett. *The Collected Dialogues of Plato, including the Letters*. Ed. Edith Hamilton and Huntington Cairns. Princeton: Princeton University Press 1961. 1151–1211.

Pritchard, James, ed. *Solomon and Sheba*. London: Phaidon 1974.

Raine, Kathleen. *Blake and Tradition*. 2 vols. Princeton: Princeton University Press 1968.

Rimmon-Kenan, Shlomith. *Narrative Fiction: Contemporary Poetics*. New York: Routledge 1989.

Rivero, Albert J. "Typology, History, and Blake's *Milton*." *Journal of English and Germanic Philology* 81 (1982): 30–46.

Robinson, H. Wheeler. *Inspiration and Revelation in the Old Testament*. Oxford: Clarendon 1946.

Rosso, George Anthony, Jr. *Blake's Prophetic Workshop: A Study of The Four Zoas*. London: Associated University Press 1993.

Rothenberg, Molly Anne. *Rethinking Blake's Textuality*. Columbia: University of Missouri Press 1993.

Said, Edward. *Beginnings: Intention and Method*. New York: Basic Books 1975.

Santa Cruz Blake Study Group. Review of Erdman, ed., *The Complete Poetry and Prose of William Blake*. *Blake: An Illustrated Quarterly* 18 (1984): 4–31.

- "What Type of Blake?" In Hilton, *Essential Articles for the Study of William Blake*, 301–33.

Schwartz, Regina M. *Remembering and Repeating: Biblical Creation in Paradise Lost*. Cambridge: Cambridge University Press 1988.

Smith, Barbara Herrnstein Smith. "Narrative Versions, Narrative Theories." In *On Narrative*, ed. W.J.T. Mitchell. Chicago: University of Chicago Press 1981. 209–32.

Stevenson, W.H. "Two Problems in *The Four Zoas*." *Blake Newsletter* 1.3 (1967–68): 13–16.

Stevenson, Warren. *Divine Analogy: A Study of the Creation Motif in Blake and Coleridge*. Salzburg: Salzburg Studies in English Literature 1972.

Sutherland, John. "Blake and Urizen." In Erdman and Grant, *Blake's Visionary Forms*, 244–62.

Tannenbaum, Leslie. *Biblical Tradition in Blake's Early Prophecies: The Great Code of Art*. Princeton: Princeton University Press 1982.

Viscomi, Joseph. *Blake and the Idea of the Book*. Princeton: Princeton University Press 1993.

von Franz, Marie-Louise. *Patterns of Creativity Mirrored in Creation Myths*. Zurich: Sprung 1972.

Webster, Brenda S. *Blake's Prophetic Psychology*. Athens: University of Georgia Press 1983.

Wenger, A. Grace. "Blake's *The Four Zoas*, Night the Ninth." *Explicator* 27 (1969): item 53.

Wilkie, Brian, and Mary Lynn Johnson. *Blake's Four Zoas: The Design of a Dream*. Cambridge: Harvard University Press 1978.

– "The Spectrous Embrace in *The Four Zoas*, VIIa." *Blake: An Illustrated Quarterly* 12 (1978): 100–5.

Wittreich, Joseph Anthony, Jr. *Angel of Apocalypse: Blake's Idea of Milton*. Madison: University of Wisconsin Press 1975.

– "'A Poet amongst Poets': Milton and the Tradition of Prophecy." In *Milton and the Line of Vision*, ed. Joseph Anthony Wittreich, Jr. Madison: University of Wisconsin Press 1975. 97–142.

Young, Edward. *William Blake's Designs for Edward Young's Night Thoughts:* A Complete Edition. Ed. with commentary by John E. Grant, Edward J. Rose, and Michael J. Tolley. 2 vols. Oxford: Clarendon 1980.

# Index